An Indelible History

An Indelible History

The African and Amerindian Religious Encounter in the Caribbean

Alejandro Casas

```
     +              +
     I              I
     0              I
     I              I
     I              0
```

Otura Niko   Ogunda Fun

RESOURCE *Publications* · Eugene, Oregon

AN INDELIBLE HISTORY
The African and Amerindian Religious Encounter in the Caribbean

Resource Publications
An Imprint of Wipf and Stock Publishers
199 W. 8th Ave., Suite 3
Eugene, OR 97401

www.wipfandstock.com

PAPERBACK ISBN: 979-8-3852-4557-4
HARDCOVER ISBN: 979-8-3852-4558-1
EBOOK ISBN: 979-8-3852-4559-8

VERSION NUMBER 04/08/25

Dedicado a mi mamá,
Niovys Felicia Reyes Rodríguez

+

I

I

0

I

Irete Yero

Contents

List of Illustrations

Figure 1: Eshu Ashikuelú (See Glossary)

Figure 2: Ashiakuabú (See Glossary)

Figure 3: Orun (See Glossary)

Preface

"En Cuba, el que no tiene de Congo tiene de Carabalí"
"In Cuba, the one who does not have of Congo has of Carabalí"

—CUBAN FOLK SAYING

IT HAS BEEN FIVE hundred and twenty-nine years since the Spanish colonial presence that occasioned the annihilation of the Amerindians of the Caribbean and portions of Latin America started. Yet, Amerindian influences are still felt all over the Caribbean and Latin America. Identifying what these influences are and where they are found, however, are questions that have not been fully answered. Passing references have been made in many works to these influences, but there is no comprehensive study on the subject, especially in the Caribbean. Intrigued by this gap in the knowledge and information available, I decided to apply for a Master of Arts in Religious Studies. The idea was to pursue this inquiry and simultaneously rediscover this much-suppressed portion of my heritage. After receiving the good news of being accepted, I applied for the prestigious Dunnick Endowment Fund Fellowship for Amerindian Studies, which I also received. Being a Dunnick Scholar provided me with the freedom and financial backing to conduct this audacious and ambitious work. Hence, I am very thankful to the Dunnick Endowment Fund Fellowship for Amerindian Studies for their original support and funding.

However, although this book is based on my Master's Thesis, it has been considerably revised, edited, and expanded for its present incarnation.

Once I began immersing myself in the world of Amerindian studies, further *lacunae* started to elucidate the extent of the field's shortcomings. An equally important topic of research left unplowed was that of the Amerindian influence on the Afro-Caribbean religions. The scant literature available on the subject matter offered very little insight into the significance of the Amerindian influence on Afro-Caribbean religions, emphasizing an urgent need for a sincere and more comprehensive inquiry into this issue. As a native of Matanzas, Cuba, I was also deeply interested in the Afro-Caribbean religions, which had always been a constant presence in my childhood and had informed much of my culture without me knowing it.

Although originally, I had not questioned their importance and influence on my culture and heritage, as I grew older I became more interested in Afro-Caribbean traditions. To my surprise, I found out that even though Santeria, or the Lucumi tradition (also known as la Regla de Ocha), and Ifá had been extensively studied and researched, the equally important Abakuá and the Palo Monte religions had not. Further research illuminated the *raison d'être* for this lack of scholarship and general avoidance.

In the case of Abakuá it was due to it being highly secretive (secret society) and highly insular to the island of Cuba. On the other hand, beyond the religion being much maligned, a large portion, especially the older Palo Monte literature by non-experts and non-initiates, demonstrated far more concerning and universal themes of antipathy or deliberate distortion of adherents' beliefs and practices. Notwithstanding, I don't believe this is a case of coincidentally published discourses scapegoating Palo Monte as the quintessential manifestation of *brujeria* (witchcraft), black magic, and low magic. Rather, I deduce that these aforementioned themes stem from covert and overt tactics/maneuverings for power, control, and authority deployed in the competition for resources tied to religion-based economies.[1] Naturally, since my experience of Palo Monte was nothing like what these writings were portraying, I also became resolute to champion it and to filter the hysterical haze cast over it.

Another crucial factor in my connection with Palo is that Matanzas, Cuba, is the birthplace of Palo. Matanzas is both a city and a province that

---

1. This of course is not limited to the deeds of Christianity but includes those of all other Afro-Caribbean religions as well as Espiritismo (Spiritism).

get their name (*matanza*-massacre) from the first Amerindian rebellion in the island of Cuba. This rebellion led to a massacre when a group of Spanish soldiers were drowned in one of the many rivers[2] surrounding the port of Matanzas by a group of Amerindian fishermen who were fishing in their canoes. The Amerindians had been forcefully enlisted by the Spanish in order to cross the river with the intention of attacking an aboriginal camp on the other side. As a native of Matanzas, Cuba, I grew up with the cultural *milieu* of this creole religious manifestation as an integral part of my heritage. I name Palo as opposed to Palo Monte because although Palo Monte is currently used as an umbrella term which includes the Palo Mayombe, Palo Brillumba, and Palo Kimbisa (also known as Santo Cristo del Buen Viaje) branches, it originally referred to its own Palo branch.[3]

This branch, Palo Monte, was called Nkunia Nfinda Malongo or Sutamutokuni, and its adherents together with the other *kiyekwa* (power or potencies) of Mayombe and Brillumba came together in the first Ngwâwanu (Union) in Matanzas, Cuba. This meeting served the dual purpose of unifying these doctrines, or Reglas de Congo as they are also known, and of consecrating the first fundament of *nkisi* (spirit, force of nature) in the island of Cuba. The idea behind this union was to secure the survival and preservation of their traditions in the face of deep transformative change and the vicissitudes of slavery. Additionally, this Brillumba should not be confused with the Palo Brillumba I mention throughout the book. As explained, it represents a much older and African variant of the Kongolese indigenous religion. While the adherents of the Kongolese Mayombe variant remained highly traditional, in the sense that they did not mix with the other Kongolese and African indigenous religions, the Brillumba branch did.[4] The direct descendants of the Kongolese Brillumba branch today would be the Brillumba Congo or Brillumba con (with) Mayombe branch.[5] Nonetheless, due to its accepted

2. These rivers are the reason Matanzas is known as *la Ciudad de los Puentes* and *la Venecia de Cuba*, which translates to the City of Bridges and the Venice of Cuba, respectively.

3. Juan Rubio, *Palo Monte y La Verdad Esotérica* (1st ed. Miami: Publicaciones Miami, 2014), pp. 15–16 & 19.

4. Juan Rubio, *Palo Monte y La Verdad Esotérica* (1st ed. Miami: Publicaciones Miami, 2014), pp. 15–16 & 19.

5. For those interested in this branch of the religion, I recommend the books by Domingo B. Lage Entuala Kongo included in the bibliography.

and established nomenclature in the literature and the community I will use the term Palo Monte throughout the book in its modern meaning.

Stimulated by the personal factors explained above and driven to understand the silence and indifference towards the Amerindian influence and the Abakuá and Palo Monte religions, I began to ask experts and practitioners about this line of inquiry. This led me to talk to Dr. Alexander Fernández, Tata Viramundo Saca Empeño, who confirmed the importance of the subject, but who equally declared that no expert or practitioner truly knew the answer. Dr. Fernández even expressed that he was not sure if in fact there *was* an influence to be found, but that the folklore of Afro-Caribbean religions affirmed something akin to this. I thank Dr. Fernández for his many enlightening talks and encouragement at the beginning of my studies on Palo Monte.

Further talks with Dr. Albert Kafui Wuaku expounded on these themes and confirmed the foundational and imperative nature of such a study. However, although he encouraged me to pursue such an important and groundbreaking study and continuously demonstrated trust in my research abilities, he also cautioned me against pursuing such a challenging topic and expressed his doubts about finding enough information for a Master's Thesis. I also express my gratitude to Dr. Wuaku for his stimulating encouragement, constructive criticism, and for his countless editing suggestions and comments made on the original Master's Thesis.

I also thank Dr. Whitney Bauman for his suggestions and opportune comments about the decolonial option, which were essential for accomplishing my intended objectives. And Dr. Ana Maria Bidegain for challenging me and requiring me to pursue primary sources, which illuminated many small details that made all the difference in my investigation. Overall, I thank my mentors, Dr. Albert Kafui Wuaku, Dr. Whitney Bauman and Dr. Ana Maria Bidegain for their singular guidance. Last, but not least, I express my gratitude to Mario Paz, Tata Mallimbe, and Carlos Alberto Rojas Calderon, Tata Mulense, for their continual support, encouragement and unwavering desire to help me with my goal of preserving this beautiful religion and of becoming an expert on Palo Monte. And just as important, I am very grateful to the Kimpungulu, Orichas, Egun and Nfumbes for their trust in placing such a responsibility on me.

As for the focus of the book, it is on the Taino and Carib beliefs and practices and the signs of their influence on the Afro-Caribbean religions. I sought to privide the first full exploration of the Ameridian influence in the beliefs and practices of Afro-Caribbean religions, with a case study of Cuba. By doing this revisionary history the book attempts to challenge and dismantle many tropes and histories set up since the colonial expansion. Overall, the layout of the study will consist of five chapters recapitulated as follows: Chapter 1 is the introduction in which I arm myself with a series of questions and insights about the silence and indifference of Caribbean scholars and Afro-Caribbean scholars towards the Amerindian influence and the Afro-Caribbean religion of Palo Monte. These questions and insights are of extreme importance, because they drive the rest of the book and inform the stance from which the book takes flight. Chapter 2 discusses the conceptual framework relevant to the research and how it structures the approach I take for understanding the data (or the lack thereof) and making sense of the research findings. Utilizing the theoretical frameworks of Pierre Bourdieu and Walter D. Mignolo and Maya Deren's insight on the African and Afro-Caribbean religious habitus, I shape the skeletal framework of the book. Additional incursions by Norbert Elias' *The Civilizing Process* and Maximillian C. Forte's insights on the historical trope of Indigenous extinction necessarily supplement the aforementioned framework.

Chapter 3 will be dedicated to the exploration of the original Amerindian inhabitants of the Caribbean and their religious habitus. This exploration will be achieved in a twofold or paralleled fashion. On the one hand I will investigate (at face value) the European primary sources recounting their encounter with the Caribbean Amerindian. On the other hand, I will challenge and scrutinize these sources *vis-à-vis* the modern archeological, linguistic, and historiographical scholarship approached through the decolonial option lens.

Chapter 4 will discuss the African and Indigenous Caribbean religious encounter and its signs. This chapter comprises the meat of the study and contains the truly important findings of the book. Although they were challenging to compile and to trace, I was able to discover a plethora of influences and common themes between the Amerindian religious habitus and the African diaspora religious habitus, which ostensibly support the aim of the project: that of rediscovering and of edifying a renaissance in Caribbean and Afro-Caribbean studies based on the repositioning of the Amerindians as legitimate contributors and agents in the religious and cultural field of the Caribbean. In Chapter 5 I arrive at the conclusion that although Amerindian influences are found across all Afro-Cuban religions, such as the Lucumi, these influences are later migrations from Palo Monte to the other creole manifestations in Cuba, rather than directly from the Caribbean Amerindians. A finding that is in part due to the larger number of Kongolese slaves at the beginning of the 16th century, and in part due to the rapid decimation of the Amerindian at about the same time. I believe that this phenomenon is the reason why, when we look at the creole religion of Palo Monte, we discern many beliefs and practices which have no Kongo origin, but rather demonstrate a multiplicity of voices (Amerindian beliefs, Spiritism, Lucumi tradition, Arará tradition, and Catholicism) which speak to us today through the religious manifestation of Palo Monte.

In conclusion, the following book is the result of a variety of personal and professional experiences that led me down this research path. While the professional and personal intermingle as has been extensively detailed above, there are in fact much deeper forces at play here. Overall, the experiences leading up to the completion of this book have felt like a tapestry full of 'coincidence' or serendipitous revelations, which had a life and momentum of their own. Looking at it from the vantage point afforded by the distance and duration of continuity, this book feeds like a brook/flame does, from a stream that is Alejandro Casas, who in turn is watered/kindled by the ebbs and flows of creation, forming a clear image of the interconnectedness and causality of these 'random-events'. I humbly ask for permission and blessings of Nzambi; to all the Tatas and all the Yayis, please provide me with your blessings to write about the religion. I also ask for blessings and *licencia* (license) of Lucero, of Zarabanda, of Watariamba, of Tiembla Tierra Kengue, of Mama Chola Wengue, of Baluande Madre Agua, of Gurunfinda, of Centella, of Cobayende, of Lukankazi, of Ntala y Nzamba, and especially of Nsasi Siete Rayos and the *indio de nganga*.

Alejandro Casas
Miami, Florida
29th of June, 2022

Prelude

Invocation

Indio rojo, indio Caribe. . . ¿Indio bueno, indio bravo donde vas con esa cruz? Voy al monte del Calvario a entregársela a Jesús. Qué bonito son los indios que vienen a laborar, siete columnas de indios vienen y van diciendo gestiomán. ¡Qué alegre bailan los indios, alegre bailan los indios hay Dios! ¡Alegres y contentos vienen los indios, alegre vienen los indios! ¡Congo! ¡Alegre vienen bailando, contentos vienen los indios hay Dios!

Indio Caribe, indio rojo yo los llamo a laborar. Indio Carire, indio rojo, yo lo llamo a laborar. Que vengan los indios, que vengan los indios, que vengan los indios a laborar. Ahí vienen, ahí vienen los indios. ¡Ahí Vienen los indios! Los indios Siboneyes. ¡Ahí vienen los indios! Los indios Caribes. Los indios Siboneyes, los indios Caribes. Nsala Malekum, Malekum Nsala. ¡Ahí vienen los indios! Yo tengo un congo que viste de indio, yo tengo un indio que viste de congo. ¡Congo! ¡Aé Aé Aé los indios, Aé Aé Aé los congos! Siá kará, Siá kará, Siá kará ya vienen los indios. Palo por palo nún cambiaca. Mbiaca mbiaca o la mundo cuaba. Mucha manteca refunanbemba. Los choro choro, los palo nganga. Siete y siete ya son catorce. Son veinte y uno más veinte y uno. Palo por palo nún cambiaca. Y arriba sube y abajo suena. Mucha manteca refunanbemba. Que vengan los indios pa laborar.

—From: *Cajón pa' los muertos, Canto a los indios*[1]

---

1. Transcribed from: "Cajón Pa'l Muerto- Los Indios", *Youtube.Com*, 2022 <https://www.youtube.com/watch?v=pIwFbZXG7pU> [Accessed 6 February 2022]

Nsala Malekum

"Igi kan ko si igbo"
"Un solo palo no hace el monte"
"A single tree does not make a forest"

—EGUN BABALAWO, LUCUMI PROVERB

1

Introduction

"Okufi konso vana kamanikíni, ivana mpe kamanunuinanga"
"El que es de baja estatura, cuelga y descuelga a su altura"[1]
"The one who is short, hangs and unhangs his height"

—PALO MONTE PROVERB

PRIOR TO THE (IN)FAMOUS and historic date of October 12, 1492, the lands of the Caribbean and Latin America were populated by a diverse and advanced people. These people, the Amerindians, are usually cast aside in the historical (linear) progression and development of the 'Americas' as a primitive and backward people that died off during the Spanish colonial expansion. Due to the desire of the Spanish crown to 'save' the discovered world under the 'universal' power of Christ and Christianity, and the Amerindians' rebellion against being 'civilized', these native's influences are ignored as insignificant in the field of religious studies. However, as is evident today and is popularly recognized, the Amerindian influence is found all over the Caribbean and Latin America. Due to the fact that writing on the Amerindian religious influence on Afro-Caribbean religions is scant and mostly exists in bits and pieces in larger bodies of literature on related subjects, this project entails a synthesis of the available information. The project will research, analyze, and document the available (to the author's knowledge) literature on the subject matter for the elucidation of the Amerindian influence found in the

---

1. *Refranes de Palo.* n.d. p. 2

beliefs and practices of Palo Monte, whose origins can be traced back to the African and Indigenous Caribbean religious encounter.

Hence, the project is based primarily on archival research and investigative literature review. This entails an exploration of the available literature on the Amerindian beliefs and practices that existed at the time of the encounter with the Spanish. I conduct archival research in order to find out more details about the different African ethnicities that were forcibly transported into the Caribbean, and their encounters with Amerindian populations there. I research the various ethnic groups brought to the Caribbean with the intention of locating the proper African diaspora and its religious manifestations, directly influenced by the Amerindian religious habitus. I then explore the available literature on the Palo Monte religion in order to elucidate the evidence (if any) of the Amerindian influence on this Afro-Cuban Kongo-derived religious manifestation.

My goal here is to determine the role such influences had in changing the religious habitus and survival approach of the Kongo diaspora in Cuba. For these reasons, in this book, I will explore the archive as a site of ethnographic revisit and qualitative sociology[2], where the practitioner-scholar binary can be contested and expanded to include insider scholarship, as well as oral histories, as valid ontologies and epistemologies that are able to participate in *tandem* with a comparative methodology in the coproduction of knowledge. Lastly, the reason for the silence observed from Afro-Caribbean scholars regarding the Amerindian influence is investigated through the decolonial lens, or the decolonial option as explained by Walter Mignolo in his famous *The Darker Side of Western Modernity: Global Futures, Decolonial Options*, where he explains it as a delinking from the colonial matrix of power underlying western modernity in order to build a global and pluriversal future in harmony with the natural world (which is a central theme of the religious habitus of the Amerindians and the African diaspora).[3]

The aim of the study is to provide scholars from fields such as Anthropology, Latin American and Caribbean Studies, and Sociology and Religious Studies with a formal body of work of the Amerindian religious influence found in the Palo Monte religion. This will serve as the base point from which further (and much needed) research will be attempted.

2. Benzecry, C.E., Deener, A. & Lara-Millán, A. Archival Work as Qualitative Sociology. (*Qual Sociol* 43, 297–303, 2020). https://doi.org/10.1007/s11133-20-09466-69.

3. Walter D Mignolo, *The Darker Side of Western Modernity. Global Futures, Decolonial Options* (Durham and London: Duke University Press, 2011).

The hope is that the resulting work will also serve as a manual and guide for those seeking to do ethnographic field work in this area of study. I approach this objective by seeking answers to the following questions: What does the available literature on the Caribbean Amerindians tell us about the original Caribbean inhabitants and their religious habitus? Which Afro-Caribbean ethnic groups were most influenced by the Amerindian beliefs and practices, why, and how? What evidence is available for the Amerindian Influence on Palo Monte? Why is there a silence from scholars who write about Afro-Caribbean religions on the indigenous Amerindian religious influence?

2

Conceptual Framework

"Nlembo ulebele uvolanga nsombe"
"El dedo que no está tenso coge la larva"[1]
"The finger that is not rigid catches the larva"

—*PALO MONTE PROVERB*

IN THIS STUDY I make three related claims. The first is that the religious mindset of the Africans brought to the Caribbean during the slave trade had a pragmatic and utilitarian quality. The second claim I make is that this mindset is in fact based on the religious foundation of African societies, which emphasizes the survival needs and quotidian worries of its adherents. The third claim I make is that due to the pragmatic orientation of African spiritualities, slaves from Africa brought to the Caribbean must have appropriated symbols of spiritual power from the native Amerindian populations to augment their own indigenous sources as they battled the vicissitudes imposed upon them because of their marginal status as slaves. Consequently, there was an amalgam of African and Amerindian ritual practices and religious discourses. Afro-Caribbean religious discourses and practices then offer contexts for the survival or continuity of Amerindian religious beliefs and practices.

These arguments lead me to some theoretical insights, including those of well-respected Afro-Caribbean scholars. I will discuss these insights separately, but also note how we can place them together as a

1. *Refranes de Palo.* n.d. p. 2

coherent body of ideas that can help us to engage with the data I have rallied in this study to demonstrate my themes. The first is the theoretical framework of Pierre Bourdieu. Bourdieu's framework will serve as a point of departure, because it will offer us leads that will enable us to make some theoretical sense of how indigenous African Religions and the religions of the native inhabitants of the Caribbean became easily integrated. Particularly pertinent to the research is his concept of habitus which offers us leads in our attempt to explain how elements of African and Amerindian religions became integrated. 'Habitus' is the seat of an individual's dispositions and the filter of all that is perceived by the individual: It is a constituent of the field of social interactions, rendering it a world of meanings, while reciprocally being informed by the field, in a sort of paradoxical infinite regress of effects and their causes. Habitus informs the individual's thoughts, actions, and feelings throughout the course of their social development. However, habitus is not a static, but rather a dynamic process, where social developments get psychologized and in turn inform further social developments. Rather than consisting of a sole habitus, the field is informed by a series of habiti (plural) that structures a nexus of interdependence, interrelatedness, competition, and fusion among the agents vying for power,[2] as is the case in the Caribbean, where the habiti of the Caribbean Amerindian, the African, and the Spanish collided and coalesced into a new habitus syncretized from a pluriverse of habiti.

Habitus is not just ideas and intellect. Habitus also includes emotions and desires as well as aesthetics and things non-rational. However, I postulate that aesthetics and affects are best understood through the lens of the civilizing process as posited by Norbert Elias in *The Civilizing Process: Sociogenetic and Psychogenetic Investigations*,[3] rather than through Bourdieu's theory. Analyzing how psychology and society interact and how both are changed over time, Elias concludes that the driving force behind the change in habitus on the European continent for the duration of the 5th through the late 15th centuries (medieval period) was the process of civilization.[4] Roughly, this period of time marks for Mignolo the origin of modernity and its darker side, coloniality. The civilizing process,

2. Terry Rey, *Key Thinkers in the Study of Religion* (2nd ed. London: Equinox Publishing Ltd, 2008), p. 40.

3. Norbert Elias and Edmund Jephcott, *The Civilizing Process: Sociogenetic and Psychogenetic Investigations* (Malden, MA: Blackwell, 2000), pp. 45–172

4. Elias and Jephcott, *The Civilizing Process*, pp. x–xiv & 5–11

for Elias, is the way that emotional and rational impulses of individual people constantly interweave in a friendly or hostile way, which informs the culture that in turn moderates the drives, immediate desires, and affects (as well as aesthetics) of the agents vying for power in the field.[5]

The civilizing process creates a new type of rationality, a new logic of the royal court as the new center of political negotiation, where the symbolic power of the king or queen as the centralization of power leads to new tools weaponized in the jockeying for power, those of civility and proper behavior. This behavior was codified with a myriad of proper/acceptable cultural and religious manifestations, which included aesthetics and affects, and the control of these behaviors was recognized as the mark of civility. Although these represent the sociological processes (and their causes) of the European royal courts, these civilizing processes led to the formation (psychologized) of a new European habitus where affects and aesthetics were socially and culturally constructed, and imposed upon society and by extension upon those deemed 'uncivilized'.[6] In conclusion the unplanned processes of civilization and of becoming 'civilized' inform the structural or systematic quality of the process of civilization that moves human society along by forces they do not control or necessarily comprehend (Mignolo's colonial matrix of power).[7] Much as the darker side of modernity is coloniality, meaning that there is no modernity without coloniality, equally there is no coloniality without the civilizing process. The civilizing process represents the secular pillar of the logic of coloniality and its matrix of power during the Colonial period whose origins can be traced to the royal courts of the 5th through the late 15th centuries. This process also led to the arbitrary demarcation of those deemed uncivilized (non-European) and those deemed civilized (European), which led to much bloodshed and abuse in the name of civilization's promise and moral right to 'progress' and 'development', a questionable promise that Elias himself falls prey to on the preface of *The Civilizing Process*.[8]

Maya Deren's characterization of Vodou provides a description of a habitus that is typical of indigenous African religions and one that lends to African-derived traditions, such as Palo Monte, a tendency to appropriate elements from similar traditions, making these traditions

5. Elias and Jephcott, *The Civilizing Process*, pp. 436–47

6. Elias and Jephcott, *The Civilizing Process*, pp. xiv, 365–67 & 379–421

7. Elias and Jephcott, *The Civilizing Process*, pp. 365–67 & 379–421

8. Elias and Jephcott, *The Civilizing Process*, pp. xiv

eventually their own. Offering an illustration of the dispositions a religion such as Vodou inculcates in its adherents, Deren writes, "The man of such a culture [a nation in which daily life is full of acts of endurance] must be, necessarily, a pragmatist. His immediate needs are too insistent, too pressing and too critical, to permit the luxury of idealism or mysticism, and they must be answered rather than escaped from. He has neither time, energy [,] nor means for inconsequential activity. His religious system must do more than rationalize his instinct for survival when survival is no longer a 'reasonable' activity. It must do more than provide a reason for living; it must provide the *means* for living. It must serve the organism as well as the psyche. It must serve as a practical methodology not as an irrational hope".[9]

Although these observations are frequently made and comprehended by most modern scholars in the field of African and African-derived religions, the way in which Deren manages to encapsulate it necessitates a direct quotation to drive home her points. The quoted passage by Deren also demonstrates (as mentioned above) why the habitus of African religions lend to their agents and followers an intrinsic ability to easily absorb similar elements from other religious traditions. I argue that this would explain why upon their encounter with the indigenous religions of the Caribbean and Latin America, these African religions selectively picked elements from these religions and incorporated those that resonated strongly with their own religious habitus. These have remained important portions of these Afro-Caribbean religions, even after their decimation of the Amerindian owners, but because these Amerindian beliefs and practices are so similar to indigenous African religious beliefs and practices, only a careful investigation can unveil their Amerindian provenance.

The question of the survival of Amerindian religio-cultural elements, which is a theme I develop in this study, leads me directly to Walter D. Mignolo's decolonial option project. In keeping with the traditions of decolonial and post-colonial scholars, Mignolo pushes for approaches to Amerindian studies that would reverse the malicious consequences of the European historical project. He argues that history is written by the winners (in this case Europeans) and therefore to accept this history is to embrace the First World order and Western modernity with its growing inherent secularism. My efforts at reconstructing the Caribbean Amerindian religions and investigating the signs of their influences on

---

9. Maya Deren, *Divine Horsemen: The Living Gods of Haiti* (Kingston, New York: McPherson & Co, 2004), p. 73.

African derived religions of the Caribbean such as Palo are in keeping with Mignolo's argument and approach. Grounded in this framework we can observe through the decolonial and post-colonial lens how the silence on—or the lack of scholarly attention to—the Amerindian religious traditions, especially their influences on African derived religions, stem from hegemonic European narratives about the 'other', which in this context includes Amerindian people.[10] Particularly poignant here is the 'historical trope of indigenous extinction'. This trope was the weapon, which European historians and writers deployed in the process of the elimination or scriptural genocide of the Amerindian culture. In doing so they were simply promoting their discourses and performances of modernity and coloniality.[11]

The uncovering and highlighting of these traditions is also part of Mignolo's decolonial option project. The process of bringing to light and of unearthing the connection of worlds is essential for decolonizing Latin America and the Caribbean. After all, it is not possible to negate the effect and affect colonization had on the Afro-Caribbean religious and cultural habitus. An example of this is the often-quoted rationalization that the African diaspora suffered the vicissitudes of slavery for the sake of preserving their religion. The Afro-Caribbean diaspora claims that the observable degeneration of traditional indigenous practices in Africa today, giving way to the religious hegemony of Christianity and Islam, supports their insight. This normalization of the transformations that Afro-Caribbean religious beliefs and practices (such as the borrowing of Catholic saints to depict Orichas) underwent is one such effect colonization has had on the Afro-Caribbean traditions. Another important influence colonization had on the Afro-Caribbean Habitus is the syncretic process of transculturation that their beliefs and practices endured. The religious encounter between the Amerindian, African, and Spanish led to the newly constructed creole religious manifestations observed today. Out of this encounter, Afro-Caribbean practices were molded to the needs of the environments and its politics, fusing with Spanish and Amerindian religious beliefs and practices. Although the syncretic borrowing from the Spanish Catholic habitus has been extensively recorded

10. Mignolo, *The Darker Side of Western Modernity*, pp. 101–3.

11. Maximilian C. Forte, 'Extinction: The Historical Trope of Anti-Indigeneity in the Caribbean', *Issues in Caribbean Amerindian Studies* VI.4, 1–2 <https://indigenous-caribbean.files.wordpress.com/2008/05/forteatlantic2005.pdf>.

and demonstrated, the Amerindian transculturation has not. This book pursues this line of inquiry in concordance with Mignolo's project.

These two theoretical frameworks and Maya Deren's characterization of Vodou construct the path from which I will route my discourse of the Caribbean Amerindian influence on the Afro-Caribbean beliefs and practices. What follows is a thorough examination of these two theoretical frameworks and Maya Deren's insight as they apply to my investigation of the Amerindian influences upon the Afro-Caribbean diaspora.

Applying the above understanding, posited by Maya Deren, to the theoretical framework of Pierre Bourdieu is the logical next step, since the theory (as explained by Terry Rey) of Bourdieu and its conceptual tools for explaining religion theorize successfully the development of the Caribbean diaspora religious beliefs and practices, as they have taken flight from Amerindian beliefs and practices. Bourdieu's critical and scientific analysis of the influence social structures have on individuals, and his explanation of what they do and why they do what they do, and reciprocally, how what they do affects the very same construction of the social and its influences (as a form of generative structuralism) on the individual[12] is the most applicable theory available to the chaotically complex development of the highly variant and syncretic religious beliefs and practices of the creole manifestations observed in the Caribbean. His use of the conceptual tools *field*, *habitus*, and *capital*, as well as *symbolic violence* in the field of power are particularly instructive in the explanation of the origins from which the religious beliefs and practices of the Caribbean diaspora emerged and how the Amerindian influence came about.

Where *field* is a space of action and a space of struggle over the different forms of capital (depending on the field and what is arbitrarily determined as capital), and the actions taken towards producing that capital, the consumption of that capital and the jockeying for positions among agents (the consumers of capital) and institutions (which produce the sought after capital) within the field form this structured place of social forces and struggle.[13] The influence of Marx is easily discernible, but while Marx gets stuck on capital and material needs, Bourdieu moves beyond materiality and cements his theory in a much wider context. Habitus, on the other hand, is the seat of an individual's dispositions and filter of all that the individual perceives (a Kantian-derived ontology),

12. Rey, *Key Thinkers in the Study of Religion*, p. 40.
13. Rey, *Key Thinkers in the Study of Religion*, p. 40.

which constitutes the field as a meaningful world, while reciprocally being informed by the field, in a sort of paradoxical infinite regress of effects and their causes (resembling Thomas Aquinas'"first mover' argument), occurring to the individual throughout the course of the individual's social development.[14] Capital equals resources, but as mentioned above, the resources are not only material, they are also symbolic and this symbolism is used as a source of power in the field in which the agents move, which is the sense pertinent to our use of this theory when it comes to religious beliefs and practices.

Ultimately, the different forms of capital determine the location in society of the individual, or in some cases a group of individuals sharing some arbitrary quality, ultimately defining their position in the power relations that constitute the field of power. The dark, or rather, more subtle form of manipulation in which this takes shape is the use of this symbolic capital as an instrument of power, while simultaneously being a stake in the struggle for power, with the aim of maintaining the status quo of those in power in the field in which it is being used.[15] An important further observation worth exploring before moving on to the actual application of this theory in the Caribbean (which will serve to illustrate the point more clearly later on) is the fundamental paradigm model used by Bourdieu which provided the means by which to support his social theory. This is "Weber's configuration of the religious world as an economic marketplace, in which the Church and its specialists seek to establish and maintain a monopoly in the production and administration of salvation goods. . .but small scale competitors, in the form of prophets and sorcerers, enter the religious marketplace and seek to gain adherents by marketing to them renegade or subversive forms of salvation goods, which the Church identifies as 'heretical', and the struggle over capital in the religious field thus unfolds accordingly"[16] which sets up explicitly, the notion of symbolic capital and Bourdieu's entire theory as how it applies to this book. Consequently, the theoretical frameworks and the intellectual justifications detailed above will be analyzed in the following sections in the context of the Amerindian influence on the religious beliefs and practices of the Caribbean diaspora today.

I must necessarily engage the ideas of Walter Mignolo gleaned mainly from his now famous book, *The Darker Side of Western Modernity: Global*

14. Rey, *Key Thinkers in the Study of Religion*, p. 46.

15. Rey, *Key Thinkers in the Study of Religion*, pp. 50–52.

16. Rey, *Key Thinkers in the Study of Religion*, p, 51.

Futures, Decolonial Options,[17] to offer a theoretical way of understanding why there is a silence on the contributions Amerindian traditions have made to the creole religions of the Caribbean. However, due to Mignolo's overall structural approach to the book based on what I believe is a notch against his idea of a polycentric world, all the various theoretical tools borrowed will be delineated rather than linearly engaged. What I mean is that rather than pursuing a coherent and linear logical structure, I will borrow those terms that serve my purpose and detail them according to my own research aims. With this understanding in mind, I will start with his idea of the logic of coloniality. Nonetheless, rather than simply giving the definition, it is best to engage and force his ideas into dialogues with other discourses in his book in order to understand them. Hence, what follows is a paraphrasing and reinterpretation of sections of his book, engaging these topics in a nonlinear and non-consequential manner, although these topics are undisputedly related by a chain of events anchored in the history of western civilization.

According to Mignolo, if we want to understand the historical precedent and spiritual oppression of the colonial matrix of power we need to look back at the period between the Renaissance and the Enlightenment. Mignolo claims that this period is the culprit of the conception of the history of western civilization based on the understanding of Western modernity as the point of arrival of human existence on the planet. The idea was based on the linear understanding of all prehistory and parallel histories being non-consequential and only appearing in this discourse when being influenced or conquered by the colonial promise of Catholic Universality and its Christian proselytizing mission. In other words, Western civilizations have been made the model which all 'other' civilizations have to follow or should be forced to follow through colonial expansion. This history of Western modernity also appropriated two important ideas of particular relevance to my research thesis of the Caribbean Amerindian influence on the beliefs and practices of the Afro-Caribbean diaspora. These are the idea or invention of the Middle Ages, and the idea or invention of America as 'discovered'. Mignolo concludes that we can unveil the darker side of modernity when we begin to understand that it has been materialized in the belief in the logic of coloniality as a necessity or mission of European culture and European Christianity to modernize and proselytize the barbarians, heathens, or uncivilized pagans.[18]

17. Mignolo, 2011.
18. Mignolo, *The Darker Side of Western Modernity*, pp. 101–3.

So, who made this distinction and where was it made? According to Mignolo this idea or abstract and arbitrary demarcation of the civilized and the barbarian only formed one of the two pillars constructed by the architects of the Western civilization, Western modernity and Western history. The pillar demarcating the civilized and the barbarian pertained to space, while the time-pillar pertained (and pertains) to the demarcation of the ancient and the modern. Ironically, as Mignolo astutely observes, much was borrowed from these 'ancient' civilizations, yet the discourse remains that Europeans managed to achieve similar success and progress equal and superior to that achieved by the ancients, but in only five hundred years. But how does this apply to in my research on the Amerindian influence on Palo Monte? Well, we must start by understanding that while European modernity has brought its advantages and virtues, it has also created a narrative of imperial duty to save the world and to make it an extended Euro-America (but under European hegemony). Nonetheless, although the original interpretation of the colonial matrix of power was to place Europe as the epicenter of this universal European expansionary unity, the world has developed and continues to develop into a polycentric world order under a capitalist economy that serves as the field (using Bourdieu's ideas) of competition. This commonality of the global economy and its disputes among First World, Second World, and Third World players (a cold war idea) for the control of other domains within the sphere of capitalism leads to the unintended or perhaps intended colonial matrix of power.[19]

The danger with the colonial matrix of power is that it has taken on a life of its own, and has even replaced Christianity and its universal aim of salvation or conversion as the driving force or hidden structure behind the colonial matrix of power, although originally European Christianity (including Protestantism and especially the Protestant variant, according to Mignolo) was what led to and allowed for the idea and materialization of modernity and its logic of coloniality to form. As we know, this is what led to the colonial expansion into the Americas and the Caribbean and the mass genocide of Amerindian populations (especially in the Caribbean) and to the oppression of the natives and later the African diaspora. However, this alone would not suffice to explain away the observed and felt silence by Afro-Caribbean religious scholars and other scholars engaged in the discourse of the Caribbean Amerindian and the influence these

19. Mignolo, *The Darker Side of Western Modernity*, pp. xiv-xv.

natives had on the Afro-Caribbean diaspora and even Christianity itself.[20] Consequently, I believe that this is where the idea of the colonial matrix of power and its autonomous patriarchal hold comes into dialogue with the idea or trope of extinction of the Caribbean indigenous populations.[21]

The historical trope of extinction as explained by Maximilian C. Forte gives us a window into the process of elimination or scriptural genocide performed by European historians aligned with the discourse and progress of modernity. As Forte points out, individuals brought up in the Western education system were taught, routinely, that the indigenous people of the Caribbean were wiped out during the 16th century and therefore have been extinct for the past five centuries. Utilizing Mignolo's work, one can argue that the driving force behind this discourse is in part the goal to wipe out any hint of survival or presence of indigeneity in the Caribbean for the benefit of the logic of coloniality. Moreover, I would argue that this scriptural genocide by historiographers, where they argue that the native populations of Taino and Caribs were wiped out, except for a few 'culturally diluted' and 'mixed race' remnants, can be traced back to the early period of colonial expansion and exploitation of the Caribbean by the Spanish.[22]

I believe that this trope of extinction started as a result of the efforts put forth by Bartolomé de las Casas and other Dominicans who advocated to the Queen Isabella and later to King Philip back in Spain for relief from the deplorable and sinful ways in which the Amerindians were being treated. De las Casas argued that the decimation and exploitation of the Amerindians in the Caribbean were not the intentional goal of the Queen and that she had sent an order to warrant the better treatment and conversion of the natives and to cease their exploitation and sinful decimation. However, de las Casas tells us that before the order arrived in 'the Indies' Isabella had died and been replaced by Juana and King Philip. Moreover, he explains that Philip also died shortly after and was replaced by King Hernando who was kept ignorant of the knowledge of the decimation and exploitation of the Amerindians.[23] Although this may be nothing more

20. For the most extensive, well researched and detailed book to date on the Amerindian influence on Christianity, please refer to *El Impacto De Las Religions Indígenas Americanas En La Teología Misionaria Del S. XVI* by Francisco Javier Gómez.

21. Mignolo, *The Darker Side of Western Modernity*, pp. xiv-xv.

22. Forte, 'Extinction', 1–2.

23. Lee M. Penyak and Walter J. Petry, *Religion In Latin America* (Maryknoll, N.Y.: Orbis Books, 2006), pp. 22–23.

than royal reverence and wisdom on the part of de las Casas (for his own security and to find an amicable reception of his cause by the royalty), and notwithstanding many other faults explored by Alexander Allen,[24] it is nonetheless enough to provide a plausible explanation for understanding how the trope of extinction may have been so easily accepted, promulgated and unchallenged for so long before being revisited.

However, as Forte point outs, we as Caribbean Amerindian scholars encounter some analytical problems that are not fully satisfied with this trope. As Forte questions: "Does cultural survival have a number? Secondly, do miscegenation and acculturation disqualify indigeneity, rather than admit processes of transculturation in which indigenous peoples were and are present?".[25] This understanding captures the lead I want to follow; this is the rationale behind the decolonial approach I want to engage in this study. Driven by the long-winded question: "How can we justify our complacency and conformity in believing, and hence giving power and precedence to, a few select documents and archival manuscripts written by Europeans rather than testimonies by descendants and the latest evidence from archaeology, linguistics, physical anthropology and contemporary ethnographies which have challenged these first-hand accounts written by European explorers and religious pioneers (in the Americas)?".[26] I felt obliged to investigate my own culture and to reclaim this part of my heritage.

Furthermore, there are also the epistemic and political objects of the patriarchal systems on which coloniality and Christianity were based (according to Mignolo). These epistemic and political objects can be best observed in the disputes over control of knowledge, authority, the economy of the norms which regulate gender and sexuality, and the arbitrary and ungrounded assumptions which regulate the classification of people and regions. More or less, Mignolo approaches this understanding of the system through a quasi-Bourdieusian lens but does provides us with some avenues of solution to this old dilemma. His solution is, put simply, the decolonial option. Mignolo describes his project of the decolonial option or decoloniality in its singular form as a sphere of beliefs and actions

---

24. Alexander Allen, 'Credibility and Incredulity: A Critique of Bartolomé de las Casas' *A Short Account of the Destruction of the Indies*', *The Gettysburg Historical Journal*, 9.5 <https://cupola.gettysburg.edu/ghj/vol9/iss1/5>.

25. Forte, 'Extinction', 2.

26. Forte, 'Extinction', 2.

which orient our thinking from a new ground of understanding outside the cartography of the Western history of ideas and development.[27]

The idea behind this approach is the base understanding that the current post-modern world increasingly progresses towards a polycentric world order, in which a pluriversal world order composed of a pluriverse of epicenters, determines the global future of the capitalistic system. Hence, Mignolo posits as the defining feature of the decolonial option the understanding that

> . . .the analytic of the construction, transformation and sustenance of racism and patriarchy that created the conditions to build and control a structure of knowledge, either grounded on the word of God or the word of Reason and Truth. Such knowledge-construction made it possible to eliminate or marginalize what did not fit into those principles that aspired to build a totality in which everybody would be included, but not everybody would also have a right to include. . . In a world governed by the colonial matrix of power, he who included and she who is welcomed to be included stand in codified power relations. The locus of enunciation from which inclusion is established is always a locus holding the control of knowledge and the power of decision across gender and racial lines, across political orientations and economic regulations.[28]

Thus, according to Mignolo, the Decolonial option projects stems from the objective or assumption that the only way forward and the only way to reclaim our identity as Latin American and Caribbean nations is to decenter the locus of enunciation from its modern or colonial configurations and limit it to its original scope. This then would end up erasing or dispelling the myth of universality which is grounded on the theo-politics and ego-politics of knowledge.[29] So what are the avenues by which one should start to exchange these old and expired forms of knowledge? Mignolo offers approaches that I believe are highly applicable not only to the Latin American and Caribbean situation but also to my ideas on the Amerindian influence on Palo Monte. The first approach is that of de-linking. According to Mignolo it is not enough to change the content of systematized knowledge, we must also understand the terms of conversation that have been implemented and we must change them if we want

27. Mignolo, *The Darker Side of Western Modernity*, p. xv
28. Mignolo, *The Darker Side of Western Modernity*, p. xv.
29. Mignolo, *The Darker Side of Western Modernity*, p. xvi.

to truly move away from the colonial matrix of power. Hence, we need to explore the geo-historical and bio-graphical configurations set up in the processes of knowing and understanding which would ultimately allow for a truly radical reframing of the original mechanism of enunciation on which the zero point epistemology (in other words the hubris of Eurocentrism and the assumed right to modernize and colonialize other lesser or less developed nations)[30] has been built.[31]

Next Mignolo urges those willing to enter into the sphere of the decolonial option to change the terms of conversation by committing epistemic disobedience and purposeful delinking from the disciplinary and interdisciplinary controversies and any of its conflict of interpretations (against the systematized system of Western education) that may arise. The aim of this intellectual rebellion is to call into question the modern or colonial foundation of the control of knowledge. However, as we have seen, in order to do this, we must call into question and focus on the knower rather than the known and thus we must examine ourselves and our narratives in the process. Only then, after moving beyond the controversies and interpretations within the realm of rules and terms of conversation (a Wittgensteinian language game), would we be able to reexamine and revalue directly the very assumptions that have sustained the Western locus of enunciation.[32] Hence, the need to revisit our Amerindian heritage and to locate its cultural (not numerical) influence today.

By approaching my own project through this lens, I am able to contribute to the dismantling of what Mignolo terms (borrowing from Quijano) the heterogenous historico-structural nodes, which can be explained as the nodes of logical structure that anchors the colonial matrix of power and which underlines the totality of Western civilization. Furthermore, these heterogeneous historico-structural nodes serve as the system of managerial logic which controls the actions and borders of the actors/agents within the colonial matrix of power. As observed in the paragraphs above, this system has remained, taken on a life of its own, and continued to exercise control long after the death of its creators, and has even replaced its original foundation of European Christianity and its theology of universal religion with a secularism of reason. Although these nodes, as defined by Mignolo, consist of 12 interdependently related matrixes of power and control, my project will only directly revisit

30. Mignolo, *The Darker Side of Western Modernity*, p. 188.
31. Mignolo, *The Darker Side of Western Modernity*, p. 122.
32. Mignolo, *The Darker Side of Western Modernity*, p. 123.

and challenge nodes number 8, number 10, and number 11. Node number 8 is phrased as follows: "A spiritual/religious hierarchy that privileged Christian over non-Christian/non-Western spiritualties was institutionalized in the globalization of the Christian (Catholic and later Protestant) Church; by the same token, coloniality of knowledge translated other ethical and spiritual practices around the world as 'religion', an invention that was also accepted by 'natives'."[33]

Node number 10 is delineated as follows: "An epistemic hierarchy that privileged Western knowledge and cosmology over non-Western knowledge and cosmologies was institutionalized in the global university system, publishing houses, and Encyclopedia Britannica on paper and online."[34] There is also the matter of language, explored as an important factor of cultural and religious exchange between the Amerindian and the African slave later on in the book, which node number 11 calls into question thus: "A linguistic hierarchy between European languages and non-European languages privileged communication and knowledge/theoretical production in the former and subalternized the latter as sole producer of folklore or culture, but not of knowledge/theory".[35]

Therefore, we must encounter our own border-thinking and we must move beyond it. This idea of border-thinking or border gnosis (borrowed once again from Quijano) constitutes a movement or remapping of the cartography of knowledge beyond the horizon of Western education, which constitutes the reshaping of the borders of epistemology, hermeneutics, and any other colonial institutionalized field or subject of education. Moreover, it should also be added that the current colonial wound, or the open wound upon which modernity and coloniality come into friction and which bleeds through the systematized and institutionalized matrix of power anchored in its heterogeneous historico-structural nodes, should be remapped (the latter includes the reshaping of the bio-graphic, body-politics of knowledge, while the former includes geopolitics of knowledge).[36]

The aim of border-thinking, according to Mignolo, is thus to serve as an antidote to the former imperial and colonial forms of institutionalized Western education and capitalism. Border-thinking aims at pluriversality and simultaneously inoculates us against the viral infection

33. Mignolo, *The Darker Side of Western Modernity*, p. 18.
34. Mignolo, *The Darker Side of Western Modernity*, p. 19.
35. Mignolo, *The Darker Side of Western Modernity*, p. 19.
36. Mignolo, *The Darker Side of Western Modernity*, p. xxi.

of zero-point epistemology which ultimately allows for the shift in the geography of reasoning and anchors this undertaking as a universal project for the future. Inherently, the desire is to bring this universal project from a post-modern world into a transmodern world order. By standing on the borders where colonial and imperial Western epistemology meets with its global differences, we are finally able to observe the totality and magnitude of the colonial matrix of power.

So, thanks to the project of decoloniality, I propose to move away from the comparative methodology to an imperative methodology which is defined as: "The effort at learning from the other and the attitude of allowing our own convictions to be fecundated by insight of the other."[37] By making this change and maneuvering away from the object of comparative methodology which privileged dialectics and argumentative reasoning, as in systems and architectonics, towards the imperative methodology which focuses on dialogue, praxis, and existential encounters (reasoning from the senses and from the locations of the bodies in the colonial matrix of power), it becomes possible to appropriately access and reclaim the Amerindian influence on the creole religious manifestation of Palo Monte. After all, I must necessarily move away from the institutionalized 19th-century comparative methodology which was put in place to ensure that the investigator/researcher and observer of these 'anthropological' works would remain uncontaminated and thus would ultimately guarantee the primacy or supremacy of Western epistemology over others by controlling all forms of knowledge and its production.[38]

This aforementioned secularism is what ultimately has replaced European Christianity as the structural foundation of coloniality and the colonial matrix of power driven by the ideal of capitalistic progress and freedom which has undermined any attempts at reclaiming any sort of identity tied to indigeneity and has suppressed any nativist movement. Hence, from this perspective we start to understand the silence of conformity and indifference exhibited by Afro-Caribbean and Caribbean scholars. This behavior is closely tied to phenomena created by the agents vying for power in the field in direct dialectic with the discourse of the colonial matrix of power as a response of the global entanglements and local histories which make this system so dangerous and oppressive. These are managed by the creation of symbolic powers that determine

37. Mignolo, *The Darker Side of Western Modernity*, p. 208.
38. Mignolo, *The Darker Side of Western Modernity*, p. 208.

desirable and non-desirable discourses and behaviors within the habitus of the structural social-economic system (capitalism).[39]

Therefore, following this understanding we can see how those agents that are nominated as pertaining to the peripheral or to the exterior of the colonial matrix of power may be coerced to comply and conform to the discourses presented; any other thoughts, especially those brought forth by those found on the periphery or exterior of the colonial matrix of power, are labeled as disqualified. Only those agents which are brought up on the arbitrarily designed Western mode of education, focused on technology and science, are deemed qualified and desirable, while those that come from 'outsider' educations or histories are deemed as dead (as in the past, non-relevant to the progress and development of Western modernity) and sometimes deadly to the homogeneity and the sovereign powers. After all, independent thought by such agents (and all agents I would argue) is highly and systemically discouraged by the association of these 'deviant' thoughts with the nominal brands of bad ideas and deadly ideas.[40]

Accordingly then, we need to rephrase or relocate our thinking on the geography of reasoning within the discourse of decoloniality and to approach ideas informed by the definitions of Malik Bennabi: "A dead idea is an idea whose origins have been betrayed, one that has deviated from its archetype and thus no longer has any roots in its original cultural plasma. In contrast, a deadly idea is an idea that has lost both its identity and cultural value after having been cut of its roots that are left in their original cultural universe."[41] Only then, will we start to reclaim and to understand our own identities, to honor our native heritage, and begin to understand our culture/religions. Based on this understanding, I build on the theoretical foundations of Bourdieu, Deren, and Mignolo, and engage them in dialogue as I explore the Caribbean Amerindian influence on the creole Afro-Cuban religious manifestation of Palo Monte.

39. Mignolo, *The Darker Side of Western Modernity*, pp. 101–3.
40. Mignolo, *The Darker Side of Western Modernity*, pp. 101–3.
41. Mignolo, *The Darker Side of Western Modernity*, pp. 101–3.

3

Caribbean Amerindian Inhabitants and Their Religious Habitus

"Ka Mayamba kani kayeela ko, 'Ye Ntoto ka wa mbongo ko'"
"Ka Mayamba aún no está enfermo, 'la tierra no produce nada (dice él)'"[1]
"Ka Mayamba is not (yet) ill, 'the earth does not produce (says he)'"

—PALO MONTE PROVERB

Historical Background

THE OBJECTIVE OF THIS chapter is to reconstruct, from historical sources I consider to be credible, some salient aspects of the indigenous religious beliefs and practices of the Amerindian populations at the time of their first encounter with Europeans. I will also revisit these beliefs and practices through the decolonial lens' modern interpretation of the archeological and linguistic data recently recovered. The reconstruction will hopefully offer keen insights into the religious habitus of these populations. In order to better elucidate this exposition of the extant and hidden influences of Amerindian beliefs and practices on the beliefs and practices of the Caribbean diaspora, it is fructiferous and necessary to provide a historical background of the Amerindian people. This will serve as a foundation from which to build an understanding of their beliefs and practices before pursuing the remains of said beliefs and practices.

1. *Refranes de Palo.* n.d. p. 2

Archaeological research supports the contention that various people migrated from the Central and South American mainland to the Caribbean islands as far back as 6000 years ago.[2] However, the earliest evidence of human colonization is in Cuba and the Hispaniola, which dates to 3500–4000 B.C.E.[3] The inhabitants from this time period made used of flaked stone tools just like the Amerindians of the Yucatan peninsula. This has been utilized as evidence for a possible migration occurring from the west, across the Yucatan Channel or via other routes from Central America, to these early settlements in the Caribbean.[4] Furthermore, the potential influence of Mesoamerican (Maya, Aztec, and some forms of Pre-Olmec or Olmec manifestations) beliefs and practices on the natives of the Caribbean cannot be discounted. The aforementioned should be taken into consideration when analyzing creole beliefs and practices, especially when they do not seem Taino or Carib in nature.

At around 2000 B.C.E. there was another migration, which is of extreme importance to the historical record of the Caribbean. This migration was made by Amerindians traveling from the northeast of South America through the Lesser Antilles up to Puerto Rico. Traces of their raw materials persist in the archaeological record right until the Antilles were colonized by new migrants (the horticultural wave) from South America.[5] The horticultural (and ceramic-making) migration wave occurred between 500—250 B.C.E. and consisted of people originating from the Orinoco drainage and the river systems of South America's northeast coast. However, it has been speculated that this horticultural wave was probably composed of more than one mainland group (that is, from a single point of origin), which, nonetheless, gave rise to a single culture in the Caribbean, that of the Taino Amerindians of the Greater Antilles.

These Amerindian migrants are known as the Saladoid people, due to their white and red painted ceramics, featuring a distinctive kind of zone-incised cross-hatching adornment called Saladoid, named after the Venezuelan site of Saladero from which they originated.[6] The Saladoid people are the originators of the *cemis* (religious objects investigated below) as religious objects, and this belief (and practice) can be seen in the

2. Samuel Meredith Wilson, *The Indigenous People of the Caribbean* (Gainesville: University Press of Florida, 1999), pp. 2–4.

3. Wilson, *The Indigenous People of the Caribbean*, p. 4.

4. Wilson, *The Indigenous People of the Caribbean*, p. 4.

5. Wilson, *The Indigenous People of the Caribbean*), p. 5.

6. Wilson, *The Indigenous People of the Caribbean*, p. 5.

religious manifestation of the Taino, who encountered Columbus when he arrived in the Greater Antilles.[7] Moreover, the Saladoid people introduced their dogs,[8] the *agouti* (*jutia* in Cuba), as well as the very famous and agriculturally important domesticated plant from the mainland, the *manioc* (*yucca* or cassava). Although the Saladoid people tended to settle extensively on the island of Puerto Rico, they also crossed over to the eastern end of Hispaniola where they were in contact with the first descendants of the first migrants from Central America mentioned above.[9]

Subsequently, major changes occurred in the population density and settlement of the Caribbean. These changes are seen in the period from C.E. 500–1000, when there seems to be an increase in the number of settlements in the Lesser Antilles of what the Spanish called the Caribs. These settlers were Arawakan language speakers of a different ethnic group. Meanwhile, the Saladoid people seemed to have been pushed to the interior of Puerto Rico, to a small Saladoid foothold on the Hispaniola, and the entirety of the Greater Antilles (Cuba and Jamaica). During this time the hunting-gathering people found in these places seem to have been incorporated into newly emerging societies.

The ceramic ware of these newly emerging syncretic groups is named Ostionoid, a name that was later used as the designation for the Amerindian people from this period of migration, colonization, and change. Simultaneously, the colonization of the Bahamas also starts at about this time.[10] However, not all hunter-gatherers were merged into the newly forming societies, and the evidence points to the survival of the Guanahatabey on the westernmost part of Cuba[11], which was never occupied by the

---

7. Wilson, *The Indigenous People of the Caribbean*, p. 5.

8. According to Cristóbal Colón's (Christopher Columbus) writings, which were based on his voyages to the West Indies, these dogs were a breed of barkless dogs unlike any European counterpart. In another happenstance of synchronicity, the Basenji of the Congo Basin, the only surviving breed of barkless dog, is the ancient wild dog and domesticated dog of the West Central African people; the influence of this breed in the culture of the Bantu-speaking people can be traced back to Egyptian artifacts and ancient Babylonian and Mesopotamian art. This otherwise inconsequential detail recorded by Columbus points to another potential cultural and historical meeting point of understanding between the Caribbean Amerindian and the enslaved African diaspora. See: American Kennel Club, *"Basenji Dog Breed Information"* (2021) <https://www.akc.org/dog-breeds/basenji/>.

9. Wilson, *The Indigenous People of the Caribbean*), pp. 5–6.

10. Wilson, *The Indigenous People of the Caribbean*, p. 6.

11. Modern-day Pinar del Rio, Ciudad de La Habana, and Provincia de La Habana, which is now divided into the Provincia de Artemisa and the Provincia de Mayabeque.

ceramic-using Saladoid people. The Guanahatabey were hunter-gatherers who lived in caves and spoke a distinct language from the Arawak Taino.[12] By the time of the Spanish conquest there were only a handful of Guanaha-tabey living in the westernmost part of Cuba and the southern peninsula of modern-day Haiti. Unfortunately, like their counterparts (the Taino and Caribs), they succumbed to the brutality and pressure of the colonizers.[13]

Although this is what the historical trope of extinction tells us, this idea will be revisited and reexamined in the following paragraphs. The main reason behind providing this subsection on the historical background of the Caribbean indigenous peoples is to expose the pervasiveness of this trope of historical extinction. As we can see from this subsection, part of the history of Caribbean indigeneity includes this trope of extinction. Although supported by archaeological and linguistic data, what I desire to challenge is the assumption made at the conclusion of this historical reconstruction, that is the total annihilation or genocide of the Caribbean indigenous population by the Spanish.

As is obviously portrayed in the data summarize above, the historical trope of extinction has become the standard and accepted dogma in Caribbean studies. Therefore, parting from this assumptive and erroneous conclusion, the following subsections will be dedicated to investigating and recollecting the Caribbean indigenous religious habitus as recorded through the lens of the European invaders and through the modern decolonial lens. The purpose is to challenge these assumptions and to locate these beliefs and practices in the Afro-Caribbean religions discussed in Chapter 4. This in turn will challenge the historical trope of extinction so blatantly put forth by established Caribbean scholars in *The Indigenous People of the Caribbean*,[14] a volume consisting of the proceedings of the conference held in the Virgin Islands for the 500th anniversary of the second voyage of Columbus to the Americas, which landed him in St. Croix.[15] Although I will move beyond it, it represents the *status quo* of Caribbean scholarship and (for the most part) academia in general when it comes to the Caribbean Amerindians, which I resolutely aim to challenge.

12. A. Brooke Persons, 'Reconsidering the Guanahatabey of Western Cuba', in *Proceedings of the Twenty-First Congress of the International Association for Caribbean Archaeology* (St. Petersburg: Cultural Resource Solutions, 2007, 243–51 <https://ufdc.ufl.edu/AA00061961/00914/citation> [Accessed 13 Nov 2019].

13. Ennis Barrington Edmonds and Michelle A Gonzalez, *Caribbean Religious History*, 1st ed., (NYU Press, 2010), p. 16.

14. Samuel Meredith Wilson, 1999.

15. Wilson, *The Indigenous People of the Caribbean*, pp. xiii-xiv.

Taino and Carib Religious Habitus

Amerindian Beliefs and Practices as Recounted by Europeans

The source I will utilize for elucidating the historical, anthropological and European account of the Caribbean Amerindians will be the great antiquarian monograph by Edward Gaylord Bourne titled *Columbus, Ramon Pane and the Beginnings of American Anthropology*.[16] Bourne's monograph compiles the only two extant European sources on the Taino and Carib religious habitus. Moreover, the monograph represents the reconstruction of the Caribbean indigenous' religious habitus based on a direct encounter with the Amerindian people. Another important reason I have decided to use Bourne's monograph is that it contains his own translation of the only surviving Italian copy (the Spanish copy was lost to history) of Fray Ramón Pané's *Relación Acerca de las Antigüedades de los Indios* (*An Account of the Antiquities of the Indians: Chronicles of the New World Encounter*).[17] The reason I have decided to use this translation over the modern Spanish editions is that although the manuscript by Pané was originally written in Spanish, the only surviving copy of it was in Old Italian. Since I cannot read or work on a manuscript written in Italian (especially Old Italian) I have decided to use the monograph by Bourne.[18]

Furthermore, Bourne's monograph contains a compilation of the only other two sources of information regarding the indigenous religious habitus: Columbus' own writings on the Taino, only available in Fernando Colón's[19] *La vida del Almirante Cristóbal Colón por su hijo Ferdinand*, but extant only in Alfonso Ulloa's 1570 Italian translation known by its first name *Historie*[20]; and Peter Martyr's[21] epitome of Fray Ramón Pané's treatise found in his *De Rebus Oceanicis Et Novo Orbe*[22] (in Latin). In

16. Edward Gaylord Bourne, *Columbus, Ramon Pane, and the Beginnings of American Anthropology* (Worcester, Mass.: American Antiquarian Society, 1906).

17. Ramón Pané, *Relación Acerca De Las Antigüedades De Los Indios*, edited by José Juan Arrom (México, D.F.: Siglo Veintiuno, 2004).

18. Bourne, *Columbus, Ramon Pane, and the Beginnings of American Anthropology*, p. 4.

19. Columbus' son.

20. Alfonso Ulloa, *Historie di Europa, Nella Quali Principalmente si Contione la Guerra Fatta in Ungheria Tra Massimiliano Imperatore et Sultan Solimano Re De'turchi* (Venetia: Bolognino Zaltieri, 1570).

21. Also known as Peter Martyr of Angleria; renowned Italian historian at the service of Spain during the Spanish Age of Exploration.

22. Pietro Martire d' Anghiera, *De Rebus Oceanicis Et Novo Orbe* (Coloniae: Apud

fact, these extant manuscripts survived and are known to us today in full thanks to the *Historie* translation by Ulloa published in 1570 in Venice. Another important factor in making my decision is the fact that according to de las Casas, Ramón Pané was born a Catalan and did not speak Castilian perfectly. This begs the question: how could he have composed a proper manuscript in Spanish on the Caribbean Amerindians? De las Casas also adds that he was simple-minded and that which he reported to Christopher Columbus was sometimes riddled with confused information and was of little substance.[23]

Moreover, according to de las Casas, who knew Ramón Pané, Pané was able to learn and compile this information after he was commissioned by Christopher Columbus "to collect all their ceremonies and antiquities"[24] because Fray Pané "who had learned the language of the islanders" was the most qualified individual to do so at the time.[25] Columbus first sent him to the lower Macorix, then to the Vega region, and lastly to the region controlled by king, Cacique Guarionex. The reason for this requested motility among these regions is that although Pané knew the language of the lower Macorix, it was only spoken in a small territory. On the other hand, the regions of the Vega and the regions controlled by Cacique Guarionex were much more populated, and the language was greatly diffused throughout the island. Moreover, de las Casas tells us that Pané remained on the island of Hayti for two years and this is where he collected, to "his slender abilities", his manuscript.[26] All this was conducted during the second voyage of Christopher Columbus in 1493, during which voyage Ramón Pané had gone with him to 'the Indies' according to de las Casas' *Apologetica Historia de las Indias.*[27]

Hence, obtaining all these limited sources under the careful scholarship of a well-respected historian, together with the singular fortune of having his notes and observations on the original extant manuscripts,

Geruinum Calenium & haeredes Quentelios, 1574).

    23. Bourne, *Columbus, Ramon Pane, and the Beginnings of American Anthropology*, p. 7.

    24. Bourne, *Columbus, Ramon Pane, and the Beginnings of American Anthropology*, p. 4.

    25. Bourne, *Columbus, Ramon Pane, and the Beginnings of American Anthropology*, p. 4.

    26. Bourne, *Columbus, Ramon Pane, and the Beginnings of American Anthropology*, p. 7.

    27. Bourne, *Columbus, Ramon Pane, and the Beginnings of American Anthropology*, p. 4.

make this monograph an invaluable addition and necessity for elucidating the European understanding of the Caribbean Amerindians. For
these reasons it is better for me to use this monograph than any modern
Spanish translation of Ramón Pané's work. Nonetheless, this monograph only serves as a direct source for the beliefs and practices of the
indigenous Caribbeans and does not provide us with possible influences
they may have had on the Caribbean diaspora today. However, because
Ramón Pané's work concerns itself primarily with the island of Haiti (although it was populated by Taino like Cuba), I have decided to start first
with Columbus' own observations which includes data from Cuba (or
the mainland as he called it), as well.

According to Columbus, the Caribbean Amerindians displayed
neither idolatry nor any other sect among their beliefs. The only form
of worship and religious veneration he was able to determine in their
villages was the worship of wooden images carved in relief, which they
called *cemis*. The *cemis* were placed in independent houses apart from
the village, which were reserved exclusively for the objects and their
devotion. According to Columbus, this devotional practice consisted of
a ceremonial prayer similar to those conducted in churches. Moreover,
he describes a "finely wrought table" which was round and built like a
wooden dish and on which an unknown powder was placed. This powder was then manipulated and placed on the heads of the *cemis* during
the performance of a ceremony which, he noted, he did not understand.
Subsequently, Columbus describes how they proceeded to pick up a cane
with two branches, which they placed in their nostrils with the aim of
inhaling the powder. Columbus concludes that with this powder they lost
consciousness and became as though drunk.[28]

Next Columbus describes how these *cemis* received names belonging to forefathers or grandfathers (or both) and how these *cemis* were
kept in a separated house. Sometimes these consisted of up to ten *cemis*
per *bohío* (Taino houses).[29] What Columbus describes here is the worship
of ancestors through devotion and reverence much like the ancestor veneration tradition of Palo Monte. Another curious and perhaps important
detail is the description of one of the *cemis*, which seemed to speak in
the language of the Amerindians. According to Columbus, after a voice

28. Bourne, *Columbus, Ramon Pane, and the Beginnings of American Anthropology*,
pp. 4–5.

29. Bourne, *Columbus, Ramon Pane, and the Beginnings of American Anthropology*,
p. 5.

was heard coming from one of the *cemis*, a member of the Spanish troops kicked it over and found that it was structurally hollow. Apparently, the *cemi* had been fitted with a trumpet or tube, which ran from its lower part to a dark part of the house, which was covered with leaves and branches.[30]

Columbus explains further that under the leaf and branch covering there was a hidden person, who was the one that spoke through the trumpet inside the *cemi*. According to Columbus, this person was hidden with the aim of conveying through the venerated *cemis* whatever the *cacique* wanted to communicate to his people. Columbus adds that the *cacique* did this with the intention of controlling the Taino population. Moreover, Columbus tells us that after the *cacique* discovered that the Spanish had learned about the deception, he implored them not to say anything to the other Amerindians (Columbus says "his subjects") nor to any other person because this was the way that they were able to maintain obedience.[31]

Columbus offers us insights into the privileged and superior role of the *cacique* in the Caribbean Amerindian's beliefs and practices. Columbus describes how most of the *caciques* had three stones, to which the people (and the *caciques*) paid great reverence. The religious significance of the stones was mainly agricultural. However, their power included but was not limited to helping with the prosperous fecundity of corn and planted vegetables, helping women with their childbearing (e.g. reducing child-bearing pain) and lastly in helping with invocation of rain or the sun when needed. Each stone presided over only one of these aforementioned powers.[32]

Columbus also writes about the funerary rites of the *caciques* and the common people. He identifies the differences and similitudes of the former and latter rites. Hence, he explains that when the *caciques* died, they were opened up and dried by fire so that their bodies may be preserved entirely. As for the rest of the people, only the head was preserved. However, Columbus also saw some rituals which diverged from these two forms.[33]

30. Bourne, *Columbus, Ramon Pane, and the Beginnings of American Anthropology*, p. 5

31. Bourne, *Columbus, Ramon Pane, and the Beginnings of American Anthropology*, p. 5.

32. Bourne, *Columbus, Ramon Pane, and the Beginnings of American Anthropology*, p. 6.

33. Bourne, *Columbus, Ramon Pane, and the Beginnings of American Anthropology*, p. 6.

He explains that there were others who were buried in a cave with a gourd of water placed on their heads together with some bread. However, other *caciques* were burned inside the house where they had died, but when the Taino thought that the *caciques* were on the verge of death, they would not let them finish their life by burning, but would proceed to strangle them then and there.[34] Yet others (not *caciques*) were driven out of their *bohíos* or placed on a *hamaca* with a gourd of water and bread at their head. These individuals were abandoned and never visited by the people. Lastly, there were other individuals who were taken to the *cacique* so that "he may dispense a sentence of being strangled or another command which they performed without hesitation".[35]

The last piece of information we have from Columbus' writings delves into the eschatological destiny of the *caciques* and their people. Columbus explains that he obtained the information from a *cacique* named Caunabo who reigned over territories in *Española* (modern Haiti and the Dominican Republic) who was wise, intelligent and of marked years.[36] Columbus relays that he was told by Caunabo (and others who he does not name) that after death they all go to a "certain valley" in which every principal *cacique* is situated in their own country and in which they are able to find their fathers and all their ancestors. Columbus explains further that the Caribbean Amerindians believed that each individual would have many women and all they wanted to eat as well as any pleasure and recreation they desired without limit or deprivation. Lastly, Columbus concludes this account by explaining that all these beliefs are more fully explained and extensively explored in Ramón Pané's writings on the Caribbean Amerindians; as mentioned by de las Casas, Columbus writes that he commissioned Pané to collect this information for the reasons detailed above. He also notes that his personal belief is that although the Caribbean Amerindians had a somewhat developed belief in the immortality of the soul, we should take the writings of Ramón Pané as fables from which one cannot extract anything useful or fruitful regarding their beliefs and practices.[37]

34. A very confusing explanation of the funerary rite, but I think it refers to the *caciques* who were not yet dead, but ill.

35. Bourne, *Columbus, Ramon Pane, and the Beginnings of American Anthropology*, p. 6.

36. Bourne, *Columbus, Ramon Pane, and the Beginnings of American Anthropology*, p. 6.

37. Bourne, *Columbus, Ramon Pane, and the Beginnings of American Anthropology*, p. 6.

Having offered this background information about Columbus and his reasons for commissioning Ramón Pané's work, I will now peruse Pané's work itself. In the following paragraphs of this subsection, I reconstruct the Amerindian religious habitus on the basis of Ramón Pané's account. His manuscript remains to this day the most extensive work by a European on the Caribbean Amerindian religious habitus. Pané begins his treatise by explaining that each individual Amerindian had in his house a *cemi* or various *cemis* which "they worshiped in their own personal fashion and mannerism".[38] This observation could be interpreted to mean that there was no set religious or ritual hegemony, but a multiplicity or pluriverse of practices within the Taino religious habitus.

Next, Pané explains that the Taino believe "God" to be located in "heaven" and that they are immortal, but that no one can see them.[39] The Taino creator god, named Iocahuuague Maorocon (or Yocahu Vagua Maorocoti, according to de las Casas) had a mother who had no beginning, and who was called by either of five names. These names are Atabei, Iermaoguacar, Apito and Zuimaco (the extant Italian text omits one name, Iella, which we recover from Peter Martyr's translation). However, it is worth mentioning that there seems to be an issue with Ramón Pané's collection of the five names used for the mother of the creator god, which arises from the fact that Pané's manuscript contains an almost illegible inscription of the second name of the god.[40]

Hence, we must include Peter Martyr's list of names for the mother of the creator God as a supplement to this historical loss. Peter Martyr gives the five names as Attabeira, Mamona, Guacarapita, Iella, and Guimasoa. According to de las Casas, the difference in names observed between Ramón Pané's and Peter Martyr's manuscripts stems from the illegibility of Pané's original text which said "*Atabex y un hermano Guaca*" (*Atabex* and a brother *Guaca*), but was copied by Ulloa as *Iermao* instead of *hermano* (brother), leading to this misspelling, conjecture, and misunderstanding.[41]

38. Bourne, *Columbus, Ramon Pane, and the Beginnings of American Anthropology*), p. 11.

39. The text is corrupt here, so to whom they are referring to as immortal is unclear.

40. Bourne, *Columbus, Ramon Pane, and the Beginnings of American Anthropology*), p. 11.

41. Bourne, *Columbus, Ramon Pane, and the Beginnings of American Anthropology*, p. 11.

Curiously, from de las Casas' revision we can observe how Fray Ramón Pané projected his own understanding of the European Christian theology onto the Caribbean Amerindian cosmology.[42] According to these explanations we can easily observe that the Amerindians believed in a dualistic god composed of a brother and sister pair. Among the many unfavorable descriptions of the Amerindian religions, Pané characterizes their belief as nothing more than superstition. Pané also records Taino beliefs and practices related to the dead. For example, he writes about the Taino belief that the dead could appear on roadways when the living were traveling alone, but did not appear when people traveled in groups.[43] We can take these circumstantial details as either another form of so-cial/religious type of control[44] or we can see this belief as part of a much larger Caribbean Amerindian cosmovision within an inherently social and group-oriented culture/religion. Whatever we make of this notion, it speaks to the premise of this book that Caribbean Amerindian's beliefs and practices are preserved in the Afro-Caribbean religions; this is an especially strongly held belief in Palo Monte.

Pané recounts the origin myth of the Amerindians of Española as starting in the province of Caanau or Caunana in which there is a mountain called Canta or Cauta. On this mountain there are two caves, one named Cacibagiagua or Casibaragua and the other Amaiuua or Amaisuna. Pané tells us that the Amerindians believed that the majority of the people who settled on the island came from the former cave. From these origin myths we also get the story of Marocael (Machoehael according to Peter Martyr, considered the proper spelling) who was given the responsibility of keeping watch over the cave at night. One day Machoehael was delayed going back to the mouth of the cave, which was his duty, resulting in the sun being carried off and Machoehael being turned into stone after the others had closed the mouth of the cave with him near it because they thought he had abandoned them.[45] The Taino also believed that those who had gone fishing had been turned into trees called *iobi, jobo,*

---

42. De las Casas as well, since he admonishes the Caribbean Amerindians for con-fusing the knowledge of the true Catholic God with this understanding.

43. Bourne, *Columbus, Ramon Pane, and the Beginnings of American Anthropology,* p. 12.

44. As described above by Columbus on the use by *caciques* of hollowed out *cemis* filled with trumpets.

45. Bourne, *Columbus, Ramon Pane, and the Beginnings of American Anthropology,* p. 13.

or *hobo*. Others called them *mirabolans* (*ciruela* in Cuba).[46] A good deal of the information provided by Pané is on the mythology of the Caribbean Amerindians. His accounts of these mythologies are extensive, but I will focus only on those that are pertinent to a plausible syncretization with Afro-Caribbean religions. This will be done for the dual purpose of brevity and remaining true to the focus of this book.

One myth collected by Pané concerns tobacco, detailing how it was created and for what reasons. According to Pané's account, the myth starts with the characters of the four twin brothers, progenitors of mankind, who are the sons of Itiba Tahuuaua. Itiba Tahuuaua is the god who released the oceans by accidentally destroying the gourd called Gaia. Gaia is the god who created the oceans and spread the fish in these oceans. Gaia had sealed off the oceans and the fish inside the gourd (herself) until Itiba Tahuuaua released them by accident.[47]

When the four twin brothers had gone to the house of their grandfather, Bassamanaco, to trade (according to the wishes of their grandfather) cassava bread for tobacco, there was a conflict over the trade; Bassamanaco requested the four twin brothers produce the cassava bread to be traded for the tobacco, which they refused. This led Bassamanaco to throw a *guanguaio* (a tobacco pouch) at one of the brothers, named Caracaracol, which hit him on the back. This bag was full of *cogioba* (or *cohoba* according to de las Casas), which Bassamanaco had made that day and which, according to Pané, the Amerindians had since used for the purpose of purging themselves.[48]

The Taino purged themselves by inhaling the tobacco powder through a cane, which was about a foot in length, and which contained two passages at one end. The Taino would place these two passages in their nostrils and inhale the tobacco via an opening at the other end of the cane. Interestingly, Pané observes that the myth tells of how the brothers were enraged by the fact that their grandfather had asked them for the cassava bread in exchange for the tobacco. These last observations may point to the fact that although tobacco played an integral part in Amerindian religious and ritual practices, cassava bread, which was

46. Bourne, *Columbus, Ramon Pane, and the Beginnings of American Anthropology*, p. 13.

47. Bourne, *Columbus, Ramon Pane, and the Beginnings of American Anthropology*, p. 13.

48. Bourne, *Columbus, Ramon Pane, and the Beginnings of American Anthropology*, p. 13.

eaten throughout the Caribbean, may have played a more prominent role in their lives. This is not found in Afro-Caribbean religions, where in fact, tobacco plays an integral part, but cassava bread does not.[49]

Subsequently, the myth explains how, due to being struck by the tobacco pouch, Caracaracol started to suffer from swollen scabs and much pain. Out of this swollen skin section (which was removed by the other brothers, because something was moving inside) came forth a female turtle, which they cared for and sustained in a cabin they had built for themselves and the turtle. This last addition, Pané tells us, is the only thing he was able to collect about this whole incident of the turtle springing forth from the swollen skin of Caracaracol. Notwithstanding, I believe that this information points to a plausible origin myth for the disease suffered by the men called Caracaracoli and their rough skin, which they viewed as resembling the skin of a turtle.

Pané next recounts the story of the sun and the moon, and how it is related to the story recorded by Columbus of the three stones which the Taino prayed to in order to obtain help with agriculture, child-bearing pains, and the invocation of the rain and the sun. According to Pané, the Caribbean Amerindians believed that the sun and the moon came out of a cave, which was situated in the lands of a *cacique* named Maucia Tiuuel (considered to be Manaia Tiunel by 20th century scholars).[50]

The cave was named Giououaua (Iounaboina according to Peter Martyr) and was held in high regard among the indigenous population. It was decorated with the paintings of leaves and other flora, but did not contain any figures.[51] Inside the cave rested two *cemis* made of stone, about a foot in height, with their hands tied. This Amerindian practice may be the origin of the Palo Monte practice of tying the *nganga* (cauldron) with a metal chain for the purpose of not allowing the spirit of the *nfumbe* (the dead) to escape the *nganga* and to manifest only within the *nganga*. Ergo, the practice of placing a metal chain around the cauldron of Ogun could have its origin in this Palo Monte practice, which in turn seems to have been borrowed from Amerindian beliefs and practices, since neither the cauldron nor the placing of a chain around the receptacle of Ogun is a practice observed in traditional Ifá or traditional Orisha worship in

49. Bourne, *Columbus, Ramon Pane, and the Beginnings of American Anthropology*, p. 13.

50. Bourne, *Columbus, Ramon Pane, and the Beginnings of American Anthropology*, p. 18.

51. The text does not specify whether the exclusion of figures included fauna or if it was just humans, *cemis*, idols, and gods that were excluded.

Nigeria. However, it should be said that this is one interpretation of the use of the iron chain around the cauldron and an equally and older interpretation of the practice, as explained by old Palo Mayombe practitioners, is for the purposes of tying together all the spiritual essences of the material components within the *nganga*.

This limitation is provided to the *nkisi* and the *nfumbe* inside the *nganga* in order to give it a boundary or horizon between the microcosm constructed inside the cauldron and the rest of the universe, which becomes the macrocosm that the composite inside the *nganga* tries to replicate. By doing so, the palero or palera is able to control, in spatial terms, the manifestation of the *nfumbe* to that of the physical domain of the *nganga*. Thus, the palero or palera exerts control on when and how the *nfumbe* should and could manifest outside of it via the use of the *patimpemba*. I predicate that this last point informs the pragmatic reason this Amerindian practice was taken up as a practical addition when working with *nsaras* and the *nfumbe* and reconstructs the origin of these two competing theories about the Palo Monte praxis.

Therefore, although these beliefs may seem contradictory or divergent at first glance, I believe that when properly understood and deconstructed, it demonstrates that they derive from the same origin and speak to the same practical purposes detailed above. These *cemis*, we are told, looked like they sweated and were prayed to when it did not rain. According to Pané, when the people would pray to these *cemis*, it would rain immediately after, even if there was a drought. Moreover, Pané tells us that these two *cemis* were named Boinaiel (Binthaitel according to Peter Martyr) and Maroio (Marohu according to Peter Martyr).[52]

The subsequent chapters of Pané's treatise inform us greatly about the beliefs and practices of the Caribbean Amerindians related to the cult of the dead and the figure of the medicine man. This figure, the medicine man, resonates harmoniously with the role played by modern day priests of Afro-Caribbean religions. However, let us start with what these natives believed about the dead. According to Pané, the Caribbean Amerindians believed that after death, the dead went to a place (for the dead) which was called Coaibai. This place was found on the island called Soraia, which according to Gaylord Bourne's notes means 'west'.[53]

52. Bourne, *Columbus, Ramon Pane, and the Beginnings of American Anthropology*, p. 18.

53. Bourne, *Columbus, Ramon Pane, and the Beginnings of American Anthropology*, p. 18.

An interesting observation regarding this point is that because the information provided by Pané was collected on the island of Hispaniola or Hayti, the island to the west may very well be Cuba, which had a large and predominantly Taino population. If we take this into consideration, then we may conclude that beyond the mythical story behind this belief, there was on the island of Cuba a place (a parcel of land) and a monument dedicated by the Taino as a sacred place for the veneration of the dead, or meant to represent Coaibai. If this was the case, then there would have been a strong presence of the veneration of the ancestors, and the most important *behiques* and *caciques* would have been present on the island of Cuba. I argue for this because, although there are Kongo beliefs in Haiti (as we will see in Chapter 4), along with very similar practices when it comes to venerating the dead, Haitian Vodou lacks the strong survival and preservation of Kongo or Amerindian beliefs and practices of the veneration of the dead when compared to the Palo Monte religion of Cuba.[54]

Following his record of Coaibai as the place where the dead go after death, Pané tells us that the first man who went to Coaibai was named Machetaurie-Guaiaua. Afterwards, this man became the lord of Coaibai, which led to Coaibai being established as the home and dwelling place of the dead. Hence, by this description we get the Taino lord of the dead and Coaibai: their Ἅιδης (*Hades*; Pluto for the Romans: ♀ or ♂), שְׁאוֹל (*Sheol*), or Kalunga.[55] However, not much else is given by Pané, so I am unable to provide any comparisons with Kuballende (see glossary). Next, Pané describes how the Taino believed the dead remained shut in during the day and came out during the night. Apparently, the Taino believed that the dead went walking about at night and even ate of the fruit *guabazza*, which according to Peter Martyr was *guannaba* and which the modern scholars Bachiller and Morales identify with the fruit named *guanabana* in Cuba.[56] In the Afro-Cuban traditions this belief was not

54. To those interested in these beliefs and practices please refer to the Kongo nanchon (nation) of Haitian Vodou for a preservation and presentation of these Kongo beliefs and practices, to the Petro nanchon of Haitian Vodou for a preservation and presentation of the Amerindian, especially Carib, beliefs and practices, and to the Ghede nanchon for a preservation and presentation of the beliefs and practices relating to the dead. A good set of classical reference works on Haitian Vodou are *Voodoo in Haiti* by Alfred Metraux, *Divine Horsemen: The Living Gods of Haiti* by Maya Deren, *The Faces of the Gods: Vodou and Roman Catholicism in Haiti* by Leslie G. Desmangles, and *Mama Lola: A Vodou Priestess in Brooklyn* by Karen McCarthy Brown.

55. Bourne, *Columbus, Ramon Pane, and the Beginnings of American Anthropology*, p. 18.

56. Bourne, *Columbus, Ramon Pane, and the Beginnings of American Anthropology*, p. 18.

preserved; rather the *guanábana* is utilized and reserved for the veneration of Tiembla Tierra in Palo Monte and Obbatalá in Lucumi practices
due to its white interior.[57]

Unfortunately, the text is corrupted here, and the manuscript jumps
into another section relating to the dead and their veneration. Pané tells
us the Taino liked to celebrate with their ancestors and would purposefully and ritually organize night festivals and feasts at which time the
dead would mingle with the living in their celebrations. The way that
the Taino were able to distinguish the dead from the living at night, and
especially during these festivities, was by touching their belly in search
of the navel. If the Taino did not find the navel, they would say that he/
she is *operito* (which meant dead), and thus would know their ancestors
were with them.[58]

Although this particular practice has not survived, a somewhat
similar practice is the Malongo festivities in Palo Monte. The Malongo
Kisonga Kia or Toque de Palo is performed with the aim of dedicating
a collective festivity or party (by the Palo practitioners of the *munanzo*
performing it) to the *bakulu* (ancestors) and the current of forces presiding over the magical world of Palo Monte and Palo Mayombe especially.
This festivity is so essential and central to the Palo Mayombe branch that
this *rama* is often called El Malongo by Palo Monte practitioners. Moreover, the word Malongo itself, which means *arriba en lo alto* (up there in
the heights), *barbacoa* (barbecue)[59] and *remolino*[60] (vortex; the Spanish
term here is better reflected in this word), encapsulates many secrets and
meanings of the religion within it. Where the Malongo diverges from
the Taino belief and practices is in that it is also used as a confirmatory
festivity by which the initiated person participates in a mutual rejoic-
ing with the Nkisi Malongo and the Kimpungulu in the pact just made
between them and the *nfumbe*.[61] Therefore, this is not enough to warrant

57. A. Enamorado Rodríguez and O. Barzaga Sablón, *Los mitos terapéuticos dentro
de la regla conga o palo monte: significación social y aportes a la cutura popular en el
municipio Holguín*, (Master en Historia y Cultura en Cuba, Universidad de Holguín.
Oscar Lucero Moya, 2013), pp. 60 & 93.

58. Bourne, *Columbus, Ramon Pane, and the Beginnings of American Anthropology*,
p. 18.

59. Lydia Cabrera and Isabel Castellanos, *Vocabulario Congo* (Miami, Florida: Ediciones Universal, 2001), p. 219

60. Frisvold, *Palo Mayombe: The Garden of Blood and Bones*, p. 77

61. Carlos Alberto Rojas Calderón, *Palo Brakamundo* (Bloomington: Palibrio,
2011), p. 157.

a thorough investigation of a potential common theme which otherwise may serve as possible meeting point between the Caribbean Amerindian and African Diaspora.

The Malongo ceremony also serves as a platform upon which all previous consecrations and practices become sanctified and blessed by the spiritual forces and the dead. Any initiation or ritual done for the consecration of fundaments or foundations (*ngangas, mpakas, gurunfindas*, etc . . .) of the religion devoid of this crowning festivity are considered null and not recognized by the spiritual forces and the *nfumbes* of Palo Monte. Another important aspect of the festivity, which diverges from the Taino belief is that during the Malongo ceremony the establishment of communication between the world of the dead and the living is achieved through trance and mediumistic possession of the living by the dead. One of the most important facets of the Palo Monte religion, the Malongo ceremony is where these performances are encouraged and celebrated. The importance of this manifestation lies in the Palo Monte belief that the dead serve as intermediaries in the communication between the living and the celestial forces.[62]

The situation described above however, is not the case in all branches of the religion. The Brillumba branch's beliefs are that the Kimpungulu are found at the center of the earth and represent the forces of nature.[63] This is very similar to the Lucumi belief concerning the place of residence of most Orichas. Another important observation to be made is that this hybrid form of Palo Monte (the Brillumba branch), borrows much from the Lucumi tradition, a factor that will come into play in Chapter 4. Meanwhile, the Kimbisa branch's beliefs are that the Kimpungulu are found in heaven and represent the forces of heaven, but from a Christian perspective, and not the Mayombe perspective of the universe and the heavenly bodies as the abode of the Kimpungulu.[64]

It is only in Palo Mayombe *rama* that we find this belief, which preserves the original Bantu beliefs concerning the cosmos or universe, demonstrating once more that the Mayombe *rama* is the most traditional and the most worthy of focus in this study of how Amerindian influences are manifested in African-derived religions of the Caribbean. Nonetheless, I must add that in today's practice of Palo Mayombe, and Palo Monte in general, the inclusion of the cross with four cardinal points inside the

62. Rojas Calderón, *Palo Brakamundo*, p. 157.

63. Emphasis on *represent* instead of *are* the forces of nature.

64. Rojas Calderón, *Palo Brakamundo*, pp. 160–62.

circumference of a circle, with the addition of smaller crosses and circles at each quadrant of the cardinal cross, represents the pact made between the Mayombe and Brillumba. As mentioned in the preface, this remnant of the unification of powers and mysteries of the celestial forces and the forces of nature was achieved and recorded in the first Ngwâwanu. Hence, when *firmas* or *patimpembas* contain these geometric drawings in the Palo Mayombe practices, we must understand that we are looking at the manifestation of this pact between the *ramas* and therefore, more recent practices.[65]

Now, returning to the Caribbean Amerindian beliefs and practices, we delve into Pané's description of the *bohuti* (as he calls them), or *boitius* for Peter Martyr and *behique* for de las Casas.[66] According to Pané, the popular cultural/religious belief among the Taino was that the *behique* was the individual tasked with communicating with the spirits and of knowing their secrets, and with taking away evil by means of magical incantations. Pané compares these practices with those of the Moors (Muslims) and tells us that their songs were replete with content related to fables and the laws by which they were ruled. Bourne notes that these songs are the now famous *areytos* (which I explore on Chapter 4), which Pané saw in a similar light to the recitation of the Qur'an.[67] As described above, these *areytos*, or *areitos* as they are known today, are not very similar to the Malongo festivities, which even use traditional African instruments (three drums and a bell, which is hit with a metal stick).

Ramón Pané then delves into the subject of the observances kept by the Caribbean Amerindians and what these consisted of, explaining that most individuals had more than one *cemi* and that these varied in composition. Some were made of stone while others were made of wood. Some spoke (as we saw in the description by Columbus earlier in this chapter), and others did not. Moreover, Pané confirms the writings of Columbus when he explains that some of these *cemis* were implored to for aid in growing things, while others were used for the purposes of making it rain or making the winds blow.[68] Pané also explains to us that when a *behique* would be asked to attend to an ill man, he would be

65. Rojas Calderón, *Palo Brakamundo*, pp. 160–62.

66. De las Casas' spelling became the accepted and standard form.

67. Bourne, *Columbus, Ramon Pane, and the Beginnings of American Anthropology*, p. 18.

68. Much like the specific Mpungo upon which the *nganga* is founded and which presides over specific powers of nature.

required to abstain from food and to make use of the cleansing ritual of inhaling tobacco through the nose.[69] Apparently, this was done by the *behique* for the purpose of going into trance and communicating directly with the *cemis* in order to unveil the cause of the illness.[70]

Although at first glance this may seem like the same procedure performed by the *palero* or *palera* in Palo Monte, the differences are marked enough to make it difficult for us to conclude that it is an Amerindian appropriation. It is true that the *palero* or *palera* uses the tobacco to start and to strengthen the communication link between the world of the living and the world of the dead found on his or her *nganga*, but the communication is effected through the use of the *chamalongos* rather than directly through the tobacco-induced trance. In cases where direct communication occurs, this is due to the influence of Kardecian Spiritism, and the *palero* or *palera* most likely developed the gifts of mediumship through involvement with that tradition. Hence, this should not be confused with traditional Palo Mayombe. Rather, it reflects the latest innovation of Palo Monte, known as Palo Cruzado.[71]

Pané also tells us that another preparatory procedure performed by the *behique* was to use a sort of soot or pounded charcoal, which they smeared over their faces, followed by the introduction of a piece of stringed meats (the plural is used) and bones into their mouths. After this, they proceeded to the house of the ill person and entered with only the principal or most important individuals of the household. Once inside the house they would consume *cogioba* again, but this time together with another un-described herb, which then the *behique* passed to the members of the family who had been allowed inside the hut for them to consume as well. After this, and after they had vomited, they would perform another *areito* and would light a torch, which remained lit throughout the night. The *behique* would then approach the ill person and perform a sort of tactile examination, touching all of the patient's body parts and miming the gesture of drawing out something from inside the person.[72]

---

69. Please refer to the section on tobacco in Chapter 4 for further information.

70. Bourne, *Columbus, Ramon Pane, and the Beginnings of American Anthropology* (Worcester, Mass.: [American Antiquarian Society], 1906), 18.

71. Nicholaj de Mattos Frisvold, *Palo Mayombe: The Garden of Blood and Bones* (1st ed. Dover: Bibliothèque Rouge/Scarlet Imprint, 2011), pp. 211–12.

72. Bourne, *Columbus, Ramon Pane, and the Beginnings of American Anthropology*, p. 21.

While performing this gesture of removing something from the person, the *behique* would move towards the entrance of the *bohío* at intervals and have the door closed behind him in order to speak the words, "Begone to the mountains, or to the seas or wither thou wilt", which he then followed by blowing, like one would dust or particulate matter. Then the *behique* would turn around once more and close his mouth by putting his hands together and covering it with them. Pané describes in detail how, after this performance, the *behique* would pretend that his hands were very cold and would make them tremble in front of the family members and proceeded to blow on them as before. The *behique* would then begin sucking the ill person all over their body in order to draw the illness from the body into his mouth. At this point, the *behique* would start to cough and make a face as though he had eaten something extremely bitter or sour. The *behique* followed this by spitting out the materials, which Pané tells us the *behique* had consumed before arriving at the *bohío*.[73]

The *behique* would then tell the patient that whatever it was he had brought out of his mouth was the reason why they had become ill, and if the thing removed from his mouth (apparently the items varied) was eatable, the *behique* would tell the individual to take notice of what it was, because eating it had brought about the illness. Moreover, Pané tells us that the *behique* would inform the patient that whatever he had removed had in fact been placed there by their *cemis* because they had not said their daily prayers to them and had not built them a temple or given them something of their possessions. Sometimes, stones were also 'removed' from the patient which were particularly important for the Caribbean Amerindians. According to Pané, when this was the case, the patient was instructed to keep the stone safe; if the patient was a woman, she was to ask for help with child-bearing pains. These stones, we are informed, were kept neatly wrapped in cotton and placed in small baskets in which they were given things to eat.[74]

Pané tells us that this was not only the case with these stones, but that it was also the same with the *cemis* to which the people would bring excesses of fish, meat, or bread (and many other foodstuffs). They would place all of these items in the cabin dedicated to the *cemis*, which was

73. Bourne, *Columbus, Ramon Pane, and the Beginnings of American Anthropology*, p. 21.

74. Bourne, *Columbus, Ramon Pane, and the Beginnings of American Anthropology*, p. 21.

separated from the house.[75] The next day they would share all of these meals and would eat what was offered. Although this practice is also prevalent in the Afro-Cuban traditions it is not exclusively an Amerindian influence but rather a manifestation of all indigenous or ecologically aware spiritualities.

Pané next discusses the cases in which the *behique* is unable to cure a person or is not able to intervene. In this case the family of the individual would dig a grave for the person's body and would pour over their mouth a liquid made of the *cogioba* plant,[76] which supposedly had leaves like basil. The Taino would pound these leaves into a powder with some hair and nails of the dead person. Then, when the family had poured this powder over the mouth and nose of the dead person, the corpse would start responding to the family's questions about the cause of death. These usually consisted of asking whether it was the fault of the *behique* or whether the person had not dutifully followed the regimen prescribed by the *behique*.[77] Pané even tells us that when the corpse is asked if it was alive, or how it was alive, it would respond that it was dead. Another way in which they investigate the truth about the death of an ill person is by building a big fire into which the person is placed; once the flames are burning high., the person is covered with earth and asked a series of questions related to their death. Pané tells us that when they perform this ritual, the corpse only revealed answers to ten questions and did not answer whether it was dead or alive. Pané compared this ritual process, especially the aspect that involves the burning of the corpse, to the traditional method of making charcoal among the European charcoal makers.[78]

The Caribbean Amerindians also believed that if the smoke coming from the furnace upon which the corpse had been placed and questioned rose high and a shrill cry came from the fire, followed by the smoke turning downwards towards the *bohío* of the *behique*, then the *behique* was to be blamed for the death. Pané tells us that when this occurred, the *behique* would be stricken immediately with peeling sores over his whole body. The people saw this as a sign that the *behique* had not followed the proper

75. Bourne, *Columbus, Ramon Pane, and the Beginnings of American Anthropology*, p. 21.

76. In this case *zachon* is used instead of *cogioba* as the name for tobacco, but Bourne's notes tells us it is the same plant.

77. Bourne, *Columbus, Ramon Pane, and the Beginnings of American Anthropology*, pp. 22.

78. Bourne, *Columbus, Ramon Pane, and the Beginnings of American Anthropology*, pp. 22.

preparatory procedures before succoring the ill person. In the case of the corpse denouncing the *behique* through the former means, the family would wait for the *behique* and beat him close to death with clubs, often breaking his extremities.[79] These means of retaliation tell us that although the magical and religious power lay with the *behique*, individuals and families also had access to magical powers and made use of them when needed. Unfortunately, I am not able to compare these practices with the Palo rituals linked with necromancy, since they are necessarily kept secret by *paleros*, and Palo Monte practitioners and I am not one. Therefore, whether or not there are similar practices in Palo Monte would have to be answered by initiated individuals who would like to contribute to this relatively unexplored field of inquiry.

In chapter 19 of Ramón Pané's manuscript he explains to us how the Caribbean Amerindians made the *cemis*. The *cemis* made of wood were created when an individual Amerindian was frightened by an 'unexplained' tree-phenomenon, such as the movement of its roots. This individual would then ask the tree-phenomenon who it was, and the tree would tell the individual to call the *behique* to tell him the answer.[80] Then the *behique* would arrive and would make *cogioba* next to the tree; after he finished, he would stand up in front of the tree and would give it all his titles before asking it: "Tell me who you are and what you are doing here and what you want of me and why you have called. Tell me if you want me to cut you or if you want to come with me, and how you want me to carry you and I will build you a cabin and add a property to it."[81]

The closest Afro-Caribbean practice to this found in the Afro-Caribbean religions is the preliminary ritual of Palo Monte. In Palo Monte, the priest must approach the *nganga* and must communicate with it first by providing his *licencias* (licenses), which consist of the individuals and powers that have granted him permission to work with and communicate with the powers of nature and the *nfumbes*. This is done foremost in any ritual or question and is the first process when working with the *nganga*, together with the lighting of tobacco and the use of its smoke to ritually fumigate the religious paraphernalia. Plants and trees are also spoken

79. Bourne, *Columbus, Ramon Pane, and the Beginnings of American Anthropology*, pp. 22.

80. This is according to de las Casas' text which cites this event and is considered the authoritative text over Pané's corrupt description.

81. Bourne, *Columbus, Ramon Pane, and the Beginnings of American Anthropology*, pp. 22.

to, and their blessings are sought in order to obtain their powers. These incantations and prayers are called *mambos* in Palo Monte and form an important part of the liturgy and repertoire of the *paleros* and *paleras*.[82] However, the latter practices and their concomitant beliefs are present in all Afro-Caribbean religions and most likely represent a universal respect and awareness towards nature fundamental to all indigenous religions.

The trees which were made into *cemis* were venerated and used for both good and bad charms. Beyond providing sacrifices and food to the *cemis*, rituals were also used for establishing direct communication with them, especially in cases of danger or when the clients wanted their futures foretold. The Taino established this direct communication by making *cogioba* in front of the *cemis*, inside the *bohío* built for them. Then, the Taino would begin to call the *cemis* in various ritualistic fashions, which would reach a climax with the inhalation of the *cogioba*. This inhalation of the *cogioba* would then establish the desired direct communication with the *cemis*, which would lead the Taino into a trance that would ultimately allow them to see the future or what they wanted to know. The stone *cemis* were consecrated as described by Columbus and Pané. An example of this is the ritual process described above, of the "removal" of the stone from the body of the sick person. One important note to add is that the leaves, which the Caribbean Amerindians added to the 'talking' *cemis*, looked like elm leaves and their purpose was to make the *giuca* (*yucca* in Cuba; cassava) grow.[83]

The following pages of Pané's manuscript, which I will explore briefly, are dedicated to the different deities and their *cemis*. The first *cemi* mentioned is called Baidrama (also Bugia or Aiba according to Pané, and Vaybrama according to de las Casas).[84] According to Pané this *cemi* was

82. Please see the Cuban documentary *Soy Tata Nganga* for references of these practices. Although most books contain *mambos* (liturgical songs) and information regarding the liturgy, none demonstrate the full process as well as do the beginning minutes of this documentary. Moreover, due to the highly personal and secretive process of this opening ritual, most published materials have abstained from including the use of *licencias* and tobacco smoke. The documentary can be accessed at: <https://www.youtube.com/watch?v=tF9n6FGISmY&t=120s>. See also Katerina Kerestetzi's excellent documentary on Palo Monte, *Les morts du Palo Monte*, which does an excellent job of demonstrating not only the use of *Fula* (gunpowder) in Palo Monte but also records important aspects of the religion such as spirit possession. The documentary can be accessed at: <https://www.youtube.com/watch?v=_cQHCT9fJlU>.

83. Bourne, *Columbus, Ramon Pane, and the Beginnings of American Anthropology*, pp. 24.

84. De las Casas' spelling remains the standard form.

burnt during war times and was later washed during peace times with the juice of the cassava so that it may regrow its arms, eyes, and body, making them anew. Moreover, we are told that when those who had made this *cemi* did not bring cassava for it to eat, it would punish them by making them ill, which was confirmed by the *behique*. The next *cemi* Pane tells us about is Corocote, which they placed on top of the house of Guamorete, who was an important individual in the community. The story of this *cemi* is that whenever it would come into the possession of an individual, it would lie with the women of the house in which it was placed. This *cemi*'s mark was that it grew two crowns on its head, and whenever someone would be seen wearing two crowns it was believed that they were the sons of Corocote.[85]

The next *cemi* described by Pane is Opigielguoiran (Epileguanita according to Peter Martyr and the accepted standard form). This *cemi* was owned by the important Cauauaniouaua who had many subjects. This *cemi*'s recognizable attributes were that it was said to have four feet like a dog and was made of wood.[86] This *cemi* seems to have been quite mischievous. It liked to go out at night and would need to be brought back every time. The Taino would go looking for it in the forest and would bring it back to the house and bind it with cords, only for it to escape again the next night. This *cemi* was in fact not seen by Pané, because (as he tells us) the Caribbean Amerindians told him that when the Christians arrived in Hispaniola it broke away from its cords once more, but this time it went into a swamp and was never found again.[87]

Another *cemi* explored in Pané's manuscript is called Guabancex. This *cemi* was found on the lands of the great *cacique* Aumatex. The *cemi* was considered to be a woman made of stone and was said to be accompanied by two other *cemis*. One of the accompanying *cemis*, named Guatauua, was a crier/screamer while the other was the gatherer or governor of the waters. Pané tells us that Guabancex's powers was that when she was angry, it would raise the winds and bring rain that would destroy houses and topple trees.[88] The role of Guatauua was to cry or proclaim

85. Bourne, *Columbus, Ramon Pane, and the Beginnings of American Anthropology*, pp. 24–25.

86. Sebastián Robiou Lamarche, *Tainos and Caribs: The Aboriginal Cultures of the Antilles*, translated by Grace M Robiou Ramirez de Arellano (San Juan, Puerto Rico: Editorial Punto y Coma, 2019), p. 120.

87. Bourne, *Columbus, Ramon Pane, and the Beginnings of American Anthropology*, pp. 24–25.

88. *Nota bene*: The Taino believed this *cemi* to preside over the power or spirit of the

by the order of Guabancex for all of the other *cemis* of the land to help them raise a high wind and bring heavy rain, which was associated with Guabancex (most probably talking about hurricanes, *derechos*, or northerly cold fronts in winter). As for the gatherer or governor of the waters, its name was Coatrischie. Its role or job was to gather the waters into the valleys between the mountains, which he would then let loose,[89] destroying much of the countryside.[90]

The last *cemi* mentioned in Pané's manuscript is named Faraguuaol.[91] This *cemi* belonged to a *cacique* of Hispaniola and was considered an idol.[92] According to the myth associated with this *cemi*, its origin dates back to a period prior to the discovery of the island by the Taino. The myth preserved by Pané tells us that this *cemi* was constructed when some hunters ran after an animal that had gone into a ditch. Once in the ditch the hunters saw a beam or log, which seemed alive. After this, they ran back to the *cacique*, who was the father of Guaraionel.[93] He came back with them and told them to take the log and to build a place for it. Pané tells us that this *cemi* also liked to leave the place where it was housed and travel back to the same place or near the same place it had been collected from. He noted how tying the *cemi* and binding it with harnesses and

---

hurricane, derecho (a Spanish word that means 'straight') and tornado (which comes from an amalgamation of the Spanish *tornado*, 'thunderstorm', or *tornar*, 'to turn') and not the deity or force of nature called Huracán. This misunderstanding derives from the historical impact of the Spanish colonization on the Caribbean and the Americas. The origin of this confusion derives from the Taino Arawak language word *huracán*, which simply means, 'storms'. Other, less reliable sources, indicate that this was the Taino word used for the Carib god of evil, Huricán. In turn, the Carib god of evil derived its name from the Maya god of wind, storm, and fire, named Huracán. Thus, when the Spanish razed through the Caribbean on their way to the 'Americas', they erroneously picked this name for the natural phenomena that are hurricanes, which remains in use to this day. Information obtained from Rachelle Oblack, 'Why Do We Call Them "Hurricanes"?' (2019) <https://www.thoughtco.com/where-does-the-word-hurricane-come-from-3443911>, and Gerald Erichsen, 'Where Did The Word Hurricane Come From?' (2019) <https://www.thoughtco.com/etymology-of-hurricane-3080285>.

89. This most likely refers to mudslides.

90. Bourne, *Columbus, Ramon Pane, and the Beginnings of American Anthropology*, p. 26.

91. Bourne's note tells us that the name *Taragabaol* has been suggested by modern scholars as the most likely correct spelling.

92. This most likely meant that it contained a skull. See the Chapter 4 subsection on *cemis* and *ngangas* for full discussion on this topic.

93. Either the story is corrupted, or Ramón Pané was not able to get all the information available regarding this myth, because he does not provide any more detail about the *cacique* or Guaraionel and moves rather abruptly to the remainder of the myth.

cords was not enough to keep it in the place they had built for it, for it would leave again.[94]

The next recorded information relates to the *cacique* Caizzihu, the great lord in the Taino heaven who had performed a fast in the celestial spheres. Imitating this *cacique*, the Taino would fast in honor of the *cemi* representing him. The Taino would especially fast to the *cemi* when they needed to obtain a victory over their enemies (most likely the Caribs), or to acquire wealth or anything else they desired.[95] Hence, this fast served as a sort of sacrifice by which they demonstrated that what they desired was deserving of the blessing of the great *cacique* in the sky and their *cemis*.

The chapter continues with an account of a curious and important event. Pané tells us that during one of these fasts, a *cacique* (either Cazzi-uaquel or Gamanacoel) had spoken in trance about how after his death, those who remained alive would rule over his lands for only a short time. The reason, according to the *cacique*, was that they would welcome to their country a people, who would be clothed, and who would rule and slay them. They would also ultimately die of hunger. Moreover, Pané tells us that the Taino originally thought these would be the Canibales.[96] Ultimately, after pondering the message, the Taino came to believe that the peoples mentioned in the trance and shown in the visions most likely referred to others. The Taino started to realize that the Caribs had not shown any intention of ruling them and had only plundered, kidnapped, and fled their lands once they had achieved their aim. Only later, they shared, did they realize that the visions and 'prophecy' of the *cacique* which had been induced by the *cemi* were referring to Admiral Columbus and the people he had brought with him.[97]

The reason this narrative is important for my argument is that although we cannot know whether the events described are true or not, they do inform my assumptions. If we take this event and its 'prophecy'

94. Bourne, *Columbus, Ramon Pane, and the Beginnings of American Anthropology*, p. 26.

95. Bourne, *Columbus, Ramon Pane, and the Beginnings of American Anthropology*, p. 26.

96. According to de las Casas, this was the original name of the Caribes (Caribs) given by the Taino, and which the Spanish initially used as well. The most probable reason this word has become the term used for those who eat other human beings is because of the Carib anthropophagic rite of the Celestial Barbecue in which they ate (as a community) a worthy sacrificial enemy.

97. Bourne, *Columbus, Ramon Pane, and the Beginnings of American Anthropology*, pp. 26–27.

as historically and factually true, then we must necessarily accept the historical trope of extinction put forth by European scholars up to the present day, due to its 'predestined' nature. In evaluating the discourse put forth by European writers about the Caribbean, we must reserve a certain degree of suspicion regarding this type of trope. It promulgates an unescapable finality or Christian apocalyptic understanding of the destiny of the Caribbean Amerindians and their 'heathen/pagan' ways. After all, as we have seen in the historical background described at the beginning of this chapter, the origins of the Taino and Caribs can be traced to South and Central America, and this 'prophecy' (if historically true and not anachronistic) could have made reference to a Taino legend of Maya or Aztec origin. Equally, based on information gained through exchange with Maya from the Yucatan Peninsula or rumors heard about the Aztecs, this may have been a Taino legend about the potential invasion of their land by the Maya or the Aztec, whom they knew wore clothing and other accessories.

Either way, we must be careful when assigning such a deterministic end to the Caribbean Amerindians. This type of belief may be telling us more about the Spanish (and European in general) mindset and their colonial efforts than about the Caribbean Amerindian habitus. I support this position with facts taken from the pages of Ramón Pané's manuscript which follow this legend. They are dedicated to the efforts and 'success' of the friars in baptizing and proselytizing the indigenous populations, and their eventual conversion (*en masse*) to the 'true religion' as ordained by the promise of God instituted in the Christian Catholic faith. With this claim I conclude this section of the chapter, noting to the readers that the additions and divergences of importance observed in the epitome from Peter Martyr and the quotations by de las Casas have been noted throughout this subsection and do not merit further exploration. Next, I would like to analyze the Amerindian beliefs and practices through the decolonial lens. Although not as rich in anecdotal and witness account of the Caribbean Amerindian beliefs and practices, the reliability and unbiased investigation of the archaeological and historical data does provide a much-needed revisionary retrogression before we spring forward with my investigation of these beliefs and practices as accurate and factual.

Amerindian Beliefs and Practices Revisited
Through the Decolonial Lens

In this subsection, I will examine the modern data on the Caribbean Amerindians. However, most of these sources use the information provided by Ramón Pané, which I have summarized above. Therefore, for the sake of brevity and focus, I will only offer a summary of the hypotheses, theories, and conclusions that have recently been drawn out from the well of data collected through archaeological and historical means. Any information repeated, or which supports what has already been recorded in the previous subsection, will be omitted and only those hypotheses, theories, and conclusions that are not reflected in Ramón Pané's manuscript will be included here. In lieu of antagonism, I want to correct and reclaim a proper understanding of the Caribbean Amerindian habitus, hence, the conciseness and directness with which I will treat the subject matter here.

The first important information, shared by Sebastián Robiou Lamarche, is that the Taino myth of the creation of the universe describes how creation occurs in several eras. The myth recounts the beginning, or the time of origin of the universe, where *Yaya* was the only existing being or entity, and its emanation in the universe. Robiou Lamarche explains that according to the work of José Juan Arrom, the word Yaya is the superlative duplication of 'Ia' which in the Arawak language means *spirit*, *cause*, and *essence of life*. Hence, Yaya can be considered a Supreme Spirit (whose name was unknown) and who seemed to have been an equivalent of the creative first cause for the continental Arawaks. However, as Mircea Eliade had hypothesized regarding original supreme beings,[98] Yaya eventually evolved into the practical name Yúcahu Bagua Maórocoti, which means Being of the Yuca, Sea, and Without Male Predecessor.[99]

Robiou Lamarche also delves into the names of the mother of Yaya,[100] which were given by Pané in his manuscript and explored in the previous subsection, but which were only superficially explained. The first name

98. Mircea Eliade saw the evolution of supreme beings in 'primitive' or agricultural societies, cultures, and religions progressing in status from this creative primacy and privileged position (in terms of worship or veneration) until eventually they are forgotten and transformed over time into an atmospheric-fertilizing gods, or gods of vegetation. Information obtained from: *Nine Theories of Religion* by Daniel L. Pals.

99. Robiou Lamarche, *Tainos and Caribs: The Aboriginal Cultures of the Antilles*, pp. 106–7.

100. It must be said that since the Taino believed Yaya to have had no beginning, its mother must not be thought as begetting him.

mentioned is Atabey, who is considered to be the Mother of the Waters. As for the other names, they also seem to have had lunar-aquatic connotations. The important implication of this mythology is that beyond establishing the hierarchy of this powerful feminine deity in the Taino pantheon, it also had the effect on Taino society of establishing a divine order, which was based on the feminine principle at the apex of its hierarchy. This divine order was projected onto Taino society as the social and cultural practice of matrilineality.[101]

The following myth, explored by Robiou Lamarche, is that of the son of Yaya, Yayael. This myth is particularly important due to it representation of the first funerary rite observed in the Taino religious/cultural habitus: that of hanging baskets with the bones of the ancestors. According to Robiou Lamarche's recounting of the story, Yayael wanted to kill Yaya, and for this reason Yaya initially banishes him for four months but ends up killing him when he returns from his exile. Then, we are told that Yayael's bones were placed inside a *higüero* (a variety of gourd from the calabash tree, *Crescentia cujete*) and hung from the roof of Yaya's hut. Inside the gourd, Yayael's bones then magically transmuted into fish by themselves. This gourd, which in Ramón Pané's manuscript was called Gaia, was accidentally knocked down and then put back in its place by the four twin brothers after they had eaten some of the fish inside it.[102] The gourd then became the ocean and all the creatures within it. Hence, Yayael can be considered as the first victim, or sacrifice, of the Taino religious habitus.[103] I argue that this myth also codifies the meaning of existence as being necessarily preceded by sacrifice, which is in much alignment with Central American Amerindians' cosmology[104] and its related mythology.[105]

101. Robiou Lamarche, *Tainos and Caribs: The Aboriginal Cultures of the Antilles*, pp. 107.

102. This recollection by Robiou Lamarche demonstrates how the manuscript by Ramón Pané and his understanding of the mythology and religious habitus of the Caribbean Amerindian was as fragmentary and erroneous as de las Casas pointed out, as explored above. While the myths do not necessarily contradict, Pané's manuscript lacks this important addition of a possible Taino osteophagic rite. Also, the importance of *higüero* as an ossuary of religious significance rooted in the mythology of the Taino cannot be overstated as a potential source of influence on the beliefs and practices of Palo Monte, a fact explored in the subsection of Chapter 4 of this book, 'Ancestral Dead, Cult of the Dead, Cemis, Hanging Calabash, Gurunfinda, Cotton Idols and Nganga'.

103. Robiou Lamarche, *Tainos and Caribs: The Aboriginal Cultures of the Antilles*, p. 107.

104. For an example of this please refer to the Maya *Popol Vuh*.

105. Robiou Lamarche, *Tainos and Caribs: The Aboriginal Cultures of the Antilles*,

Robiou Lamarche tells us that the four brothers detailed in Ramón Pané's manuscript and researched above can be seen as the four cardinal points of the *ceiba*.[106] The four twin brothers, and the four cardinal points for which they stand, represent the expansion of space-time in the four cardinal directions. With this myth and the myth of the female turtle spawning from Deminán Caracaracol, the first stage of the cycle of Taino creation is complete. This stage can be encapsulated as the quadrant of time prior to the existence of the Taino.[107]

The second stage of the Taino cycle of creation relates to the creation of the Taino universe and its mythical geography. However, as explained in the section reserved for the examination of Ramón Pané's manuscript, these myths represent a retelling of Pané's work and do not inform much of this book. For this reason, I will not include the second stage of the Taino creation cycle here. However, for a concise representation of the caves, the underworld, and the movement of the sun through the four quadrants of existence, read Robiou Lamarche's representation of the Taino cosmos on page 112 of his *Tainos and Caribs: The Aboriginal Cultures of The Antilles*.[108] This is also the case for stage three of the Taino creation cycle, with perhaps the only important addition being the identification of the mythical *cacique* Anacuya and his association with the Polaris or the North Star and its linkage with the Big Dipper.[109] This correlation was utilized through the morning cycle of the Big Dipper around Polaris, which the Taino seemed to have used as a sort of climatological calendar.[110]

In Chapter 8 of *Tainos and Caribs* Robiou Lamarche further informs us that although we do not know much about geomancy in the Taino religious habitus, it informed an important part of their cultural and practical lives. The Taino used geomancy for the purpose of selecting the

---

p. 107.

106. See Juan Rubio's exploration of this myth in the subsection 'Geometric Drawings and their Representations', Martinez-Ruiz's exploration of the Kongo belief and the Palo Monte belief of the four winds found in Chapter 4 of this book for a thorough examination of this commonality between the Amerindian and the West Central African diaspora brought to the Caribbean.

107. Robiou Lamarche, *Tainos and Caribs: The Aboriginal Cultures of the Antilles*, pp. 107–10.

108. Robiou Lamarche, Sebastián, *Tainos and Caribs: The Aboriginal Cultures of the Antilles*, translated by Grace M Robiou Ramirez de Arellano (San Juan, Puerto Rico: Editorial Punto y Coma, 2019).

109. Robiou Lamarche, *Tainos and Caribs: The Aboriginal Cultures of the Antilles*, pp. 107–17.

110. Excellently depicted by Robiou Lamarche on page 114.

appropriate place for the construction of villages and ceremonial centers in accordance with the cosmic forces of nature. Therefore, they sought to keep the harmony of the microcosm with the macrocosm by the utilization and interpretation of markings on the ground, which formed patterns they read as signs in their method of divination. Robiou Lamarche further describes at length the patterns and behaviors exhibited by the Taino when building their dwellings and ceremonial huts,[111] which, as noted above, was directly influenced by this system of divination.[112] I recommend anyone interested and able to compare the construction of the Palo Monte *munanzo* and the Taino construction of their religious, social, and spatial structures, since I am not equipped for it as an outsider to the Palo Monte tradition.

Following Robiou Lamarche's exploration of the Taino, he delves into the Carib's world and its cosmology and related mythology. This section of the book is perhaps the most important contribution of Robiou Lamarche's book to my investigation. Since, as we have seen, Ramón Pané did not record any myth or cosmology of these peoples, and they remained stigmatized as cannibals and looters without much sophistication. Although originally they were the inhabitants of the Lesser Antilles and this book is concerned with the Caribbean Amerindian influence on Palo Monte, a Cuban creole religious manifestation, the Caribs were transported all across the Caribbean as forced labor.[113] Therefore, if we want to trace the Caribbean Amerindian influence on the creole religion of Palo Monte, which came about during the colonial period, we must necessarily include information on the Caribs' beliefs and practices.[114]

Since the Kallinago warriors coming from South America became engaged in a transculturation process of incorporating the Taino worldview, there must have been a synthesis of these two systems of beliefs and practices that, over time, cross-pollinated each other through the common tongue, Arawak. This occurred because during their raids on Taino chiefdoms, Caribs kidnapped Taino women, who they took as wives. These women in turn transmitted their language to their sons and

111. Robiou Lamarche, *Tainos and Caribs: The Aboriginal Cultures of the Antilles*, pp. 122–32.

112. Robiou Lamarche, *Tainos and Caribs: The Aboriginal Cultures of the Antilles*, p. 125.

113. See Chapter 4 for more on this practice by the Spanish.

114. Robiou Lamarche, *Tainos and Caribs: The Aboriginal Cultures of the Antilles*, p. 125.

daughters and busied themselves with the construction of pottery and domestic utensils which infused Carib culture with the Taino worldview. However, the first point of divergence between the Taino and the Caribs was found in their institutionalized social hierarchy or their lack thereof.[115]

Whereas the Taino chiefdoms legitimized their systems of social hierarchy as models or representations, which reflected the truths of the divine hierarchy, the Caribs had in fact quite the opposite conception. The Caribs did not have a defined social hierarchy, and as a consequence did not require the existence of a model for their social structures. The Caribs had no ruling class and in fact there were no commonly accepted deities within their worldview. As I explained above, the Caribs' social structure consisted of men and women of different ethnic backgrounds, which resulted in a worldview whose principles lay in animistic and individualistic conceptions of the world. In the Carib religious habitus, each person had a personal protective spirit, which they claimed as their personal god. There were different words for this god based on gender, with the words Ichetriku and Nechemeraku used for men and women respectively, and which became the namesake of their personal gods.[116]

Further subdivisions were prevalent in the Carib religious culture. Men called the soul *akambue*, while women called it *opoyem*, which seems to have been related to the Taino word *opia*, used to describe the soul of a person after death. There was also a name reserved for the spirit that performed good deeds; this was Icheíri if it was for a male and Chemyn or Chemíjn if it was a spirit of a female Carib. The word for women's beneficial spirits derives from the Arawak word for the Taino *cemi* of that name. On the other hand, the word for the spirit that caused chaos and performed malevolent deeds such as disruptions and upsets was called, for both men and women, Mabouya, Mapoya, or Maboya. Much like the Africans, the Caribs did not believe in evil spirits, but rather saw spirits as being potentially good or bad, and only defined as such when their behavior corresponded to one of these extremes.[117]

The Island-Caribs, as they became known in order to differentiate them from the South American Caribs due to their ethnically diverse

115. Robiou Lamarche, *Tainos and Caribs: The Aboriginal Cultures of the Antilles*, p. 125.

116. Robiou Lamarche, *Tainos and Caribs: The Aboriginal Cultures of the Antilles*, p. 216.

117. Robiou Lamarche, *Tainos and Caribs: The Aboriginal Cultures of the Antilles*, p. 216.

social constitution,[118] believed that the human body had three 'souls'. Maboya, the third of these souls, originated in the arms and was thought to move, after the death of the person in whose body it was residing, to the woods in order to become the spirit of the forest. This third soul of the body, the Caribs believed, transformed into the "evil spirits to which they attributed everything sinister and ill-fated"[119]. The second spirit or 'soul' present in the human body was called Uméku and was located in the head. This spirit went, after the death of the individual in which it re-sided, to the edge of the sea with the aim of wrecking boats.[120] This spirit may have been particularly important to the Caribs due to the pivotal role that seafaring played in their cultural and religious habitus, since, their warring and nautical lifestyle informed their centermost beliefs and practices grounded in their cosmology.[121]

The first spirit or 'soul' of the human body was called Yuanni or Lanichi and it was considered the main spirit of the human body. This spirit resided in the heart, and it moved to the otherworld after the death of the person in which it was residing. This otherworld for the Caribs was a place found in the distant west, much like the Taino belief of Coaibai (Coaybay for Robiou Lamarche).[122] Once more, I claim that the repre-sentation on earth of this place most likely should have been located on the island of Cuba, the farthest west of the islands found in the Antil-les, underscoring the importance of the veneration and propitiation of

118. However, following the standard nomenclature of Caribbean and Amerindian scholarship, I will use the term Caribs instead of Island-Caribs throughout the book as the name for these people.

119. Robiou Lamarche, *Tainos and Caribs: The Aboriginal Cultures of the Antilles*, p. 217.

120. Robiou Lamarche, *Tainos and Caribs: The Aboriginal Cultures of the Antilles*, p. 216.

121. Robiou Lamarche, *Tainos and Caribs: The Aboriginal Cultures of the Antilles*, pp. 219–24.

122. Robiou Lamarche, *Tainos and Caribs: The Aboriginal Cultures of the Antilles*, p. 216.

the ancestors through a religion[123] or cult[124] of the dead on the island of Cuba. Furthermore, the Caribs believed (much like the Vikings) that if the deceased person had been a courageous warrior in life, his main spirit would go to idyllic islands where there was abundant food, spending his time in dances, games, and parties, and where he would have Taino slaves as servants. On the other hand, if the deceased person had been

123. The sense of the word 'religion' I am trying to convey here (and throughout the book) is related to its potential pre-Christian origin rather than its modern Christian or monotheistic meaning. Although it has been clearly and definitively demonstrated that the most plausible origin for the word religion is the Latin *religio*, which the early Christian fathers, notable among them Augustine of Hippo, and modern scholars, such as its biggest proponent Emile Durkheim, have established as deriving from *religare*, which means to re-bind or to tie again, this seemingly and conveniently obviates or intellectually circumnavigates the work by Cicero on the origin of the word *religio* itself, which the Roman orator Marcus Tullius Cicero stated was derived from *relegere/religere*, which means to re-trace or to re-collect. This in turn referred to the practice of divination as one of the three pillars of Roman religion, the other two pillars being prayer and sacrifice, which are also the three pillars of all 'pagan' religions or, more appropriately, all ancient aboriginal religions, including pre-Christian European religions. I mean to use the term aboriginal in its etymological sense from the Latin word *aborigines*, which means the first inhabitants (especially of Latium) that in turn derives from the amalgam of *ab origine* (from the beginning). The reason I avoid the usage of 'pagan' is due to its historical precedent and original meaning, deriving from the Latin *paganus*, which means a country dweller or rustic individual. Although at first glance it may not seem controversial or to have any negative undertones, the word was used in antiquity as a derogatory term for those practicing polytheistic faiths as backwards and 'uncivilized' people who had not converted to the true and sophisticated monotheistic religion of Christianity. Moreover, to some modern-day spiritual descendants of these 'pagan' traditions, the word also carries emotional baggage related to the unjust crusade made again them. These 'pagans' and their traditions were persecuted in antiquity (and until recent times) by Christians after the Roman Emperor Constantine the Great or Constantine I recognized Christianity as *religio licita* (a legal religion) in 313, and later were persecuted more overtly when the Roman Emperor Theodosius I instituted Christianity as the official religion of the Roman Empire with the Edict of Thessalonica in 380. Hence, from this brief historical reconstruction rises my aspiration to call these polytheistic faiths 'religions', and to replace the word pagan for these traditions with the term 'aboriginal religions' in all subsequent scholarship of non-Abrahamic religions. Information obtained from: <https://www.newworldencyclopedia.org/entry/paganism>; <https://pemptousia.com/2017/10/emperor-constantine-and-the-theology-of-christianity-1/#:~:text=Neither%20Constantine%20nor%20Licinius%20proclaimed%20Christianity%20as%20official,the%20history%20of%20the%20Roman%20Empire%20until%20then>;   <https://www.britannica.com/biography/Theodosius-I>;   <https://www.etymonline.com/word/aborigine>; and 'The Occult Does Not Exist: A Response To Terence Ranger', *Africa*, 79, by Gerrie ter Haar and Stephen Ellis.

124. In the original sense of the word, not the modern one and its related connotations. That is: a system of religious veneration and devotion directed toward a particular figure or object.

a cowardly or timid warrior in life, his main spirit would go to a desert region where the Taino enemies reigned.[125]

Although there was no social structure and no ruling class, the Caribs had a *behique*-type figure in their communities. Their shamans[126] were called *bóyez*, *boyez* or *boye* and were in charge of the spirit world, for which they earned much respect. In fact, the *boyez* was a very distinguished and well-known person among the Caribs. The process of initiation and selection occurred while they were quite young. It was a voluntary process by which the young man would decide at an early age that he wanted to dedicate his life to being an intermediary between the spirits of the otherworld and the Caribs. The consecration occurred in the Carib *carbet*, which was a big hut used as a sacred space where the Caribs would meet when they decided to celebrate festivities or rites and which also served as a neutral space, dedicated to diplomacy with non-Carib representatives of other villages and European nations.[127] During the consecration of the *boyez*, a small opening called *tourar* was left in order to allow the *coribib chemin*[128] in, which was seen as a messenger of the afterlife and symbol of the *boyez*.[129] (See Chapter 4, subsection '*Maboya, Ndoki, the Coribib Chemin and the Lechuza*', for more on this topic).

Another festivity or ritual which was performed in the Carib *carbet* was the *caouynage*. This ritual or festivity had much in common which the Taino *areito*. However, although it was used to mark important milestones in the lives of the Caribs, it also served as a tool or platform upon which internal discords and tensions were balanced out or resolved among the Caribs, who celebrated a multiplicity of milestones and socially significant events. Examples of these events were the celebration of a male firstborn, the initiation of a warrior, the cutting of a son's hair, celebrations due to the preparation of a type of orchard they planted, the

125. Robiou Lamarche, *Tainos and Caribs: The Aboriginal Cultures of the Antilles*, pp. 216–17.

126. To use the appropriate modern terminology for these indigenous medicine men.

127. Robiou Lamarche, *Tainos and Caribs: The Aboriginal Cultures of the Antilles*, pp. 213–14.

128. A species of small owl found in the Caribbean. Scientific name: *Spéoyto cunincularia*.

129. Robiou Lamarche, *Tainos and Caribs: The Aboriginal Cultures of the Antilles*, pp. 216–17.

capture of a turtle,[130] and the construction or the launching (for raids) of canoes, among others. These *caouynages* sometimes lasted as many as eight days, such as when it used to celebrate the appointment of a captain (naval captain) and the formation of a council to oversee the plans and preparations necessary for going to war (a council of war), or for securing a safe return from war.[131]

The *caouynage* was summoned by the *ubutu* (chief) of the village,[132] which led to the gathering of about two hundred to three hundred people. These people were led by the performance of songs, the playing of *coulouras* (flutes made either of bone or wood), and were accompanied by *maracas* and drums made from hollow trees. Moreover, when the *ubutu* had called for the *caouynage*, the women would be tasked with organizing the tableware and the preparation of the cassava as well as the *uicú*, which was an intoxicating drink they drank for this purpose. Meanwhile, men were tasked with bringing fish and iguana to eat. Both men and women painted their entire bodies with different colors and designs used solely for the caouynage. Men also adorned themselves with crowns of feathers, *caracolis* (adornments made of shell), and necklaces. There were other men who smeared themselves with some sticky liquids so that when loose feathers were blown over them and they would adhere to their bodies.[133] Other than the common sense understanding that they did this for the purpose of imitating what was most likely a sacred bird, there is no recorded explanation by the French chroniclers for this behavior. As we can see from the description of the *caouynage*, this ritual performance or festivity shared some similarities with the Taino *areito*. However, the Carib ritual seemed to have been much more complex and to have been a more useful tool in Carib society than the *areito* ritual was for the Taino.

Meanwhile, inside the *carbet*, the Caribs placed offerings of fresh cassava and *uicú* over a small table called *matutu*. These offerings were part of the ritualistic veneration of the family spirits. As for the *boyez*, the elder among them was tasked with conducting a ceremony in the dark

130. This celebration's origin is curious in the face of the Taino myth of the Cara-caracol and the female turtle springing from his wound as symbols of Taino mythology.

131. Robiou Lamarche, *Tainos and Caribs: The Aboriginal Cultures of the Antilles*, pp. 213–14.

132. Not to be confused with the *caciques* who owned vast lands and were seen as powerful semi-divine entities.

133. Robiou *Tainos and Caribs: The Aboriginal Cultures of the Antilles*, pp. 213–14.

of night in which he sang mournful songs, blew tobacco smoke, and entered into a trance in the center of the *carbet*. This *boyez* invoked a god who seems to have been a much-purified god that required of the *boyez* and the entire Carib community to conduct rigorous fasting before being called upon. Moreover, the *boyez* presented the offerings while lying on a *hamaca* (hammock). If the person for whom the sessions were being conducted was a man, then this god presented itself as male, but if a woman, then this god would present itself as a goddess. Beyond these practices there are no reported religious activities among the Caribs. Along with the lack of temples and sacred figures, according to Robiou Lamarche there was an overall lack of sophistication or elaborate performance of religious belief among the Caribs. The only religious offerings recorded by the French chroniclers of the Lesser Antilles were that of the cassava, which they called *anacri*, and of the first fruit harvest that each villager could perform in the privacy of their own homes.[134]

Perhaps the only communal ceremony that united the main ideological values of the Caribs was the sacrifice of an enemy warrior. The Carib anthropophagic rite of an enemy warrior was the central ritual around which and for which Carib society revolved. It was acknowledged, even by the early French chroniclers, that this rite was the apex of an annual cycle of festive rituals performed by the Caribs and amounted to their feast of feasts. For the Caribs, all social activities were oriented towards this rite, which in their eyes manifested a communal climax of celebratory festivities. As mentioned in Ramón Pané's manuscript, this explains the lengths to which the Caribs went in order to capture enemy warriors, even sacrificing their lives in the process.

Nonetheless, the anthropophagic rite of the Caribs should not be understood as a practice aimed solely at consuming human beings, but as a complex ideology, which was informed by multiple religious and socio-cultural values. These can be condensed to the memory of their myths of origin, the commemoration of their ancestors by avenging enemies' past insults,[135] and the cyclical reaffirmation of traditional values with the objective of maintaining the social cohesion of the Kalinago[136]

134. Robiou Lamarche, *Tainos and Caribs: The Aboriginal Cultures of the Antilles*, pp. 217 & 219.

135. Due to the Caribs' lives lost in battle, which they redeemed through consuming the enemy warriors in their anthropophagic rite of the Celestial Barbacoa (Carib word from which barbecue originates).

136. Modern alternative word for Carib.

warrior lifestyle. I have included this paragraph in order to address their most important religious ritual, which constituted the zenith of their religious calendar and as mentioned above, the *axis mundi* on which their entire socio-religious habitus revolved. Simultaneously, I wished to address the continually expressed misconceptions about the Caribs' cannibalistic practices and supposedly belligerent disposition, which contradicts their observed amicability towards the French and other village representatives during peacetimes.[137 & 138] However, due to the nature of this book, this ritual will not merit further discussion, because it does not seem to have any parallel or replication in the Palo Monte liturgy.[139]

The Carib *boyez*, as a tribal shaman, was concerned with controlling the spirits rather than appeasing the gods. He played four main roles within Carib society. Mainly, the intervention of the *boyez* was sought when he was needed to cure an illness, to avenge a wrong received by someone seeking his consultation, to declare his inspired decision about the appropriateness of pursuing war, and lastly to declare his powers over the spirits in order to expel an evil spirit tormenting a villager. Unlike the Taino, the Caribs did not go to see the ill man or woman, for fear of exacerbating their illness. Therefore, the services of the *boyez* played an essential role in the ordinary lives of the Caribs. The healing ceremony performed by the *boyez* was much like that of the *behique*, with the difference being that an extraction of either stones of particulate matter (bound together) was not performed. Although the *boyez* did rub the skin of the sick person he was attending to, and blew and sucked on the patients like the *behique* did, their aim was directed at extracting or removing the spirit that had caused the disease and not the stone or particulate matter.

137. Robiou Lamarche, *Tainos and Caribs: The Aboriginal Cultures of the Antilles*, pp. 213–14.

138. Robiou Lamarche, *Tainos and Caribs: The Aboriginal Cultures of the Antilles*, pp. 226–30.

139. For a more profound and insightful philosophical exploration of the role and function of sacrifice, and limit experiences like cannibalism , as recorded in Carib society, please refer to Georges Bataille's *The Accursed Share: An Essay On General Economy (Volumes I, II & III)* and *Erotism: Death & Sensuality*.

They also did not make use of the *cohoba* or *güeyo*.[140] Instead, they used the tobacco smoke as a *panacea*.[141]

The rest of the information preserved on the Carib worldview (its mythologies and practices) is directly related to the cosmic forces and the celestial bodies. Due to the high complexity[142] of these belief systems and their focus on the celestial bodies and primacy of these forces as the center of their practices and views, I will not delve deeply into their cosmology. Although the Palo Mayombe branch sees the origin of the supernatural forces giving life to the *nganga* and the *nfumbe* as celestial,[143] its cosmology (although equally advanced and scientifically admirable) differs greatly from that of the Caribs in its explanation and outlook on these forces.[144] Hence, what follows is a short summary of the Carib reli-

140. Although Robiou Lamarche does not provide a description of this plant, I was able to find a historical note by the great Cuban anthropologist and ethnologist Fernando Ortiz about a plausible modern day equivalent of this substance used by the Caribbean Amerindians. On page 176 of the second edition of *Contrapunteo del Tabaco y el Azúzar: Advertencia de sus Contrastes Agrarios, Económicos, Históricos y Sociales, su Etnografía y su Transculturación* he writes: '*Entre los indios de las Guayana el tabaco suele ser mascado, para lo cual se mezcla con ciertas cenizas de gusto salado que se obtienen de una especie de alga (Mourera fluvialis, Aubl.) que recogen junto a las cascadas de los ríos, llamada por los indios "weya".*' [Translation: Among the Guyana Amerindians (South American Arawak speakers), tobacco is usually chewed. Before they chew on it however, they include an admixture of some specific ashes they obtain from a species of algae (*Mourera fluviatilis*; the correct Latin binomial nomenclature based on Linnaean Taxonomy), which gives a salty taste to the final mixture. These algae are found next to river cascades from where they collect it. The Guyana Amerindians call it '*güeya*'.] Although referring to the Amerindians from Guyana of South America, these indigenous people (as explained in the historical introduction of the chapter) are the living descendants of their common South American ancestors. Also, as Arawak speakers like the Taino and the Caribs (to some extent), their culture and language pose a plausible linkage to the intellectual and material culture of these insufficient historical, linguistic, and archaeological reconstructions. Yet other more modern scholars have concluded that the *güeyo* most likely referred to the coca plant (*Erythroxylum coca*); please refer to 'Españoles y Hoja de Coca a Mediados del Siglo XVI en el Antiguo Perú-I: Contacto con la Coca', *De re Metallica* (Madrid), 29, by Enrique Orche García for a concise exploration of this possibility.

141. Robiou Lamarche, *Tainos and Caribs: The Aboriginal Cultures of the Antilles*, pp. 217 & 219.

142. In my opinion, which goes against Robiou Lamarche's opinion of Caribs' religious beliefs and practices as being less sophisticated than the Taino.

143. Rojas Calderon, *Palo Brakamundo*, pp. 160–61.

144. For a further and more thorough explanation of these cosmological belief systems see Robiou Lamarche's *Tainos and Caribs: The Aboriginal Cultures of the Antilles*, pages 231 through 261, for the Caribs' cosmological belief system, and Kimbwandende Kia Bunseki Fu-Kiau's *African Cosmology of the Bantu-Kongo: Tying the Spiritual Knot*,

gious habitus provided for the benefit of the scholar reading this book, in case there are commonalities I may have missed.

First, we must keep in mind that due to the syncretic process by which Carib society was built over time, there are shared beliefs and practices between them and the Taino. However, due to the second wave of migrating of Kalinago warriors from South America, who brought with them their traditional views,[145] the Carib systems ended up being the first syncretic experiment of the Caribbean. Overall, they shared an animistic religious habitus, but with a highly developed and sophisticated cosmological basis. Although there was a belief in the spirits of nature (as we have seen) among the Caribs, there were also other beliefs that played a critical role. An example of this was the belief shared by the Caribs of the celestial Great Serpent found in the constellation of Bakámo.[146] This constellation was what is today referred to as the astrological constellation of Scorpius, although in its entirety it stretched from Scorpius ($\mathbb{M}$; ♀ or ☿) through Sagittarius ($\nearrow$; ♃) and ending in Capricorn ($\mathrm{v}\mathrm{s}$; ♄), which constituted the head, body, and tail respectively of the Great Serpent they referred to as Bakámo.[147]

The importance of this cosmology for understanding the beliefs and practices of the Caribs is directly tied to the *boyez*; according to the Caribs, the Great Serpent was associated with the *boyez*. For this reason, it received veneration and tobacco offerings. The Caribs believed that the Great Serpent was the bearer of the magic plant called *toúlála*.[148] Caribs believed they had acquired this plant, the essence of which was the benevolent forces of nature, directly from the Great Serpent. Hence, from this plant they made amulets, which they wore as protection against the malignant forces of the Maboya.[149] They were also able to make a sort of antidote against the poisonous arrows used by the Taino, which bolstered their beliefs about the divine origin of the plant.

Principles of Life & Living for the Bantu-Kongo and Palo Mayombe cosmological belief system.

145. With some modifications that seemed to have occurred over time.

146. Robiou Lamarche, *Tainos and Caribs: The Aboriginal Cultures of the Antilles*, p. 262.

147. Robiou Lamarche, *Tainos and Caribs: The Aboriginal Cultures of the Antilles*, pp. 248–49.

148. The arrowroot, *Maranta arundinacea*; a small and edible tuber.

149. Robiou Lamarche, *Tainos and Caribs: The Aboriginal Cultures of the Antilles*, p. 262.

Moreover, the location and movement of the celestial bodies and stars informed and directed the social life of the Caribs. The main idea shared by the Caribs was that these celestial bodies and the cosmos in general was the place of residence of the spirits of earthly things. Hence, they saw these celestial bodies as analogous to objects, plants, animals, and their ancestors. Therefore, when these celestial bodies were visible from earth, the Caribs saw them as spirits descending to earth to visit them.[150]

The cosmology of the Carib religious habitus focused on the origin of things in the celestial bodies, constellations, and stars. It informed and governed the social structure and life of the Carib people. For example, the presence of the Celestial Turtle (Catáluyuman) was the source of the spawning ability of the sea turtles. Another example of this was the departure of the Big Dipper, the Celestial Canoe (Lukúni-yáruba), which marked the beginning of their expeditions and their raids on enemy villages.

Nonetheless, the Carib religious habitus contains a contradictory and yet interdependent system of beliefs, which played a complimentary role in their social life. This can be seen in the Carib beliefs explaining the absence or disappearance of celestial bodies. An important example of this is when the absence of the Isúla[151] in the sky indicated that the ban on felling the *ceiba* for the purposes of building a canoe was lifted, and the *ceiba* could be cut once more after it had lost all its leaves. Another important contradictory and complementary belief within their religious habitus is the Carib myth of the Maboya eating the moon and sometimes a piece of the sun. According to the Caribs, the Maboya, which had a human origin, went through a transformation inside the forest once it had left the human body, after which it elevated itself to the sky or celestial spheres in order to perform an act of cannibalism in which it ate pieces of the moon and sometimes the sun.[152] This in turn brought about a cosmic imbalance, epitomized by an eclipse, which represented the negative aspect of cannibalism with its antisocial potential.[153]

Although the *ceiba* was seen as the World Tree by the Caribs and was respected as much as it was in the Taino and Maya society, the Caribs

150. Robiou Lamarche, *Tainos and Caribs: The Aboriginal Cultures of the Antilles*, p. 262.

151. The celestial constellation that marked the beginning of the Celestial Barbecue when present in the sky, and permission to fell the *ceiba* for building canoes when absent.

152. I imagine this myth was created to explain lunar phases and rare solar eclipses.

153. Robiou Lamarche, *Tainos and Caribs: The Aboriginal Cultures of the Antilles*, p. 262.

differed in their beliefs about it. Mainly, the *ceiba* was seen in connection with Acáyouman (Cayman), which was in turn inherently related to the Milky Way. Acáyouman was the mythical character who provided the basis for the anthropophagic rite of the Caribs. This mythical character in turn is based on the first Kalinago naval captain who arrived in the Eastern Antilles and who ate and exterminated all the natives of these islands. After his death, at the hands of his own children and grandchildren who poisoned him for his cruelties,[154] he became a monstrous fish called Akeuman, a term that means 'he still lives in a river full of life'.[155]

The word Akeuman[156] corresponds to the word *acáyouma*, which means Cayman. Through this mythical story, the historical ancestor became the mythical character Acáyouman, who became known as the father of the Kalinago lineage and was immortalized as a monstrous fish in the celestial vault (♌ ♉). The river full of life, in which the mythical character was said to reside, was none other than the Milky Way. The Caribs conceptualized this Celestial River as the origin of creation that connected and communicated with the sky and the earth.[157]

Thus, Acáyouman[158] was likened to the established anthropophagic rite practiced by the Caribs during the months of September and October. Caribs called this month[159] *mubé*, which was also the name they gave to the Caribbean *jobo* tree. The reason they named the *jobo* tree *mubé* was because that was the season in which the tree bore fruits. The *jobo* tree also had an important mythological basis in the religious habitus of the Caribs. Carib mythology tells us that when Acáyouman needed a tree to sculpt his daughter, he made use of the *jobo* tree. In contrast, the *jobo* tree in Taino mythology was the tree from which asexual beings descended

154. Such as torturing, eating, and adorning his throne room with the spiked heads of his enemies as well as Kalinago warriors he thought had disobeyed, failed, or betrayed him.

155. Robiou Lamarche, *Tainos and Caribs: The Aboriginal Cultures of the Antilles*, pp. 231–32.

156. This story was collected in and originates from modern day Dominica, the place where he was said to reside and which seems to have had a dialect of the Kalinago language.

157. Robiou Lamarche, *Tainos and Caribs: The Aboriginal Cultures of the Antilles*, pp. 231–32.

158. The Celestial Cayman and the Spirit of the Old Father, which represented the Milky Way, and which was seen in the sky during the months of September and October.

159. The two Gregorian months of September and October were interpreted as one station of the celestial and/or ritual calendar.

and which was later carved by the Inriri (woodpecker) into women. For these reasons, Robiou Lamarche concludes that the anthropophagic rite practiced by the Caribs can be traced back to the legend of Acáyouman, which, as his name may suggest, was the father of the lineage that established anthropophagy as well as the beginning of warrior expeditions in canoes across the Caribbean Sea.[160]

In this respect, the *ceiba* was associated with Acáyouman, since, as we have seen above, the canoes the Caribs used during the months of September and October were made from it when the Isúla was absent in the night sky. These canoes served as the vehicles by which the Caribs could purposefully conduct raids across the Antilles for the sole purpose of capturing enemies in order to perform the cannibalistic ritual for which they became so famous and stigmatized. However, the *ceiba* was also seen as the abode of the Great Spirit of the Trees and was much respected and guarded for this reason.[161] Notwithstanding, these were not the only sources of contradiction in the Carib religious habitus.

Other interdependent, contradictory, and complementary belief systems were manifest through the variations of Carib worldview recorded among the different islands of the Lesser Antilles. An example from Dominica, which demonstrates the differences in the dialect of the Kalinago language, is that of Olubera, the Great Serpent. As explored above, for the rest of the Caribs outside Dominica this serpent was called Bakámo and was seen as an all-around beneficial and benevolent force of the universe. However, for the Caribs of Dominica, Olubera was both beneficial, but could also kill if specific terms of devotion and sacrificial propitiation were not followed. This duality observed in the mythology of the Caribs from Dominica may result from their closeness to the actual historical figure Acáyouman, which as I mentioned above was ultimately killed by his male descendants due to his tyrannical reign. I deduce that the distance in time and space offered to the other Caribs from spatially separated islands was the potential for a gradual progression of exaltation by which this historical figure developed from a tyrannical ruler to a mythologized and romanticized deity. I conclude that this process most likely occurred due to sentimental longing or from nostalgia for their

160. Robiou Lamarche, *Tainos and Caribs: The Aboriginal Cultures of the Antilles*, pp. 231–32.

161. Robiou Lamarche, *Tainos and Caribs: The Aboriginal Cultures of the Antilles*, p. 262.

perceived golden age of seafaring and warring expeditions, resulting in a total distortion of the true historical individual.[162]

Other examples include the *juluca* (rainbow), which was interpreted as evil if seen on land because it could cause death, but which was also interpreted as beneficial if seen at sea. According to Robiou Lamarche, this difference most likely arose because the navigational season of the Carib naval warriors followed the Atlantic hurricane season, which is one of the rainy seasons, and a rainbow would have meant the end of these storms on the seas. Solar or diurnal birds such as the *guaraguao* (the red-tailed hawk; *Buteo jamaicensis*) and the *yeretté*,[163] which were associated with life, were also seen in contradiction with the *coribib chemin*, the messenger bird of the afterlife and a nocturnal animal. Yet another important contradictory opposition found in the worldview of the Caribs was between the *toúlála* plant and what they considered its rival, the poisonous plant, *mancenillier* or *manchineel* (*Hippomane mancinella*), which informed the war and peace aspects of the Carib worldview and its complex practices.[164]

Although Roberto G. Muñoz-Pando's paper on the mortuary beliefs of the Taino and Caribs contains a large amount of previously explored information, there are a few things the author was able to compile about their mortuary beliefs that have not been included above. Once again, instead of providing all the information found in his paper, I will only add those details that are relevant to my investigation, and which have not been previously discussed. Since the paper was supervised by Sebastián Robiou Lamarche and deals solely with the mortuary beliefs and practices of the Taino and Caribs, exploring this paper was the logical next step in my investigation of the Caribbean Amerindian influence on the Afro-Caribbean religions. Also, since the cult of the dead, the veneration and propitiation of one's ancestry, and mortuary rituals are an integral part of the Palo Monte religion, exploring these rituals and beliefs may open previously untrodden paths of influence found in this creole religious manifestation. Therefore, Muñoz-Pando's paper will be used as the last

---

162. Robiou Lamarche, *Tainos and Caribs: The Aboriginal Cultures of the Antilles*, pp. 254 & 262–63.

163. The Caribbean hummingbird of which there are four distinct species; of importance due to the myth of the ascendency of Luna (the moon) to the sky and the hummingbird bringing its daughter Híali, a product of an incestuous relationship with her brother, which is rewarded by Luna's father.

164. Robiou Lamarche, *Tainos and Caribs: The Aboriginal Cultures of the Antilles*, pp. 254 & 262–63.

source of information on the Caribbean Amerindians before we move on
to the actual investigative research on their increasingly plausible influence on the beliefs and practices of modern Afro-Caribbean religions.

The first important piece of information provided by Muñoz-Pando
not yet investigated above is his archival recovery of Dr. Agustín Stahl's
investigation of Gonzalo Fernández de Oviedo Valdés, known simply as
Oviedo, who related that there was a *cacique* (necessarily Taino due to his
title) who died and was interred with two of his still-living wives. Apparently, Oviedo writes, this was done against their will. Although I have this
book in its original form,[165] it is rather illegible due to its font and archaic
form of Spanish, which I am not able to fully comprehend. However, as
Muñoz-Pando tells us, Stahl believed that we should not trust this story
as credible. Stahl believed it represented a joke on the gullible Oviedo.
Moreover, Stahl believed that this story was nothing more than the wea-
ponizing of a false story by the Spanish as a propaganda tool in order to
exterminate the supposedly savage and barbaric Caribbean Amerindians.[166] I agree with Stahl's observation because it falls directly in line with
our decolonial project of disentangling the historical trope of indigenous
extinction in the Caribbean.[167]

Muñoz-Pando writes about another finding by Stahl in which we
are told that when the *caciques* died, they were wrapped from head to toe
in a tight-fitting cotton shroud. Then the Taino would make a hole in the
earth with wooden walls as support, where they would sit the dead *cacique* on a small bench made of wood. The hole contained the bench, victuals, armaments,[168] and adornments[169] for the journey or life after death.
Apparently, the Taino did this so that the body of the *cacique* would be
interred in a sort of funeral vault, a process they would ceremonially follow with performance of *areitos*.

Although this is recorded as a ritual done for a *cacique* (both male
and female), the fact of the matter is that it is not known whether this was

165. G. Fernández de Oviedo y Valdés, *Sumario de la Natural Historia de las Indias*
(Toledo: Biblioteca Nacional de España, 1526).

166. Which I find remarkable for a work published in 1889: Agustin Stahl, *Los Indios Borinqueños. Estudios Etnográficos.*

167. Roberto G. Muñoz-Pando, *Creencias Mortuorias de los Aborígenes Antillanos,
Taínos Y Caribes,* Estudio Etnohistórico Y Social. Análisis de los Taínos y Caribes: et-
nohistoria, arqueologia y literature oral (San Juan, Puerto Rico: Centro de Estudios
Avanzados de Puerto Rico y el Caribe, n.d.), 6.

168. Including *macanas* (a surviving Taino word) as well as bows and arrows.

169. Including lithic rings and jewels.

a practice that was reserved only for the *caciques* or if it included *naborías* (common man or woman), *nitaínos*,[170] and the *behiques*. Nonetheless, Stahl concludes that the most likely scenario was that these social classes within the Taino social hierarchy probably had less elaborate burials, which were done on the outskirts of the *yucayeque* (the Taino villages). A practice we can say with absolutely certainty (according to Stahl) was not part of the Taino religious and cultural habitus was the practice of cremation. Although there are no known Taino cemeteries, a practice such as cremation would have been too scandalous (according to Stahl) for the early Spanish chroniclers, because it went against the Christian funerary practices of the epoch.[171]

As for the Caribs, their funerary rituals were apparently better preserved through multiple extant documentations written by French chroniclers, who were more conscientious than the Spanish chroniclers were when it came to the Taino. For example, it was recorded by the French chroniclers that when a Carib warrior died in battle, his compatriots would do everything humanly possible to recover his body so that it would not be eaten by the enemy. They would rather sacrifice all the spoils of war and even their own lives for the religious necessity of burying the body of their own in their own lands, something that went beyond the concern that the dead warrior would be cannibalized. The Caribs practiced a highly complex funerary ritual, which fortunately has been preserved. First, the Caribs would make a pit in the middle of the *bohío*, which was three feet in depth. Then they would wash the body, the feet, and the head of the deceased, and rub it with oil as well. Later, they would wrap the body in a newly made cotton shroud, which they would then put in the pit in a fetal position with the feet pointing downs toward the center of the earth. Apparently, unlike the Taino, the Caribs did not place victuals or armaments in the tomb of the deceased. After the corpse was placed inside in the aforementioned manner, a big plank of wood was placed over it.[172]

The Carib funerary rituals also consisted of a various cultural displays of emotions or lack thereof. These consisted of an exaggerated

170. A sort of royal or noble class of warriors, much like the medieval knights of Europe.

171. Muñoz-Pando, *Creencias Mortuorias De Los Aborígenes Antillanos, Taínos Y Caribes*, 6–7 & 9.

172. Muñoz-Pando, *Creencias Mortuorias de los Aborígenes Antillanos, Taínos Y Caribes*, 6–7, 9 & 14.

wailing performance by the women, while their husbands would console them in a stoic and expressionless matter. Gloomy songs would also be sung by the women, while some of them threw earth over the pit with their hands. Once it had been sealed, the Caribs would construct a fire over the pit in which the clothes of the deceased were burnt, if they were not given away by the family. Moreover, those family members close to the deceased would cut their hair as a sign of mourning. If the deceased had slaves, they would either be killed or be freed at the discretion of the family. Another important practice performed by the Caribs was that of fasting. Apparently, this was not done for the benefit of the deceased, but for the benefit of the living so that they may continue to experience good fortune.[173]

If there was a family member who was unable to attend the funeral, it was obligatory for them to visit the tomb at a later time.[174] On the anniversary of the death of the individual and once the corpse had decomposed, the close family members of the would gather together again in order to go through a second cultural display of mourning and remembrance. This consisted of wailing, dramatic bouts of fits in which the women would hit the floor, and a somber presence by the men. However, on this one-year anniversary of the death of the deceased Carib, the entire community would partake of the ceremonial and intoxicating drink called *uicú*. The French chroniclers tell us that they drank this beverage for the purpose of easing their miseries and memories of the deceased. Although the Carib cultural and religious habitus was based on a gerontocracy informed by oral traditions, much like the Taino, this seems to have been the only recorded tribute or veneration of the ancestors performed by the Caribs. This absence of Carib rituals relating to the veneration and appropriation of the ancestors runs in sharp contrast to the Taino practices relating to the dead, a fact that remains baffling to Caribbean and Amerindian scholar to this day.[175] In conclusion, the funerary beliefs and practices of the Taino and Caribs consisted of highly elaborate rituals infused with codified cultural and religious meanings that we are not able to decipher today. Although in the Afro-Caribbean religions there are funerary rites reserved for the *santero/santera*, *babalawo*, and *tata nkisi* or *ngangulero*,

173. Muñoz-Pando, *Creencias Mortuorias De Los Aborígenes Antillanos, Taínos Y Caribes*, 6–7.

174. In order to pay respect to, and to attract good fortune and blessings to/from the dead.

175. Muñoz-Pando, *Creencias Mortuorias De Los Aborígenes Antillanos*, 11 & 13.

called Itutu (cooling) and Llanto (crying) respectively, do not resemble the Caribbean Amerindian practices, but rather seem more like Lucumi and Kongo preservations.[176]

176. Please refer to *Muerte, muertos y "llanto" palero* by Ana Stela de Almeida Cunha for a somewhat extensive treatment of this funerary ritual of Palo Monte. Also, please refer to *Itutu: El Libro De Los Muertos* by Cecilio Pérez Obá Ecún for the most extensive book on the *Itutu* funerary rites.

4

Religious Syncretism

Amerindian Contributions to the Afro-Caribbean Kongo-Derived Religion of Palo Monte

"Maza matia keyokanga nlele ko"
"Agua hirviendo no quema la ropa"[1]
"Boiling water does not burn clothes"

—PALO MONTE PROVERB

Introduction

FOR A STUDY OF the Amerindian influence on the religion of Palo Monte to be complete, it is essential to begin with a historical reconstruction of the context in which these two communities encountered each other. This should lead us to a history of the African and Amerindian marronage and the creation of *palenques* as alternative societies or counterhegemonic cultures offering opportunities for both communities to preserve their traditions in colonial Cuba. By communicating and cohabitating freely and away from the predatory behavior and the prying eyes of the Spanish and their Catholicism, the African runaway slave and the Amerindian native were able to share and exchange their religious habitus with one another. Their purpose was to increase their chances of survival by finding similar ground upon which to build their codependent existence. Based on the elements of the religious habitus of the African and the

---

1. *Refranes de Palo.* n.d. p. 2

Caribbean Amerindian, it is not difficult to comprehend how the most important contributions to the Afro-Cuban religion of Palo Monte from the Amerindian natives should have unfolded in the bowels of these self-contained *palenques*.

Confronted with the present need for survival and adaptation to the new flora and fauna of the Caribbean, and the new socio-political context, the Kongo Maroons most likely saw refuge in the cosmogony, cosmology, and cosmovision of the native Amerindians. My hypothesis is that the Kongo Maroons fused the Caribbean Amerindian religious habitus with their own traditional beliefs and practices, especially where these equipped them or served them with the appropriate tools for dealing with life and its new demands in the Caribbean landscape. Following this line of thinking and based on information provided by Chinea in his excellent academic paper,[2] I have identified some signs of the Amerindian influence on Palo Monte and its contemporary expressions among descendants of the Kongo Maroon in Cuba. It would seem to be a profitable approach if we start with the history of the Maroons and their *palenque* societies as spaces of dialogue and fusion of religious and cultural goods.

Entangled Histories: African and Amerindian Cultural and Religious Connections

Cimarronaje, Cimarrones, Palenques, Behiques, Boyez, Paleros and Santeros

The phenomenon of marronage[3] was a common tool used by both communities in the Caribbean and the Americas. The Caribbean Amerindians and the African slaves brought to the Caribbean used this form of resistance as a last resort attempt to reclaim their freedom. This diasporic

2. Jorge L. Chinea, 'Diasporic Marronage: Some Colonial and Intercolonial Repercussions of Overland and Waterborne Slave Flight, With Special Reference to the Caribbean Archipelago', *Revista Brasileira Do Caribe, Associação Caruaruense De Ensino Superior Brasil* X (2009), 259–84 <doi:1518–6784>.

3. For the most extensive and well researched book on the *palenques* and the phenomenon of marronage in Eastern Cuba during the 18th and 19th centuries, please refer to *Los Cimarrones de Cuba* by Gabino la Rosa Corzo. The reason why I have not used this excellent book in my investigation is precisely because of its emphasis on the eastern part of Cuba and its late date range. Hence, the data in the book does not represent the actual manifestation of the phenomenon of marronage across the entire island of Cuba. Nonetheless, it is the best book to date on the subject matter and I recommend it as further reading.

marronage (as Chinea names it) constituted an important part of the colonial era, both for the Spanish (in a negative sense) and for the Indigenous and African slaves (in a positive sense). The phenomenon of marronage across the Caribbean challenged the Spanish hegemony (in both religious and authoritative terms) via the establishment of *aldeas/ palenques* on the outskirts (mostly in the mountains and forests) of town in which were created social and economic networks with slaves, pirates, contrabandists, and representatives of other competing colonial and rival nations.[4] Most interesting and informative about these rebel societies is the etymology of the word *cimarrón* (maroon) itself, which originates from the amalgamation of the Hispanicized Taino expression *cima* (used for undomesticated plants and animals) and the Spanish word for the peak of a mountain.[5] Hence, by the utilization of this word we can perhaps conclude that the cohabitation and establishment of these *palenques* by both the Caribbean Indigenous and African Maroons was a common feature of the colonial era.

The overall picture of the Maroons today is a split one, with some writers declaring these individuals as heroes, warriors, masters of the wilderness, freedom fighters, and keepers of African spiritual values,[6] and others, especially European writers, describing them as harassers, kidnappers, killers, and robbers who stuck stubbornly to their 'primitive' ways in their *palenques* in complete disconnection from the rest

4. Chinea, 'Diasporic Marronage: Some Colonial and Intercolonial Repercussions of Overland and Waterborne Slave Flight', 259–62.

5. Chinea, 'Diasporic Marronage: Some Colonial and Intercolonial Repercussions of Overland and Waterborne Slave Flight', 263.

6. For a historical source that reveals the African diaspora habitus, its resulting position (as described), and its inevitable manifestation as the phenomenon of marronage and the Maroons, please refer to *Biografía de un cimarrón* by Miguel Barnet and Esteban Montejo. It preserves the testimonial narrative of Esteban Montejo, a former slave, Maroon, and later soldier of the Revolutionary Wars, as told to Cuban ethnographer Miguel Barnet. The book provides the best first-hand account of the phenomenon of marronage, Maroons, slavery, sugar plantations, sugar mills, and *palenques*. Invaluable information about the language, religion, music, and customs of the 19th-century African diaspora in Cuba are also provided.

of the civilized world[7, 8] Chinea observes that, as a mode of survival, much of the dissemination of African culture in the Caribbean occurred thanks to the efforts of the black Maroons to throw the Europeans off their trail by traveling long distances by land and water and setting up communication networks with different members of the strata of society (including sympathizing Whites). Moreover, this diasporic marronage included the curious phenomenon described by David Waldstreicher as 'self-fashioning', which consisted of African Maroons impersonating free Blacks, mestizos, and (more importantly for our research) Amerindians. According to Rubén Silié, this included adopting the cultural markers of these individuals and hence through performance, integrating their cultural beliefs and practices through embodied cultural performance.[9] See Yolanda Covington-Ward's introduction to her book *Gesture and Power: Religion, Nationalism, and Everyday Performance in Congo*[10] for a full discussion of this theory as applied to African and Afro-Caribbean religions and the Congo religious landscape in particular.

The aforementioned performative phenomenon seems to have been formally recorded in the liturgy of Palo Monte. This is evident in my transcription of the spiritual invocation song at the beginning of the book titled *Cajón pa' los muertos, Canto a los indios* (Box Drumming for the Dead, Singing to the Amerindians), where the following phrase *Yo tengo un congo que viste de indio, yo tengo un indio que viste de congo* translates as 'I have a Congo who dresses like an Amerindian, I have an Amerindian

7. For a historical source that reveals the Spanish habitus and its resulting position on the phenomenon of marronage and the Maroons (as described) please refer to *Diario del Rancheador* by Cirilo Villaverde. However, I would like to mention that although the book is historically ascribed to Cirilo Villaverde (author of *Cecilia Valdés*), the diary was originally orally dictated by *rancheador* Francisco Estévez to his daughter, later copied in 1843 by Cirilo Villaverde, and only published in 1982. The book provides the best account of the institutionalized persecution of Maroons and its manifested systemic racism, brutality, and cruelty promulgated and perpetrated by the Spanish. The reason why this diary is particularly poignant is that the figure of the *rancheador* (runaway slave–hunter or Maroon herder) embodies the microcosm of the entire Spanish macrocosm of dispositions towards marronage and Maroons. The 1976 movie *Rancheador* by Sergio Giral is based on the book and can be found at: <https://www.youtube.com/watch?v=dq9aPz8pWGY>.

8. Chinea, 'Diasporic Marronage: Some Colonial and Intercolonial Repercussions of Overland and Waterborne Slave Flight', 263.

9. Chinea, 'Diasporic Marronage: Some Colonial and Intercolonial Repercussions of Overland and Waterborne Slave Flight', 265.

10. Yolanda Covington-Ward, *Gesture and Power: Religion, Nationalism, and Everyday Performance in Congo* (Durham, NC: Duke University Press, 2018).

who dresses like a Congo'. Hence, if we take performance theory as a foundation for understanding the diffusion and survival strategy of the African Maroons in escaping the European attempts at eradicating mar-ronage, together with the fact that they had set up establishments in conjunction with Caribbean Amerindians, it would not be a stretch to conclude that the adoption and fusion of Amerindian beliefs and prac-tices was much more pervasive than we would otherwise imagine.

As a side note, it is worth mentioning that the original language, *habla bozal*, used in the song performed in the actual liturgical cycle of Palo Monte refers to the Carib Amerindians as Carire and Cariré rather than Caribe (as I have it in my transcription). This highly creolized Palo Monte liturgical language is called *habla bozal*, which is a Spanish term. The term *bozal* (the noun 'muzzle') refers to the apparatus that is fastened around the nose and mouth of an animal so that it may not bite; both in Spanish and in English it also has another level of meaning, as the process by which a person or a group is prevented from expressing them-selves and their opinions freely. Here the word *bozal* (the verb 'muzzled') demonstrates the scars left by the colonial wound (   ). The word *habla* means speech, speak, or language. This reminder unfortunately supports the Spanish language being enforced by the Spanish secular and religious hegemony and leaves no doubt as to the impact it had on the Amerindian and African socioreligious experience.

In Spanish, the word Caribe is both the word for the Caribs and the Caribbean. El Caribe (the Caribbean) took its name from the Caribs which was itself the name given to these people by the Taino and which the Spanish used to label them and the Caribbean territories. This conclusion is also supported by the used of Carire in the spiritual invocation song at the end of the book titled *Toque de Palo Monte, Buena Noche* where the following phrase, based on my own transcription, *¡Mundo Nuevo Carire!* *¡Mundo Nuevo Carire!* translates as 'Caribbean New World! Caribbean New World!' demonstrating the versatility and twofold meaning of the word in the *habla bozal* Conga.

Although one may be tempted to proclaim that this mispronuncia-tion of the Caribs is the result of the broken Spanish spoken by the Kongo slaves, which ended up being preserved throughout the generations, I conclude otherwise. The reason for my revisionary attempt is based on the understanding of the stigma surrounding the Caribs. As was explored in Chapter 3, the Caribs were stigmatized and nominalized as less-than-human cannibals, whose rights as legitimate human beings were refuted on the basis of their cannibalistic practices. By contrast, the Taino, which in the spiritual invocation song are referred as Siboney (a term used to differentiate the Taino of Western and Central Cuba from the Taino of Eastern Cuba, Hispaniola, and Puerto Rico, known as Classical Tainos), were extended (to a limited scope) these rights and were seen as superior and more sophisticated than the Caribs in the eyes of the Spanish. The fact that the Taino are named properly in the spiritual invocation song, while the Caribs are not, supports my conclusion.

This stigma represented a dilemma for the Kongo descendants whose practices were already under the watchful and scrutinizing eyes of the Spanish. Hence, beyond veiling their Kimpungulu with Spanish Catholic Saints, they must have also changed the name of the Caribs in their practices to that of Carire or Cariré with the aim of diverting any potentially dangerous or injurious suspicion and association with the Caribs and their practices. Following this line of thinking then, it is extremely propitious and of paramount importance to investigate the Palo Monte liturgy El Mundo Nuevo Carire (The Carib New World). I proclaim that under this thin veil of mispronunciation the entire Carib religious habitus was preserved. As the title suggests, this sub-nation of Palo Monte seems to have preserved the entirety of Carib beliefs and practices under the liturgy of Palo Monte. As I have been able to glean from Osvaldo Sesti's YouTube channel[11], this sub-nation of Palo Monte has its own liturgy (although closely related to the traditional liturgy of Palo Monte) complete with its own names for the Kimpungulu as well as its own *patimpemba*.

Unfortunately, this sub-nation remains highly veiled, and to my knowledge, nothing has been written on it. Therefore, I encourage those experts and practitioners who are knowledgeable of El Mundo Nuevo Carire to investigate it using my book as a guide so that these Amerindian beliefs and practices can be reclaimed and preserved under their proper Amerindian provenance. For these reasons, when I was completing my transcription of the song I decided to 'fix' the historical necessity of us-ing the misnomer Carire or Cariré instead of the proper name Caribe in order to decolonize the liturgy. In doing so, I hope to restore the Caribs as legitimate contributors and agents in the religious and cultural field of the Caribbean.

11. *https://www.youtube.com/user/OsvaldoSesti*

Now, returning to the main findings being discussed in this chapter, we also need to know something about the nature of these *palenques*. According to George Brandon, *palenques* consisted of scattered cabins with attached plots of cultivated land (resembling the *conucos*[12] of the Amerindians). These communities hidden in the belly of the wilderness depended on a defense strategy utilizing pits full of hardwood poles sunk into the ground, which were deliberately forked and sharpened to a knifepoint. The Maroons also depended on their ability to secure pistols and rifles from white contrabandists, pirates, and representatives of other colonial nations which wanted to support the insurrection of these runaway slaves against their former masters. Following this, Brandon tells us that although some *palenques* may have constituted an ethnically

---

12. Taino term that means plots of cultivated land, which are generally small and consist of small mounds of buried agricultural goods and staves protruding from inside a mound. I conjecturally extrapolate that the current practice of constructing a *nganga* inside the cauldron, utilizing varied types of earth, combined with the *palos* (sticks) placed inside the *nganga* in much the same manner as in the *conucos* which become the spiritual staves of the *nkisi* and the *nfumbe* and serve as the structural skeleton or conduit of the forces of nature manifested in the *nganga* and the universe, derives from this Amerindian agricultural practice. As support I use the anecdote recorded by Pané regarding the Taino who on one occasion stole several Christian images and threw them upon soil that was to be cultivated, covered them with earth and urinated on them. Though Pané never uses the word *conuco*, I conclude that these images to be their *conucos*. Apparently, Pané tells us that while doing this fertility ritual they said "now your fruits will be good and great" (page 138 of Robiou Lamarche's *Tainos and Caribs: The Aboriginal Cultures of the Antilles*). Although this observation is worth mentioning due to the influence this Amerindian agricultural practice and fertility ritual may have had on the Palo Monte practice of the constructing a *nganga*, this is not seen or recorded in the traditional Kongo or more general Bantu religious habitus, where the *nganga* is the name of the Bantu medicine man and whose art or praxis is called *kinganga* (from *Death and the Invisible Powers: The World of Kongo Belief* by Simon Bockie). In the traditional Bantu religious habitus the medicine man or the priest embodies the *minkisi* and the powers of the ancestral dead. Meanwhile, in Palo Monte, this name and role was replaced by the cauldron and the use of the *palos*, the *kiyumba* or *kiyumbas*, earth, and a multiplicity of mineral, animal, and vegetal items that resemble a microcosm of the planet earth and, on a bigger scale, the universe. Therefore, my inclination is that the construction of the *nganga* as it is done today in Palo Monte was highly influenced by these Amerindian fertility and agricultural practices, which demonstrate (according to Pané's anecdote) the same utilitarian mentality as that of the African, and would not have seemed very foreign or difficult to incorporate or assimilate into the religious habitus of the Kongo diaspora in Cuba. Nonetheless, I refrain from including it as a standalone common theme in the discourse due to the lack of further support regarding these Amerindian fertility and agricultural practices. I prefer to leave it as an observation worthy of noting and sharing, that it may tempt other interested scholars and practitioners who are better educated and informed on the subject to follow this potential lead.

homogeneous community, the majority of them seem to have been populated by a varied and heterogeneous set of culturally diverse inhabitants
who were seeking refuge away from the common evil of Spanish slavery.
Nonetheless, Brandon believes that it is difficult to conclude which form
and what level of acculturation were achieved within these *palenques*.
Hence, the religious practices and beliefs of the Maroons cannot be elucidated. The nature of this religiosity remains a mystery with the only
historical (and biased) note on the structural system of these communities arriving via the works of Francisco Perez de la Riva which tell us
that these *palenques* were constituted by "Men and women [who] lived
in absolute promiscuity and were dominated by their leaders (who they
called Captains [*Capataz* in Spanish]) and by the sorcerer or *santeros*,
who would at times function as witch doctor."[13]

However, Brandon points out that the use of the word *santeros* here
points to an anachronism, and that de la Riva himself proclaims that
this word was not in fact used by the Maroons themselves to describe
their priest, doctor, or sorcerer. Brandon traces this usage of Santeria in
Cuban historical/anthropological works to an umbrella term for all Afro-
Cuban religious forms. We must conclude that the religious landscape
of these *palenques* was dominated by these types of ritual specialists. A
santero/santera did not necessarily denote specifically a Yoruba, a Congo,

---

13. George Brandon, *Santeria from Africa to the New World* (Bloomington: Indiana
Univ. Press, 2000), pp. 65–66.

a Mandinga,[14] a Gangá,[15] or an Arará[16](among others) priest/doctor/sor-cerer but an indigenous and traditional form of religious medicine, as embodied in the medicine man. Therefore, as we have seen in Chapter 3 on the Caribbean Amerindian religious habitus, we can include the practices and beliefs of the Taino and Caribs in this admixture, since, the only thing that can be concluded about the religious landscape of these *palenques* is that beyond the fact that they were utilizing a traditional or 'primitive' form of religious manifestation, we are not able to determine the origin or its form.[17] After all, the intercessions, prominence, and simi-

14. Umbrella term for Afro-Cuban ethnoreligious groups that descend from the Mandinka or Mendé people of Niger, Senegal, and Gambia in West Africa. It also in-cluded other neighboring ethnic groups such as the Bambara, Diola, and Yola. These peoples were highly influenced by Islam and the Arabic habitus, which they brought to Cuba during the colonial period. I believe that these Muslim Mandingas with their Muslim faith healers, which they also syncretized with indigenous healing practices, are the origin of the Palo Monte use of the salutatory phrase *Nsala Malekum* and its response *Malekum Nsala* (see Glossary). I support this by the fact that the Kingdom of Kongo was a Catholic Kingdom and the first in Africa to adopt Christianity. Also, prior to the relatively modern incursion of Islam to West Central Africa, there is no record of this salutation being used in the Kingdom of Kongo. Hence, this phrase, which has baffled to most Palo Monte scholars, most likely resulted from the borrowing of the Congo in Cuba from their Mandinga counterparts. Please refer to *Cultura Afrocubana Tomos I-IV* by Jorge Castellanos and Isabel Castellanos. Also, for an example of a mod-ern syncretic practice of Muslim faith healing and indigenous practices in Senegal, please refer to *https://www.youtube.com/watch?v=GlKSp2HoVow* (7:13- 12:24) by Ze-inab Badawi.

15. Afro-Cuban ethnoreligious group that descends from Sierra Leone, Libya, and Côte d'Ivoire in West Africa. This group preserved its own religion, culture, language, and identity, which are separate from those of the other extant Afro-Cuban peoples. For an excellent source on the only Gangá community extant in Perico, Matanzas, Cuba, please refer to *Los Gangá en Cuba: La Comunidad de Matanzas* by Alessandra Basso Ortiz. Also, for an article that describes the serendipitous discovery in 2013 of the origin of this Gangá-Longobá (as it is now known) community to a small village in the north of Sierra Leone please refer to 'Josefa Diago and the Origins of Cuba's Gangá Traditions' by Emma Christopher Alonso.

16. Afro-Cuban ethnoreligious group that descends from the Ewe and Fon of the Old Kingdom of Dahomey in West Africa. This group preserved its own religion, culture, language, and identity, which are separate from those of the other extant Afro-Cuban peoples. For an excellent source on the Kingdom of Dahomey and the Dahomey Slave Trade, please refer to *Dahomey and the Slave Trade: Reflections on the Historiography of the Rise of Dahomey* by Robin Law. Also, for the most complete and well researched sources on the Arará, please refer to: *Los Ararás en Cuba: Florentina, la Princesa Dahomeyana* by Guillermo Andreu Alonso and *Situated Narratives and Sa-cred Dance: Performing the Entangled Histories of Cuba and West Africa* by Jill Flanders Crosby and J.T. Torres.

17. Brandon, *Santeria from Africa to the New World*, p. 66.

larities in role and function which the *behique*, the *boyez*, the *palero*, and the *santero* manifested/performed within the community of their respective societies are overwhelmingly parallel to each other and point to the most easily marked meeting point of these cultures.[18]

Proximity as Catalyst for Cultural Encounter between Caribbean Amerindians and West Central Africans

Consequently, this leads us to the following theme found across the Caribbean diaspora, which was the swift extermination and subjugation of the Amerindian population in the Caribbean. The heinous and unforgivable practices and ideology imposed on the natives of these islands, together with the decimation of the rest of the surviving population due to the European diseases introduced into them, are vividly recorded in the writings of Bartolomé de las Casas. De las Casas' (now) seminal works, such as the *Brevísima relación de la destrucción de las Indias* and *Historia de la Indias* are exemplars of the recorded atrocities committed by the Spanish in their colonies. Because of this complete decimation, our only recourse is to examine the earlier African diaspora communities in these Caribbean spaces, as these communities had encounters with the native inhabitants of the Caribbean and appropriated aspects of their cultures. Through a reconstruction of the histories of these earlier African diasporic communities in the Caribbean we hope to identify Amerindian cultural and religious survivals in creole religions of the Caribbean and the processes through which the African communities appropriated them.

The data from the colonial period can be accessed in the work done by Linda M. Heywood. Heywood's Appendix 1[19] is particularly informa-

18. The reason why I do not include *babalawos* as a part of these indigenous medicine men or priests in the *palenques* is because the Ifá religion was introduced to Cuba in the 19th century, which would have made it impossible for them to cohabitate and interact with the *behique* and the *boyez*. For more information on the subject please refer to Natalia Bolívar Aróstegui and Valentina Porras Potts, 'Cuba. Una Identita in Movimento—Ifá: Su Historia en Cuba' (2009) <http://www.archivocubano.org/ifa_historia.html>; Arnaldo Varona, 'SANTERIA: A Brief History of The Babalawos (Babalaos) in Cuba. + Santeria: Breve Historia de los Babalaos en Cuba' (2021) <https://www.thecubanhistory.com/2015/12/santeria-a-brief-history-of-the-babalawos-babalaos-in-cuba-santeria-breve-historia-de-los-babalaos-en-cuba>; and Ile Yoruba Esoterica, 'Historia de IFA en Cuba: Testimonio de un Sacerdote' (2021) <https://ileyoruba.wixsite.com/ileyoruba/religion-yoruba-en-cuba>.

19. Linda M. Heywood, *Central Africans and Cultural Transformations in the American Diaspora* (New York: Cambridge University Press, 2002), pp. 64–69.

tive with regards to the light it shines on the ethnic composition of the slaves brought to the Caribbean during the slave trade, starting from the 16th century (right after the discovery of the West Indies). In table *A. Slaves Boarded from Central Africa, by Decades*,[20] we see that the predominant ethnic group being exported at the beginning of the slave trade was from Central Africa. Trade in the West African population was not significant until the period between 1690–699 (although this analysis only looks at the Portuguese records). On the other hand, table *E. Slaves from Central Africa (Embarked) as Proportion of Total Atlantic Trade, by Quarter Centuries*[21] gives us a better understanding of the composition of the slave trade during the early colonial period of the Americas. From 1519–1600, 82.7% of the total Atlantic trade was from central Africa, and from 1601–1650 that number increased to 92.8%. Lovejoy's academic paper puts these numbers into perspective by providing a percentage of the total number of enslaved Africans (identified) as 409,000 or 3.6% (of the total known population of slaves taken from Africa from 1450 to 1867) for the period 1450–1600 and 1,348,000 or 11.9% for 1601–1700.[22] This data sheds greater light on the Kongo diaspora in Cuba and the Amerindian religious influence on Palo Monte in particular.

Moreover, Lovejoy puts the number taken from West Central Africa during the period of 1601–1650 at 51,775 or 73.38% (of the total known population of slaves brought during this period).[23] Lovejoy's account establishes that the West Central African diaspora was the biggest source of enslaved Africans brought during the early period of the transatlantic slave trade. Moreno Fraginal's account puts the number of enslaved West Central Africans of Kongo origin working in sugar plantations during the 1760–69 period at 30.30% (of the entire ethnic compositions of slaves working in the sugar plantations) or 1,305, and 25.31% or 1,090 as Carabalí[24] in origin, with the rest of the ethnic groups forming only incidental

20. Heywood, *Central Africans and Cultural Transformations in the American Diaspora*, pp. 64–65.

21. Heywood, *Central Africans and Cultural Transformations in the American Diaspora*, p. 67.

22. Heywood, *Central Africans and Cultural Transformations in the American Diaspora*, pp. 64–69.

23. P.E. Lovejoy, *The "Middle Passage": The Enforced Migration of Africans across the Atlantic* (Toronto: York University, 2007), 2–3 <https://educacioncivicamep.files.wordpress.com/2015/04/lovejoy_middle_passage_the_enforced_migration_of_africans_across_the_atlantic.pdf>.

24. Spanish term for the Afro-Cuban ethnoreligious group, also known as the

amounts.[25] This data points to the fact that not only did the West Central African diaspora represent the largest source of slaves during the first century of the transatlantic slave trade, but also that their presence and prominence extended well into the 18th century, which points to the continuity and preservation of their beliefs, no matter how fragmentary.[26]

Moreover, I believe that the Cuban folk saying *En Cuba, el que no tiene de Congo tiene de Carabalí*, which translates to *"In Cuba, the one who does not have of Congo has of Carabalí"*, utilized at the beginning of the Preface of this book, reflects these findings and speaks to the true historical and existential experience of the creole individual in Cuba, which by extension includes the Amerindian natives and the European invaders. As observed above, the numbers demonstrate a greater Congo and Carabalí presence right up to the 18th century, which demonstrates the greater chances of Cuban creole miscegenation happening with one of these two ethnic groups and thus constitutes the greater part of the Cuban genetic and sociocultural heritage. Therefore, I deduce that like most folk sayings, this Cuban folk saying preserves a long-forgotten history and deeply ingrained folkloric wisdom about the genesis and heritage of Cuba, being recuperated and reclaimed in this book. Overall, the above information, together with the writings of de las Casas and Maya Deren's observations about the decimation of the Amerindian populations in Haiti by 1667, point to the fact that if there are any surviving Amerindian beliefs and practices in the Caribbean (and beyond) they would be found in the religious beliefs and practices of the creoles of Central African (Kongolese) descent. Any surviving beliefs and practices outside of those originally Kongolese must have been transferred via syncretism into the creole manifestations of these Kongolese practices in the Caribbean.

Abakuá, that descends from the Calabar capital found on the coast of the Cross River State of Nigeria. Also known for their religious institutions or secret societies called *juegos* (games) or *potencias* (potencies), which are brotherhoods or fraternities where they preserved their own identity, language, culture, and religious manifestation. Please refer to *La Sociedad Secreta Abakuá: Narrada por Viejos Adeptos* by Lydia Cabrera and to *Voice of the Leopard: African Secret Societies and Cuba* by Ivor L. Miller.

25. For a complete analysis of these numbers in their full original investigative and interpretative empirical context, please refer to Manuel Moreno Fraginals' masterpiece *El ingenio: Complejo Económico Social Cubano del Azúcar Tomos I-III*.

26. Manuel Moreno Fraginals, 'AFRICA IN CUBA: A QUANTITATIVE ANALYSIS OF THE AFRICAN POPULATION IN THE ISLAND OF CUBA', *Annals of The New York Academy Of Sciences*, 292.1 (1977), 187–281 (p. 190) <doi:10.1111/j.1749–6632.1977.tb47743.x>.

Language, Maracas, Baobab and the Ceiba

According to Deren, the meeting ground (beyond the spatial location) between the imported Africans and the Amerindians was the Spanish language.[27] The aforementioned observation makes sense on the grounds that being enslaved and conquered by the Spanish would lead both groups of people to seek the opportunity to communicate in the mutually enforced language of the conqueror. Furthermore, due to the common hatred of the oppressor both groups would have felt the need to work together in order to fight and survive under the yoke of the Spanish colonizers. The Spanish language, then, would be a good indicator of the remains of Amerindian beliefs and practices in the surviving creole manifestations of the Caribbean diaspora. As Deren rightly claims, even though the French (in Haiti) began importing Africans after 1677, Spanish would have still remained the sacred and ritual language of the religious practices contributed by the Amerindians, because of the fact that they were almost extinct by the time the French period of colonization began.[28]

The legacy of the Amerindian language in the Caribbean today is too extensive to cover in this book, and merits its own independent study.[29] However, since the goal of this study is to trace the influence the Amerindian beliefs and practices had on the Afro-Caribbean Diaspora specifically, I will focus on these instead. In Cuba, the tradition of Palo Monte is full of Bantu and Spanish-language words and songs[30] and on first inspection we might be led to believe that the absorption of the Amerindian beliefs and practices by the Central African diaspora in Cuba was restricted to the Spanish portions. However, on further investigation we start to see some signs of the Taino and Carib language legacy. The

---

27. Deren, *Divine Horsemen: The Living Gods of Haiti*, p. 271.

28. Deren, *Divine Horsemen: The Living Gods of Haiti*, pp. 271–72.

29. Please refer to *Language of the Voiceless: Traces of Taino Language, Food, and Culture in the Americas from 1492 to the Present* by Leonardo Wilson Nin.

30. As explained previously, this highly creolized Palo Monte liturgical language is called *habla bozal*, which is a Spanish term. The term *bozal* (the noun 'muzzle') refers to the apparatus that is fastened around the nose and mouth of an animal so that it may not bite; both in Spanish and in English it also has another level of meaning, as the process by which a person or a group is prevented from expressing themselves and their opinions freely. Here the word *bozal* (the verb 'muzzled') demonstrates the scars left by the colonial wound ( ). The word *habla* means speech, speak, or language. This reminder unfortunately supports the Spanish language being enforced by the Spanish secular and religious hegemony and leaves no doubt as to the impact it had on the Amerindian and African socioreligious experience.

name of the Mpungo Zarabanda, which is the name of one of the seven Kimpungulu (the pure or ideal form of the *nkisi*: force, spirit or energy),[31] seems to be one of these borrowings from the Amerindian language directly related to their beliefs. While the rest of the Kimpungulu have Spanish or Bantu names—Lucero, Vence Bataya (also called Watariamba, its Bantu name), Siete Rayos (also called Nsasi, the Bantu name), Mama Chola, Centella, Baluande (Bantu in origin), Cobayende (also called Koballende or Kuballende), Gurunfinda (Bantu in origin), Lukankazi (Bantu in origin) and Nganga Kissi (Bantu in origin),[32] Zarabanda seems to be an amalgamation of the Amerindian word *zara*, meaning 'corn'[33] and *banda*, the Spanish word for 'band' or the Bantu word, *banda*, meaning 'to go up' or 'goes up'.[34]

In Palo Mayombe, *munansos* are also called *bateys*, like the Taino courts for playing ball.[35] The *batey* was the central plaza in the village, where communal practices such as the ceremonial ball game (called by the same name) and *areitos* took place. *Areitos* consisted of the entire community joining in singing, dancing, and chanting the religious repertory of the tribe.[36] The practice of Espiritismo del Cordón (a form of Spiritism which derives its name from its central ritual in which participants move in a circle or chain called the *cordón*)[37] in the east of Cuba has elements of the Taino *areito* practice.[38] Although the inclusion of the *maiohauau* (or *maiouauan* according to Brasseur de Bourbourg), which was a sort of drum of about 45 inches long and 22.5 inches in breadth that

31. Nicholaj de Mattos Frisvold, *Palo Mayombe: The Garden of Blood and Bones*, 1st ed. (Dover: Bibliothèque Rouge/Scarlet Imprint, 2011), p. 44.

32. Frisvold, *Palo Mayombe: The Garden of Blood and Bones*, p. 81–126.

33. Deren, *Divine Horsemen: The Living Gods of Haiti*, p. 280.

34. Lydia Cabrera and Isabel Castellanos, *Vocabulario Congo* (Miami, Florida: Ediciones Universal, 2001), p. 159.

35. Tukuenda, 'NSUNGA, TABACO', *Caribbean Spirituality and Understanding in the Diaspora*, (2010) <caribbeanspiritualityandunderstanding.blogspot.com/2010/11/nsunga-tabaco. html>.

36. Wilson, *The Indigenous People of the Caribbean*, p. 166.

37. Christine Ayorinde, *Afro-Cuban Religiosity, Revolution, and National Identity* (Florida: University Press of Florida, 2004), pp. 20–21. Also see page 121 of Robiou Lamarche's *Taino and Caribs: The Aboriginal Cultures of the Antilles*.

38. Jorge Luis Morejón, 'From the Areíto to the Cordon: Indigenous Healing Dances', *Revista Brasileira De Estudos Da Presença*, 8.3 (2018), 563–91 (p. 564) <doi: 10.1590/2237-266069826>.

resembled "the shape of the pincers of a farrier" and had at its opposite end a club-shaped form, was lost, this was not the case with the *maracas*.[39]

The *maracas*, which the Caribbean Amerindians used—a gourd with a long neck (as Ramón Pané described it),[40] and the plant seeds inside—have become a staple of Afro-Cuban religions (except Palo Monte) and form an essential part of the ritual paraphernalia and process of the *santero* and *babalawo* in Cuba when calling and working directly with the Orichas. The African form of the percussive instrument which is used in a similar fashion in music is called *axatse* in Ghana, and *shekere* more generally throughout Africa, was made using a hollowed calabash. It was dressed with a lattice work of Job's Tear (*Coix lacryma-jobi*) seeds (or other seeds of similar composition; beads and cowrie shells are also used sometimes) and to which a thick and rather short handle was glued.[41] Although they may sound similar, the composition and sound of these instruments are rather different: the Caribbean Amerindian *maracas* are much louder, more versatile, and are deeper-sounding than the African equivalent. This can be observed in the note made by Ramón Pané himself when he describes the *maracas* (although he does not use this Amerindian term preserved in Cuba) as "so loud a sound that it is heard a league and a half [away]".[42] In the same vein, the *ceiba*, a Taino word meaning the giant silk-cotton or kapok tree (a word completely transferred to other languages today),[43] and which was also the tree of life for the Maya of the Yucatan Peninsula and the region of Guatemala, is another example of the ritual objects African-derived traditions of Cuba made their own. The belief in the sacrality of trees or plants in general in the indigenous Americas is equally prevalent on the African continent. For example, the Carabalí and their descendants in Cuba with their Abakuá practice incorporated into their own beliefs and ritual praxis the *ceiba* and the royal palm as sacred trees that are fundamental for their

39. Bourne, *Columbus, Ramon Pane, and the Beginnings of American Anthropology*, pp. 19–20.

40. Bourne, *Columbus, Ramon Pane, and the Beginnings of American Anthropology*, pp. 19–20.

41. 'Axatse or Shekere', *Africa Heartwood Project*, (2015) <https://www.africaheartwoodproject.org/product/axatse-or-shekere/>.

42. Bourne, *Columbus, Ramon Pane, and the Beginnings of American Anthropology*, p. 20.

43. Wilson, *The Indigenous People of the Caribbean*, p. 160.

religion.[44] Moreover, the African *baobab* is equally important for the Yoruba and the Fon of Dahomey.[45]

The *ceiba*, known in Palo Monte as Sanda Naribe or Sanda Fumandanda[46] (and Pikinako Ofuma Ndoki in el Oriente de Cuba,[47] the eastern

44. For the most thorough and beautiful book on the Abakuá, please refer to *The Light Inside: Abakuá Society Arts and Cuban Cultural History* by David H. Brown. For a presentation of the actual beliefs and practices explored above and more please watch the excellent YouTube documentary 'Un Plante Abakuá' published by D Ritmacuba, filmed, edited and collected by Daniel Chatelain, José Betancourt and Patrice Banchereau respectively. See: <https://www.youtube.com/watch?v=2_Df4cSGkzg>. And for two excellent sources on the Fon of Dahomey, please refer to *The Fon of Dahomey* by P. Mercier and to *The Fon of Dahomey: A History and Ethnography of the Old Kingdom* by W. J. Argyle.

45. Juan Rubio, *Palo Monte y La Verdad Esotérica*, 1st. ed., (Miami: Publicaciones Miami, 2014), p. 365.

46. Rubio, *Palo Monte y La Verdad Esotérica*, p. 365.

47. Literally translates to the Orient of Cuba. I believe that the phrase *el Oriente de Cuba*, which has become a formal name, betrays a somewhat accepted vestige of the colonial era. To put it into context, this phrase, although used as a formal name for the easternmost provinces of Cuba (Las Tunas, Granma, Holguín, Santiago de Cuba, and Guantánamo), is also used, especially in the western provinces of Cuba (Pinar del Río, La Habana, Ciudad de La Habana, and Matanzas and the municipality of la Isla de la Juventud), as a nominal demarcation that carries racist connotations and condescending undertones. Consequently, this phrase becomes charged with an expressed and inherent sentiment of superiority that is weaponized against the natives of the eastern provinces. This superiority complex stems from a complicated history of the demographics and geography of power in Cuba, a complex history that can be best deconstructed and understood by the postcolonial revaluation and which is encapsulated by the term Orientalism. And to add insult to injury, there is another common derogatory phrase used to describe a native from these easternmost provinces: Palestino/Palestina. This word is the Spanish term for Palestinian, which clearly demonstrates a further segregating and belittling attempt based on a religious background of Judeo-Christian hegemony in Cuba, that 'others' and minimizes the youngest of the Abrahamic faiths, Islam, and its Muslim believers. Equally important here are the issues of territoriality or land contestation arising out of the history of the Jewish and Palestinian conflict which I deduce are implicitly carried through this Cuban phrase. However, a proper investigation of these matters goes well beyond the scope of this study. Therefore, I have decided only to frame and to focus this colonial manifestation through the appropriate lens and will challenge sociologists and Cuban scholars who may be interested in this wholly unique phenomenon to pick up the proverbial mantle. Ideally this would lead to a proper investigation in which this colonial vestige is finally countered and this issue, worthy of exploration, is ultimately brought to light. For a landmark study of postcolonialism that first unveiled the issue of the Orientalism, please refer to *Orientalism* by Edward Said. Also, for two excellent sources that delineate the history of the Jewish and the Palestinian peoples please refer to *Jerusalem: The Biography* by Simon Sebag Montefiore and to *A History of Palestine: From the Ottoman Conquest to the Founding of the State of Israel* by Gudrun Krämer and Graham Harman. For an excellent and thorough analysis of the ways in which Judaism, Christianity, and Islam compare and contrast

part of Cuba[48]), is the *axis mundi* of Palo Monte and is essential for the training of initiates in the tradition, since they have to sleep under it for seven when initiated.[49] Overall, the views of the Bantu-speaking people and their descendants in Cuba are that the *ceiba* or baobab (as is known in Africa) is a sacred tree. Some believers even declare that it was planted on earth by the gods themselves. This is so that it may guide the human race and its ethnic roots as though they were its own roots, because in the *ceiba* or baobab is found the secrets of creation (according to Bantu beliefs). Moreover, for the ancient Pángolas it was the temple of the gods and where they lived. More importantly for our study of Palo Monte is the belief that the *ceiba* marks the four cardinal points of the universe (Kizimbi—north, Kimbundo –South, Bukulu—east and Nganga—west)[50] or the four winds as they are known. We will revisit the importance and significance of this in the section on 'Geometric Diagrams and Their Representations' below.[51]

For the Taino, the *ceiba* was the sacred tree which presided over and was the sentinel of the forest. It was the daughter of Yaya and the sister of Yocahú and faithful maid of Atabey, who knows her secrets and mysteries. Even the indestructible Guabancex with her strong winds cannot harm the *ceiba*. They also believe that Guataba, the god or spirit of lightning, did not dare strike the *ceiba* lest it provoke the fury of Yaya. The Taino also believed that the *ceiba* served as the vehicle or the link between the underworld and heaven. This was based on the belief that its roots went all the way down to the kingdom of the dead and the ancestors, its branches led to the kingdom of the great celestial spirits, and its location in our world allowed for direct communication of the three planes of the universe. The Taino would also place their hands over its trunk, branches, and superficial roots in order to obtain strength and resistance when needed (such as in illness or in war), and place their foreheads on it so that they may obtain answers to their questions and problems.[52]

---

and how they have affected each other's faith, please refer to *Judaism, Christianity and Islam: The Classical Texts and Their Interpretation, Volumes I, II and II* by F. E. Peters.

48. Rojas Calderon, *Palo Brakamundo*, p. 166.

49. Joseph Hartman, *The Ceiba Tree as a Multivocal Signifier: Afro-Cuban Symbolism, Political Performance, And Urban Space in the Cuban Republic* (Texas: University of North Texas, 2011), pp. 22 & 26.

50. Rojas Calderon, *Palo Brakamundo*, p. 162.

51. Rubio, *Palo Monte y La Verdad Esotérica*, pp. 365–67.

52. Rubio, *Palo Monte y La Verdad Esotérica*, pp.365–67.

Juan Rubio also provides an extended discussion of the Maya in which he touches on their beliefs and practices. My sense is that he uses this account as an opportunity to discuss the mysteries of Palo Monte, which he is not otherwise able to discuss. I base this inference on the observation that, as explored in the historical section, there were continuous contacts between the Yucatan Peninsula and the Caribbean which lasted right up to the Spanish colonial invasion, and the fact that the colors and other characteristics attributed to the four cardinal points by the Maya are extremely similar to those of the Bantu explored in the 'Geometric Diagrams and Their Representations' section below. Nonetheless, Juan Rubio focuses on certain aspects of Maya beliefs and omits others that are equally important, which suggests to me that these are the most pertinent to his book on Palo Monte and its esoteric teachings (which had not touched upon the Amerindian religious habitus until that point in the book).[53] Also, because much is not known about the Taino and Carib beliefs concerning the *ceiba* beyond the points explored above, and because similarities in religious and cultural habitus have been found between the Maya and the Taino and Caribs, I will venture to use Rubio's observations to demonstrate the Amerindian influence on Palo Monte.

According to Rubio, the Maya believed the cosmos to be structured and divided into three levels. The superior level was composed of thirteen celestial realms, the middle level consisted of the world in which we live and was represented by the sacred mountain Ritz, and the inferior level was generally considered to be inherently related to the aquatic world and its nine realms, resembling the Bantu and Palo Monte belief of Kalunga. The concept of Kalunga refers to the ocean (the means for the middle passage); as the passage to the kingdom of death and ancestry it represents a metaphor of death and the fluid immanence of death itself.[54] The middle level (where we live) was the place that sustains life and where the sacred corn was cultivated as food, and was the opposite of the inferior level. The Maya believed that the branches of the *ceiba* supported the weight of the heavens or celestial realms, while its roots served as a means of communication between the world of the living and the underworld. This aspect was explored in the Malongo ceremony in the previous chapter and which I suggest can still be detected in the reference to a new initiated person as a *pino nuevo* and to the branches

53. Rubio, *Palo Monte y La Verdad Esotérica*, pp. 365–67.

54. Frisvold, *Palo Mayombe: The Garden of Blood and Bones*, p. 2.

of the religion as *ramas*.[55] Furthermore, Rubio explores the funerary rites of the Maya and explains that they exhibited a high degree of respect and reverence for the dead. The Maya were accustomed to placing funerary offerings which they considered to be of utility in life after death. These offerings varied depending on the social status of the individual, but usually consisted of polychrome ceramics and sacred objects such as jade, obsidian, and shells, which were interred with the individual, whose body was placed in the ground in an extended position, with its head turned towards the north.[56]

Recalling Columbus' explanation of the *caciques* being venerated through the *cemis* explored in Chapter 3, we learn that the Maya interred their leaders in tombs which were placed inside their temples (which mirrored Ritz, the sacred mountain). They did this to obtain their leaders' continual support and blessing after death, where they would serve as mediators between the gods and their people (like the cotton idol with the skull, which Rubio is most probably referencing here as the practice of placing the *kiyumba* on the *nganga*). I am referring here to the construction of the *nganga*, which is a process done in the *nkimba*. Nkimba is a word that comes from the Bantu word Kinkimba, which was the Kongo preparatory school for the future *ngangas*. Nkimba is also known as *rayamiento*, which literally means 'scratching', due to the incisions made. This initiatory rite of Palo Monte is one of the most complex and highly veiled aspects of the religion, but based on what I have been able to collect from the scant literature available, I was able to reconstruct or reverse engineer some parts of the ceremony; it goes as follows.

Foremost, it has to be said that there are variations in this initiatory rite, with some Tatas requiring the neophyte to be blindfolded for the duration of the rite, while others don't. Yet others make this decision based on the spiritual path of the neophyte. If the neophyte has a path as a Tata Nkisi, then the second rite, performed after one year and one month has passed, is done without blindfolds, but if the person is only to remain a Ngueyo, then he goes through the initiation blindfolded. Prior to any initiatory event, the neophyte, with the help and guidance of the Tata, has to obtain a *nfumbe* from the cemetery. This process is done at two different times, depending on the aim and wishes of the *palero* or *palera* going through the ceremony. Those who wish to work the nganga

55. Frisvold, Nicholaj de Mattos, *Palo Mayombe: The Garden of Blood and Bones,* p. 52–53.

56. Rubio, *Palo Monte y La Verdad Esotérica,* pp. 365–67.

Cristiana pursue the dead, and the ceremony is to be continued just after 12:00PM, while those wishing to form a pact with a malevolent spirit and desire to build a nganga Judía perform the ceremony just after 12:00Am. Also, because in Palo Monte the masculine is represented by the sun and the feminine is represented by the moon, women can only be initiated at night (just after 12:00PM).[57, 58, 59, 60 & 61]

This *nfumbe* will serve as the main *nfumbe* of the *nganga*, which is composed of up to seven other *nfumbe* and the dead with whom the neophyte makes the blood pact, and becomes the chief or commanding spirit of the *nganga*. This pact starts between the neophyte, the Tata, and the *nfumbe* in the cemetery, where the neophyte and the Tata try to buy or to convince the dead to serve as the chief *nfumbe* of the *nganga*. Usually, the *palero* and the neophyte try to buy the cooperation of the dead through conversation and offerings of rum or any other sort of strong spirits, seven *kilos* (seven American pennies or seven British pence), and tobacco; if the neophyte does not have any money, he uses seven grains of corn. Once the dead has been bought or convinced, four lit candles are placed on the four cardinal points of the cardinal cross of *los cuatro vientos*. In the left-hand part of the cardinal cross a hole is made, and all of the items mentioned above are poured in while calling on the name of the dead who has been bought from Centella, the one who determines whether the desired *kiyumba* of the dead can be taken out and used in the *nganga*. Once the *kiyumba* has been taken home, it is fed with the blood of the neophyte and an animal, at which point, with the use of many *mambos* that serve as the incantation of the plants and blood spilled, the pact has been made.[62, 63, 64, 65 & 66]

57. González-Wippler, *Santeria: Magia Africana en Latinoamérica*, pp. 129–38

58. Cañizares, *The Book on Palo: Deities: Initiatory Rituals and Ceremonies*

59. Rojas Calderon, *Palo Brakamundo*

60. Carbonel, *Secreto del Palo Monte*

61. Also, please refer to: <*https://www.youtube.com/watch?v=MtQOxBezo7w*> for a short video recording of parts of the *nkimba* ceremony.

62. González-Wippler, *Santeria: Magia Africana en Latinoamérica*, pp. 129–38

63. Cañizares, *The Book on Palo: Deities: Initiatory Rituals and Ceremonies*

64. Rojas Calderon, *Palo Brakamundo*

65. Carbonel, *Secreto del Palo Monte*

66. Also, please refer to: <*https://www.youtube.com/watch?v=MtQOxBezo7w*> for a short video recording of parts of the *nkimba* ceremony.

Moreover, it should be said that this is the reason why the ceremony of *jubilacion* (a taboo (for traditionalists), in which an individual is initiated in Palo Monte after being initiated in the Regla de Ocha), is performed. The ceremony of *jubilacion* is where the crowning of the Oricha that serves as el Angel de la Guarda (Guardian Angel) is retired or reversed, which is performed by some modern *paleros* or *paleras* in order to initiate someone crowned with an Oricha into the Palo Monte religion. The problem with this is that el Angel de la Guarda does not accept the spillage of *menga* (blood) of the crowned initiate as well as the modification of his astral nature, which is why this ceremony has come under scrutiny and has been heavily opposed by more traditional Palo Monte practitioners, since the traditionalists believe that these *paleros* or *paleras* do not truly understand the extent and meaning of the blood pact being made with the *nfumbe*. These traditionalists confirm that when a neophyte gives his blood to the *nfumbe* and the *nganga*, this act has repercussions that extend to the astral plane of the individual, forever marking them in the spiritual world with the fate and spiritual paths of both the Ngueyo and the *nfumbe* becoming intertwined forever through any successive incarnations in the material plane.[67, 68, 69, 70 & 71]

However, this *kiyumba* then needs to be taken to another tree (what type of tree varies according to the main Mpungo giving the vital force of the *nganga* being consecrated) where it is interred once again for nine days. Here el Angel de la Guarda also comes into play in Palo Monte. When a *palero* wishes to build a *nganga* of any of the Kimpungulu, he needs to make sure to buy or persuade a spirit of the dead who, when alive, was the son/daughter of that particular Mpungo. For example, if a *palero* wants to build a *nganga* of Zarabanda, then when he goes to the cemetery to buy or persuade the roaming spirit of the dead he wishes to work and make the pact with, he must make sure that his Angel de la Guarda was Zarabanda/Ogun when they were alive. Then, after the nine days, the *kiyumba* is brought back to the *munanzo* and is placed inside the *nganga* together with a plethora of items and *kiyumbas* from the animal, mineral and vegetal kingdoms. However, before the construction of

67. González-Wippler, *Santeria: Magia Africana en Latinoamérica*, pp. 129–38

68. Cañizares, *The Book on Palo: Deities: Initiatory Rituals and Ceremonies*

69. Rojas Calderon, *Palo Brakamundo*

70. Carbonel, *Secreto del Palo Monte*

71. Also, please refer to: <*https://www.youtube.com/watch?v=MtQOxBezo7w*> for a short video recording of parts of the *nkimba* ceremony.

the *nganga*, the neophyte is marked with incisions that vary according to his potential spiritual path within the religion as either an Ngueyo for life, or his potential involvement as a *ngangulero*.[72, 73, 74, 75 & 76]

Also, the tool used to do the scarification can also vary with a *nchufla* (blade) being the most common, but chicken spurs, the thorny side of a plant, or a purposefully made spiked end of a plant, as well as any knife or sword with a white handle can be used. Meanwhile, the neophyte is made to kneel for a long period of time, which is done as a test, while he holds a cross made out of clay or terra cotta. Once the incisions have been made, they are smeared with sperm and with some plant infusions, meanwhile the Tata sings *mambos* (incantations) and the Yayi inspects the *mbozos* (incised signs) made for any prophesies or revelations offered through them, which are also wholly unique to each individual and are informed by the *nfumbe* with which he has made the pact. Moreover, usually these signs contain karmic meanings and messages that need to be relayed to the Ngueyo. These incisions are usually made on top of each nipple, one in the back part of the neck, two in each foot, two in each hand, and some do one on top of the heart, especially when he has a path as a Ngueyo, but it is usually two on top of the heart. After this the Ngueyo is given his own *firma* that is unique to him and a *patimpemba* of Cobayende is drawn in order to gain the power and acceptance of the Mpungo due to his role as Lord Death. At this point the neophyte is required to sleep with his *nganga* under the *ceiba* for the duration of seven nights. After he has gone through this procedure, he is given new clothes and told to take them to the cemetery, where he is supposed to bury them in a tomb previously selected. The clothes will be left interred for the duration of three Fridays or twenty-one days.[77, 78, 79, 80 & 81]

72. González-Wippler, *Santeria: Magia Africana en Latinoamérica*, pp. 129–38

73. Cañizares, *The Book on Palo: Deities: Initiatory Rituals and Ceremonies*

74. Rojas Calderon, *Palo Brakamundo*

75. Carbonel, *Secreto del Palo Monte*

76. Also, please refer to: <https://www.youtube.com/watch?v=MtQOxBezo7w> for a short video recording of parts of the *nkimba* ceremony.

77. González-Wippler, *Santeria: Magia Africana en Latinoamérica*, pp. 129–38

78. Cañizares, *The Book on Palo: Deities: Initiatory Rituals and Ceremonies*

79. Rojas Calderon, *Palo Brakamundo*

80. Carbonel, *Secreto del Palo Monte*

81. Also, please refer to: <https://www.youtube.com/watch?v=MtQOxBezo7w> for a short video recording of parts of the *nkimba* ceremony.

During this period of waiting, the neophyte has to be washed or more appropriately cleansed inside and out with a brew made out of *palos*, leaves of the *ceiba*, and a variety of different plants. After the neophyte has done this, he has to be left outside to dry in the open air; they cannot be dried in any other way. Thence, he is taken by his Palo Monte godfather (main Tata of the *munanzo* where he is being initiated) together with other *paleros* of the *munanzo* that serve as witnesses of the initiation of the neophyte, back to the *ceiba* where they call on the spirits, the dead, and the spirit of the *ceiba* so that they can also witness and approve the initiation; this is the *Malongo* ceremony. At this point, the ritual possession or altered state of mind of the Ngueyo is expected; in order for the ceremony to be complete the Ngueyo has to be mounted or possessed by the chief *nfumbe* of the *nganga*. After the possession has been completed and the *nfumbe* provides prophesies and advice to the *paleros* present about the new life of the Ngueyo, a white plate with a lid candle and a wrapped tibia is given to him as a symbol of his power and vision over the reign of the dead and the underworld.[82, 83, 84, 85 & 86]

Meanwhile, caves were considered essential for communicating with the underworld and the bodies of the dead were placed, with their offerings, in the cavities of limestone, where they were supposed to start their journey through the underworld and its nine realms to their final destinies. This last reason explains why time and space are of extreme importance for Amerindians and I will venture to say, the Congos in Cuba as well,[87] since their belief is that by seeking assistance from the world of the dead we are able to receive vital information about our lives and the world due to the remoteness of the dead from the limitations of time and space imposed on corporeal beings. Also, it is worth remembering that as people who had at one time lived on earth, their familiarity with the conditions of the living also enables them to make very well-informed decisions or offer good advice. This last point is my own and should be taken with a grain of salt since I am neither an initiated person nor one who communicates with the dead.

82. González-Wippler, *Santeria: Magia Africana en Latinoamérica*, pp. 129–38

83. Cañizares, *The Book on Palo: Deities: Initiatory Rituals and Ceremonies*

84. Rojas Calderon, *Palo Brakamundo*

85. Carbonel, *Secreto del Palo Monte*

86. Also, please refer to: <*https://www.youtube.com/watch?v=MtQOxBezo7w*> for a short video recording of parts of the *nkimba* ceremony.

87. Rubio, *Palo Monte y La Verdad Esotérica*, pp. 365–67.

The last point of similitude pointed out by Rubio which I want to explore is that of the sacred cycle of corn, the colors identified with each of the cardinal points located on the *ceiba*, and the cycles or human life and its stations. These perceptions of the world formed an integral part of the belief system of the Maya and, I believe, the Kongos in Africa and their diasporic descendants, the Congos in Cuba. Although fusion between these far-flung communities cannot be determined, I conclude rather that these representations are informed by the cyclical conception of the universe prevalent in 'primitive' communities. Only with the advent of the Abrahamic religions and their eschatology of the messiah do we get the first transformation of the understanding of time from a cyclical universe to a linear one. This point is a part of the myths of creation within the Maya worldview and its cosmogony. Their religious system was tied to the celestial bodies, which in turn were tied to supernatural deities with whom they coexisted and performed devotions to (usually through sacrifice). The Maya associated the color red with the east, white with the north, black with the west, and yellow with the south, thus representing the cycles and the four cardinal points located on the *ceiba*. As explored in the section 'Geometric Drawings and Their Representations' below, these colors assigned by the Kongo traditional religious system and Palo Monte practitioners in Cuba to each of the cardinal points of the four winds resemble in meaning, form, and cosmogony, the views, beliefs and practices of the Maya.[88] Hence, this semblance demonstrates another point of contact that can lead us to conclude that through contemporary Palo Monte practices some Amerindian beliefs and practices have survived.

Lastly, I want to focus on what will be a controversial theory for some, but at least from my viewpoint will be equally as valid an interpretation of the name Palo Mayombe as those accepted by the majority of Palo Monte practitioners and scholars. There are three *reglas* (rules; also known as branches) in the Palo Monte tradition: these are La Regla Mayombe, La Regla Brillumba/Vriyumba and La Regla Kimbisa. The Regla Kimbisa (formal name: La Regla Kimbisa del Santo Cristo del Buen Viaje) was a truly syncretic creation of Andres Facundo Cristo de Dolores Petit (known as Andres Petit or Andres Quimbisa) in that it combines elements of Abakuá, Espiritismo,[89] Freemasonry, Regla de Ocha (Santeria),

88. Rubio, *Palo Monte y La Verdad Esotérica*, p. 365–67.

89. I make this separation regarding Spiritism and Espiritismo because of the divergent evolutionary development of these forms. When I use the term Spiritism, I am referring to the original Kardecian and 'scientific' form of Spiritism that arrived in

and Christianity with a Congo religious foundation center stage and om-
nipresent. However, the name itself derives from a more arcane Kimbisa
rama (branch) related to the Abakuá secret society. The Brillumba or Vriyumba *rama* derives its name from the Kikongo word *yúmba*, meaning,
'spirit of the departed one' and the Kikongo word *vili*, which both denotes
a native of Angola, but also means 'works'. Subsequently, that leaves us
with the Regla Mayombe. The popular and scholarly consensus is that
the Mayombe branch is a continuation of a particular tradition from the
hills of Mayombe in the areas of Cabinda and Calabari in Kongo that was
brought to Matanzas, La Habana, and Pinar del Río in Cuba. However,
as Lydia Cabrera and Natalia Bolivar have suggested, the meaning of the
word Mayombe is, rather, 'superior' or 'chief', in the sense of someone

---

Cuba during the 19th century and was very popular with the Cuban aristocrats and
middle-upper class. The term 'scientific' was a name used by Kardecian Spiritists to
distinguish themselves from the 'other, less sophisticated' forms of folk Spiritism found
in the island. These forms, which I call Espiritismo due to its creole and Cuban provenance, were considered rustic and incoherent forms of Spiritism lacking the European
essence of progress and what is called today Scientism. Ironically, this folk or popular
form of Spiritism (Espritismo) is the main or only form of Spiritism now found in
Cuba, a fact that may have been influenced by the takeover of the Cuban Communist
Revolution and its related discourse of societal reformation chiefly concerned with the
center-stage reframing of the *vox populi* as the core of society. Also, the reason I make
this arbitrary demarcation is that this form of folk Spiritism, namely Espiritismo, has
been heavily influenced by the Afro-Caribbean religions of Cuba. Consequently, this
resulted in its theory and praxis having been remolded to fit the tapestry of the Cuban
religious landscape. Espiritismo has weaved itself in to such an extent that it has managed to ingrain itself in the ladder of Cuban spiritualities. Espiritismo has become such
an integrated creole manifestation in Cuba today that it has even been established as
a requisite step on the Afro-Caribbean ladder of initiation. I mean by this that rituals
such as *la misa de investigación* (investigation mass of the *cordón espiritual* of the person being studied by the Spiritist; please refer to the glossary) and *la misa de coronación
del muerto* (coronation or crowning mass of the chief spirit accompanying the person;
please refer to the glossary) are considered standard, if not required, steps prior to any
initiation in Palo Monte and the Lucumi Tradition. Please refer to *The Mediums' Book:
the Mediums' and Evokers' Guide*; *The Spirits' Book: According to the Teachings of Spirits
of High Degree and Transmitted Through Mediums*; *The Gospel According to Spiritism*;
Genesis: Genesis-Miracles and Predictions According to Spiritism; and *Heaven and Hell*
by Allan Kardec for a proper understanding of the traditional form of Scientific Spiritism. Also please refer to *Developing the Dead: Mediumship and Selfhood in Cuban
Espiritismo* by Diana Espírito Santo and *Espiritismo, Variantes Cubanas* by José Millet
Batista for a proper study and presentation of *Espiritismo* in Cuba. Lastly, please refer
to *Irna: Un Encuentro con ca Santería* by Heriberto Feraudy Espino for an in-depth
study of a religious figure (Irna) who was initiated and has gone through all these steps
(except becoming a *babalawo*) of the Afro-Cuban religious ladder, and who practices
these creole manifestations through a highly unique and syncretic stance.

who is dominating the cult, nature, and the *nfumbe,* while replicating the status of the *manikongo.*[90]

The *nfumbe* is the Palo Monte term for the spirit of the dead. Usually referring to those found inside the Palo Monte cauldron used in their necromantic practices. It must be said that although the *nfumbe* are spirits of the dead who aid the palero and palera, and even though they may be working with a nganga Cristiana (see glossary), the Palo Monte spirits are materialized spirits of the dead and thus by nature constituted those spirits that are attached to material things and tend to be less spiritually illuminated. Therefore, they serve as a stark contrast to the illuminated spirits of the *cordón espiritual* of the person, and are those spirits with which the *espiritistas* tend to work in their practice. Therefore, to *espiritistas* and those individuals who were born with or developed the ability of second sight, these Palo Monte spirits of the dead usually manifest as dark entities or dark clouds of energy, no matter their type of nganga. Also, depending on whether the palero or palera mainly focuses on good or bad *nsaras* (magical works), it tends to speed or retard the illumination of the chief *nfumbe* of the *nganga* with which he has made the pact. Usually, the normal process for those spirits still roaming this plane is to progress from *anima sola* to their eventual return to and integration with the abysmal waters of Kalunga ($\mathcal{H}$; Ψ). Therefore, depending on the *palero* or *palera,* the pact may be retarding its natural progression as a potential spirit or *bakulu* (venerated ancestor), which is supposed to occur after one year and one day of the *nfumbe*'s passing.[91 & 92]

Following the insights of these two ethnographers of the Congo tradition in Cuba, I will posit an alternative theory of the meaning of the name Palo Mayombe. *Palo* is the Spanish word for 'stick' (can also be interpreted as 'tree') and, as we have seen, the tree is present in all the *ramas* of the various *reglas,* as well as las Reglas de Congo (Congo Rules), Palo Monte. Mayombe, although it is the name of the Maiombe

90. Frisvold, *Palo Mayombe: The Garden of Blood and Bones,* pp. 49–51.

91. This summary is of my own making and was synthesized from the many years of audiovisual teachings offered up by Osvaldo Sesti at: *<https://www.youtube.com/user/OsvaldoSesti>.*

92. And for a well written and concise explanation of these beliefs in Haitian Vodou, which have much in common with Palo Monte beliefs (no surprise since they derived from the same Kongo origin), please refer to Chapter 1, 'Vodun and Social Transformation in the African Diasporic Experience: The Concept of Personhood in Haitian Vodun Religion' (authored by Guérin C. Montilus) of the book *Haitian Vodou: Spirit, Myth, and Reality* edited by Patrick Bellegerde-Smith and Claudine Michel.

Hills in the Northern delta of the Congo River in the province of Cabinda in modern day Angola,[93] could also be a derivation of the Carib word *mayombo* which refers to a stick which could magically beat any other stick.[94] The meaning of the Carib word not only reflects the insight expressed by Lydia Cabrera and Natalia Bolivar, but also the belief that the Mayombe *rama* is the principal and most powerful *regla*. Although Cuba was a Taino geographical settlement, Amerindian multitudes from every shore and atoll of the Caribbean were carried in slave ships to all parts of the Caribbean where labor was needed, and a fusion of the various Amerindian cultures occurred in these territories. Caribs were specially affected by this, since Spanish law permitted enslavement in the new world only of 'cannibals' (the word cannibal comes from Carib), while the other Amerindian groups became serfs on their own land.[95] Therefore, the possibility of the Carib word, *mayombo*, being used as the name for this creole reinterpretation of Kongolese beliefs and practices in their new manifestations (with Amerindian beliefs and practices) is not implausible.

Geometric Diagrams and Their Representations

The symbolic designs used in the African religious diaspora of the Caribbean are perhaps the most magnificent and complex forms of religious artistry preserved of what seems like an admixture of Kongo and Amerindian original forms. Since these specific geometric, artistic, and ritualistic designs have not (yet) been identified as purely originating from Africa,[96] it has been assumed that they represent Amerindian contributions. When we look at the *vevè* of Haitian Vodou and the *patimpembas* of Palo Monte and their central use in the religious beliefs and practices of these African diasporic groups (both which have origins in the Kongolese diaspora), there is no denying the plausible influence of the petroglyphs representing Amerindian beliefs and practices. Their similarities, and the fusions of the intricate drawings of the Kongo and Caribbean Amerindians, are particularly enlightening.[97] In this way we can see how the structured

93. Manuel Álvarez Ferrer, *Raíces del Palo Monte en Cuba* (Unos & Otros Ediciones, 2012), p. 9.

94. Deren, *Divine Horsemen: The Living Gods of Haiti*, p. 285.

95. Deren, Maya, *Divine Horsemen: The Living Gods of Haiti*, p. 67.

96. Deren, *Divine Horsemen: The Living Gods of Haiti*, p. 276.

97. Deren, *Divine Horsemen: The Living Gods of Haiti*, p. 276.

visual language of the BaKongo (and Bantu-speaking people in general) plays an integral role in the inherent system of communication of daily life directed at establishing interactive communication channels between humans and the natural and spiritual worlds. The purpose of the evolution of these forms of visual writing was to preserve and transmit cosmological and cosmogonical beliefs systems.[98] This is particularly evident in the Congo diaspora in Cuba today as seen through the practice of Palo Monte and its complex, structured visual code system.

Similarly, Taino art with its various manifestations is directly tied to the Taino mythology, cosmology, and cosmogony. The Taino artistic manifestations related to their beliefs and practices go beyond simple pottery-making and decoration; Taino craftsmen incorporated their religious/cultural art into their work with stones, bones, and shells. These materials were necessarily infused with the magical power of the *behique*, whose knowledge of the spiritual world was represented through the hands of the specialist Taino who worked with these materials. These 'artists' made use of bone chisels, natural abrasives, flint, and fiber threads that were mixed with water and sand in order to carve their beliefs and practices into rock. Their goal was to construct with these materials and these instruments petroglyphs and *cemis*, their ultimate objects of veneration and sources of power.[99]

Nonetheless, these forms of visual representation did not include the codified language of the geometric drawings. The Taino geometric visual language is tied by modern scholars to the symbolic code associated with the religious worldview of the chieftains (the *caciques*). According to Robiou Lamarche, this Taino geometric system of codified language consisted of a canon of writing, which was systematized with some rules and proportions that gave it its characteristic Taino quality. Overall, Taino geometric designs have a symmetrical quality to them, which is laid out in geometric patterns that form labyrinth-like complexes.

Some curious conclusions that have been reached concerning the commonly utilized motif of a circle at the center point of the pottery or sculpture, which contained these geometric designs.[100] According to

---

98. Barbaro Martínez-Ruiz, *Kongo Graphic Writing and Other Narratives of the Sign* (Philadelphia: Temple University Press, 2013), p. 1.

99. Robiou Lamarche, *Tainos and Caribs: The Aboriginal Cultures of the Antilles*, pp. 165–66.

100. Robiou Lamarche, *Tainos and Caribs: The Aboriginal Cultures of the Antilles* (San Juan, Puerto Rico: Editorial Punto y Coma, 2019), 165–66

Robiou Lamarche, this center most likely demonstrated religious beliefs associating the conceptual Center with divinity itself. Other related details that have been observed in this geometric system and which are appropriate to my research is the group of parallel lines or a line with a point at both ends, which was carved in a horizontal, vertical, or inclined position. There is also the use of the 'S' in an inclined or intertwined form, which curiously resembles the 'S' utilized in the *patimpembas* of *Zarabanda* which, as we have seen in the language section, possibly derives its name from an amalgamation of the Taino word '*zara*' and the Bantu or Spanish word '*banda*'.[101] There is also the consistent use of semicircles,[102] circles (others than those alluded to above),[103] concentric circles,[104] the triangle,[105] or the 'V' inverted with or without a characteristic point.[106] Unfortunately, beyond this archaeological understanding (only recently reconstructed) there has not been a satisfactory reconstruction of the codified language and its meaning. Hence, the original purpose of this system of language has not been decoded, and the key for deciphering the meaning codified in the geometric drawings[107] remains elusive.[108]

Since the Amerindian (especially the Taino) visual language has not been deciphered and its code has not been unraveled, we must look to the Kongo influence on the *firmas* of Palo Monte. By reverse engineering the preservation of Kongo symbols and graphic writing system preserved in Palo Monte, we can determine whether the similarities observed above truly derived from an Amerindian background or whether they just represent coincidences. According to Ruiz-Martinez, the historical archeology of graphic and pictographic writings of the BaKongo extends back to ancient times (a specific timeline cannot be determined due to its antiquity) and played an essential role in communication during the early period of migration across the forests and savannas of West Central

101. See page 94 of Frisvold's *Palo Mayombe* for similar patterns on the *firmas* of the *Kimpungulu,* as well as a pictorial representation of the *firma* containing this 'S'.

102. Frisvold, *Palo Mayombe: The Garden of Blood and Bones,* pp. 102 & 110.

103. Frisvold, *Palo Mayombe: The Garden of Blood and Bones,* pp. 80, 86, 91, 94, 99, 112, 116, 120 & 124.

104. Frisvold, *Palo Mayombe: The Garden of Blood and Bones,* p. 105.

105. Frisvold, *Palo Mayombe: The Garden of Blood and Bones,* pp. 80, 91 & 124.

106. Frisvold, *Palo Mayombe: The Garden of Blood and Bones,* p. 102.

107. See pages 171–76 of Robiou Lamarche's *Tainos and Caribs* for pictures of these geometric drawings.

108. Robiou Lamarche, *Tainos and Caribs: The Aboriginal Cultures of the Antilles,* pp. 170–71.

Africa by these pioneering Bantu settlers. Another important aspect of the BaKongo graphic writing system was the fact that it served as an important tool of universal language among the BaKongo, which included written symbols, religious objects, oral traditions, and body language integrated under one structured system of graphic writing.[109] Hence, the Kongo graphic writing system contains the most integrated and the most important source of information regarding the cultural and religious beliefs of the Kongo and their descendants. This last point is particularly poignant to the creole religion of Palo Monte, since the *firmas* or *patimpembas* graphic visual system is considered the most important tool of communication between the *nganga*, the spiritual world, the dead, and the Palo Monte practitioners.

Moreover, these highly complex drawings are said to contain the secrets of the religion as well as its power and are jealously guarded from non-initiated people and even other *munanzos* of the religion due to their supreme value to the *palero*. This evidence builds on the fact that when *paleros* write books on the religion and they include the *firmas* of works or the *Kimpungulu*, they never include the complete *firma* and leave important details out of the published drawings. Another important phenomenon related to this is the fact that when an initiated person is given the *firma* of the dead person with whom they have made the pact, it remains the knowledge of only that person receiving the *nganga* and the godfather *palero* from whom his *nganga* was born. The secrecy of these *firmas* is so important to the initiated that practitioners believe that showing other practitioners these *firmas* would mean the loss of the dead with which they have made the pact, and that other *paleros* would take control of their dead via the secret *firma*. This last point is also used as a mechanism by some godfather *paleros* to control godchildren who are perceived to be manifesting deviant and rebellious qualities in this highly traditional religion.[110]

109. Martínez-Ruiz, *Kongo Graphic Writing and Other Narratives of the Sign*, pp. 72–73.

110. This information was not obtained directly from any book but rather forms my synthesis of many videos by Osvaldo Sesti, Tata Iraka, who has delved into this topic many times throughout his ten-year project towards preserving the traditional Palo Mayombe religion via audiovisual teachings. These teachings are aimed at showing initiated and non-initiated individuals the way to perform *nsaras* or *bilongos* while providing a vast amount of knowledge on all things Palo Monte. As a side note, his contributions to the preservation of the religion and his openness (to an allowed degree that does not reveal the mysteries of the religion) in showing the practice of the religion within the confines of his *munanzo* are unparalleled and should be nominated

Martínez-Ruiz's interpretation of the data regarding the Kongo influence on the Palo Monte *firmas* is based on his use of Gerhard Kubik's term 'graphic writing systems' for this kind of visual language, together with his subdivision of the units composing these codified graphic systems (Ideograms<Pictograms or Pictographs<Cosmograms). Moreover, the author also seeks to provide a continuation to Robert Farris Thompson's work while providing a more thorough and detailed understanding of the Kongo system of graphic communication in both Africa and the Caribbean. The first link Martínez-Ruiz establishes between the Palo Monte *firmas* and the Kongo graphic writing system is that of the *dikenga*, which is the cosmogram depicting the conception of all living beings in the universe as well as the energy of the universe and the forces of all existence and creation. This is also known, when represented in a form similar to the Christian cross, as the *yowa* (Kongo Cosmogram) or *kilisu*, and it is almost always present (at least in the *yowa* form, the cross of the four cardinal points) in the Palo Monte *firmas*. However, the *dikenga* is also used in Cuba and is known by *paleros* as *nkuyu* or 'the abstract thing from Congo' and has a meaning more or less equal to that described above.[111]

The *yowa* is the Kongo's and Congo's most important projected symbol. This symbol depicts the synthesis of the entire belief system of the Kongo and Congo in Cuba; it is their Cosmogram.[112] I would like at this point to bring to the attention of the readers the similarities this Kongo Cosmogram has with the zodiac wheel. As mentioned above, the initiated person has gone through a process of alignment with the four stations and the four elements of the universe, fire, water, wind, and earth, and spring, summer, fall, and winter (built around the spring equinox, summer solstice, fall equinox, and winter solstice) in a period of waiting that consists of one year and one day. These stations are marked at each of the cardinal points on a circle, and each of the quadrants of the circle depicts the corresponding station or element.

---

as representative of Palo Monte practice for the UNESCO list of Intangible Cultural Heritage of Humanity. You can find his YouTube Channel at: <*https://www.youtube. com/user/OsvaldoSesti*>.

111. Martínez-Ruiz, *Kongo Graphic Writing and Other Narratives of the Sign*, pp. 71–72.

112. Martínez-Ruiz, *Kongo Graphic Writing and Other Narratives of the Sign*, pp. 71–72.

The astrological cardinal cross of Aries (♈; ♂), Cancer (♋; ☽), Libra (♎; ♀) and Capricorn (♑; ♄), as it is known in the west, parallel these Palo Mayombe beliefs and cosmological principles of the universe, with each representing and manifesting the elements of fire, water, wind, and earth as well as spring, summer, fall and winter respectively. Overall, these Palo Mayombe beliefs demonstrate the paramount role of the astral plane and of the heavenly spheres in conjunction with the rest of the universe as points of spirituality and the origin of the forces of the universe that manifest here on earth, invoked and placated by Palo Mayombe practitioners and astrologers alike. As for the center of the *yowa*, it refers to the quintessence of the universe (manifested spirit) that in this case refers to the Palo Mayombe practitioner or client who is making using of these codified graphic writing systems as divinatory technologies or instruments that project and amplify the wave of potentialities of the forces of the Universe that could manifest as paths in their lives.[113]

In other words, this 'primitive' technology (♉) is concerned with amplifying desired waves of potentiality and with changing the baseline state of the frequency of the vibratory concentric rings surrounding the body for which the *cuatro vientos* was cast, a body whose architectonic spiritual matrix enters into direct confrontation with the energies of the universe, which consequently unleashes the manifestation or the cancellation of some waves of potentialities over others, and which the *cuatro vientos* technology of the Kongo and Congo spiritual science wishes to engineer. On the other hand, in astrology there is no center, since the nucleus of the manifestation of these forces of the universe is symbolically added as the astrological symbol for the earth (⊕; not to be confused with the parts of fortune ⊗) that always appears opposed to the sun on the zodiac wheel of the casted chart. This is the main reason for the greatest difference between these two spiritual sciences. While the Kongo and the Congo in Cuba track the movement of the Ntango (sun) from the right-hand point found on the x-axis of the cardinal cross in a counterclockwise way, the astrological tracking of the sun (   ) is done in

113. Please refer to *Palo Mayombe: The Garden of Blood and Bones* by Nicholaj de Mattos Frisvold and to *Flash of the Spirit* by Robert Farris Thompson. Also, for an in depth and superb lecture on the *yowa* please refer to *Ki Kongo cosmograph, historical memory and perspective of time Professor Greg Carr* by Dr. Greg Carr at: <https://www.youtube.com/watch?v=ZtDA7FADdLA>.

a clockwise fashion, starting from the left-hand point of the x-axis of the cardinal cross.[114]

Moreover, the circular shape of *nkuyu* has been transmuted in Cuba and has come to represent the world of the ancestors, while symbolizing protection, time, perfection, the receipt of energy, balance, existence, and the realm of initiation. This circular representation is seen as the frontier between the living and the dead and as the pathway through which the initiated person has to travel in order to complete the spiritual transformation to a new life. Martínez-Ruiz also delves into the meaning of the cross within the *nkuyu* in the Palo Monte religion. He explains that the cross is best understood as a map of the forces of the universe which divide space into four parts representing the cosmos, nature, the atmosphere, and human beings and human creation. The four winds, as they are known, also serve as symbols, with the north point representing God or the almighty forces of creation, the south point, the animals, the east point, the plants and trees, and the west point, the minerals of the earth.[115] Hence, the use of the four winds across almost all *firmas* demonstrates that this graphic form of the religion was preserved from the traditional Kongo belief system, which is consistent with the archeological data recovered about the Caribbean Amerindian's geometric system.

Another important connection Martínez-Ruiz makes is between the philosophical cosmology of the Kongo and the four cardinal points of the *dikenga*. This is understood as the four points of the sun across the sky and the colors used in the drawing of the *lucero* (another name used for *nkuyu*) *patimpemba* in Palo Monte needed for the corresponding type of work to be performed. The Kongo *dikenga* understanding is as follows: "Musoni sun (yellow sun)—sun of perfection; Kala sun (black sun)—sun of vitality; Tukula sun (red sun)—sun of warning or danger and Luvemba sun (gray/white sun)—sun of death and change".[116] In Palo Monte, the colors utilized for completing the *nkandu* (contract) with the spirit world so that the *bilongo* works effectively are described as follows: "South: Yellow—fresh water, the river or Simbi spirit; North: Red—change,

114. Please refer to *Palo Mayombe: The Garden of Blood and Bones* by Nicholaj de Mattos Frisvold and to *Flash of the Spirit* by Robert Farris Thompson. Also, for an in depth and superb lecture on the *yowa* please refer to *Ki Kongo cosmograph, historical memory and perspective of time Professor Greg Carr* by Dr. Greg Carr at: <https://www.youtube.com/watch?v=ZtDA7FADdLA>.

115. Martínez-Ruiz, *Kongo Graphic Writing and Other Narratives of the Sign*, pp. 73–74.

116. Martínez-Ruiz, *Kongo Graphic Writing and Other Narratives of the Sign*, p. 70.

transformation, dangerous situation; West: White—purity, perfection; East: Black—underground or death and Center: Blue—(Egáno) inde-structible, pure energy, such as morning dew or rays of the sun, and wholesomeness. It marks the beginning of the motion of energy and the spiritual journey in the circle".[117]

Furthermore, Martínez-Ruiz tells us that overall the beliefs system codified in this image is the same for both the Kongo and the Palo Monte practitioners in Cuba, representing the Ntango (sun) and its stages across the sky. Martínez-Ruiz even points to the Palo Monte Loango branch practiced in Pinar del Río and Matanzas, in Cuba, which includes *firmas* depicting representations of the Ntango in its five critical stages.[118] Hence, this is a Kongo preservation; I will also venture to conclude that the ad-dition of the Ntango and the Ngunda (moon; ☽) in some *firmas* are also Kongo preservations. I make the aforementioned conclusion, because although the Taino and Carib cosmological and cosmogonical system was highly developed, their geometric system of graphic representation and their religious objects did not portray the sun and the moon, to say nothing of their stages.

The following piece of important information provided by Mar-tínez-Ruiz is in regard to the beginning of the Kongo system of graphic writing, which can be traced back to the rupestrian drawings found at Lovo, Mbanza Kongo, Angola. When we compare these early signs, which he provides in a table that compares the different forms of the same drawings at these locations as well as some similar drawings found in Palo Monte,[119] we can see how this codified system was truly preserved in Palo Monte. After, reviewing the large number of drawings presented in Table 4, we can conclude that the vast majority of the Kongo graphic writing system is a codified language of culture and religion which was preserved in the Afro-Cuban religion of Palo Monte as practiced by their Congo descendants. Moreover, the similarities alluded to above seem to be nothing more than this, similarities. The majority of geometric similarities observed while investigating Taino art in comparison with the *firmas* are also found the in the codified graphic writing system of

117. Martínez-Ruiz, *Kongo Graphic Writing and Other Narratives of the Sign*, pp. 76–77.

118. Martínez-Ruiz, *Kongo Graphic Writing and Other Narratives of the Sign*, pp. 76–77.

119. Martínez-Ruiz, Barbaro. *Kongo Graphic Writing and Other Narratives of the Sign*, pp. 81–81.

the Kongo people, which can be traced from the migration of the Bantu people across the Western Central African savannas, through the establishment by the *manikongo* of the Kingdom of Kongo[120], and beyond the incursion of the Portuguese and the capuchins with their brand of Portuguese Catholicism.[121, 122]

We cannot conclude that the geometric visual language of the Taino was borrowed by the Kongo diaspora. Rather, we must understand it as a meeting point between the beliefs and practices of the Taino and the Congo slaves, which informed their cooperation, cohabitation, and fusion in the Caribbean. My claim, then, is that this should be viewed as a universal language which allowed for a better cross-pollination of Taino and Congo ideas and religious and cultural beliefs for the purpose of surviving and obtaining power against the common enemy. This is particularly demonstrated by the Taino story recounted by Ramón Pané in which he tells us that on one occasion six Taino stole several Christian images and threw them on the ground, seemingly for the purpose of borrowing

120. Please refer to *Daily Life in the Kingdom of the Kongo, From the 16th to the 18th Centuries* by Georges Balandier for the best anthropological analysis of the Kingdom of Kongo as recounted by European historical sources as well to *The Kingdom of Kongo* by Anne Hilton, which also provides an equally outstanding anthropological analysis of the Kingdom of Kongo, but with a focused lens on the dynamics and change of its political, social, and religious spheres. Also, please refer to *Power and Prestige: The Rise and Fall of the Kongo Kingdom* by Kajsa Ekholm for an in-depth exploration of the history, and the *Kingdom of Kongo and to The Kongo Kingdom: The Origins, Dynamics and Cosmopolitan Culture of an African Polity* by Koen Bostoen and Inge Brinkman for a modern reevaluation of the historical, anthropological, and linguistic data through the decolonial lens, including the oral histories of the natives. Overall, this approach (which Mignolo would consider in alignment with his imperative methodology) situates and clarifies the history of the Kingdom of Kongo on a much well-balanced and deeply rooted foundation.

121. This historical encounter between the BaKongo and the Portuguese and the unfortunate events that ensued is the reason why we should be careful in assigning Spanish Catholicism as the only brand of Catholicism which influenced Kongolese beliefs and practices. Although Spanish Catholicism heavily influenced the Congo in Cuba, Portuguese Catholicism had had an equal impact on the beliefs and practices of the Kingdom of Kongo prior to and throughout the slave trade, and I argue that by extension, Portuguese Catholicism also influenced the Kongo diaspora, their Congo descendants and their las Reglas de Congo or Palo Monte religion. For an excellent investigation of these themes and more, please refer to *An Anthology of Kongo Religion: Primary Texts from Lower Zaïre* by John M. Janzen and Wyatt MacGaffey, *The Art of Conversion: Christian Visual Culture in the Kingdom of Kongo* by Cécile Fromont, and *The Kongolese Saint Anthony: Dona Beatriz Kimpa Vita and the Antonian Movement, 1684–1706* by John K. Thornton.

122. Martínez-Ruiz, *Kongo Graphic Writing and Other Narratives of the Sign*, pp. 81–88.

their power. Pané tells us that they "covered them with earth and then urinated on them, saying: 'Now your fruits will be good and great'",[123] apparently because they had buried them in a *conuco* or a farming field. This can be understood by utilizing Robiou Lamarche's insight in which he tells us that most likely this behavior demonstrated a religious habitus or a cultural mindset, which allowed for the ready adoption of spiritual symbols based on their utility. Then, by performing the fertility ritual in this way, the Taino were most likely thinking that the religious symbols which the Christian priest had brought were more powerful than their own *cemis*, and thus they readily borrowed the symbols' spiritual power for the purposes of their own survival and empowerment.[124]

Tobacco

The ritual use of tobacco in Palo Monte also reflects another point of contact of the Kongo and the Amerindian religious habitus. The Taino word for tobacco was *cohoba*. *Tabaco* (tobacco in Spanish) meant the bifurcated tube from which the hallucinatory powder was inhaled. Due to the confusion of the Spanish, there was a loss of the original meaning and a misapplication of the latter, which has since become the name of the plant in many languages.[125] The Taino *cohoba* rite was enacted by the *cacique* (chief) or *behique* (shaman) and consisted of induced vomiting for the purposes of purification. The rite also consisted of the inhalation of *cohoba* (in a powdered form) as explained above, with the aim of falling into a trance in order to communicate with the *cemis* (the spirit forces in the other world). The goal of this communication was to bring back a message from the spirit world containing instructions for the living community.[126] The aforementioned practices seem to be in harmony with the shamanistic practices seen in the Americas among other Amerindian groups.

As for the Caribs, the use of tobacco seems to have played an even bigger role in their religious rituals. In fact, unlike their Taino counterparts, the Caribs did not (according to the early French chroniclers) use any other hallucinogenic substance than tobacco for their religious

123. This is obtained from Ramón Pané's manuscript, Chapter XXVI.

124. Robiou Lamarche, *Tainos and Caribs: The Aboriginal Cultures of the Antilles*, pp. 138–39.

125. Wilson, *The Indigenous People of the Caribbean*, p. 163.

126. Wilson, *The Indigenous People of the Caribbean*, p. 167.

rituals. Moreover, the effects induced by the Taino *cohoba* seemed not to have been the same as those exhibited by Caribs when using their tobacco. Rather, they used tobacco as a communication tool through which they established links with their personal gods. This invocation by the *boyez* (the Carib medicine man) consisted of singing songs while he blew up smoke in accompaniment with the singing. The *boyez* would also manipulate the tobacco by squeezing it in his hands, and then blowing it out of his hands with an exhalation of smoke during this ritual performance.[127]

Moreover, the *boyez* would take the smoke in his mouth and blow it in puffs into the air.[128] These practices by the Carib *boyez* are closely aligned with the ritualistic performances of the *paleros* in Palo Monte. I would suggest that if there were a direct influence on the use of tobacco in the religious rituals of Palo Monte, it must have been directly borrowed from these practices of the Carib *boyez* rather than the Taino *cohoba* ritual as usually thought, which seems to have been more complex and sophisticated. Another important detail recorded by an early chronicler described how one of these *boyez* had inherited one of two gods from his father.[129] This is also a common practice among Palo Monte practitioners. When a *ngangulero* dies, his *nganga* or *ngangas* is/are inherited by either a family member or one of his godsons (it could also be disarmed if the *nfumbe* desires it).[130]

In the case of the ritualistic use of tobacco, we find that not only was this incorporated by the Kongolese diaspora, but that it was also incorporated into the West African creole religious manifestations. The Caribbean Amerindians cultivated tobacco for recreational use, but it was also incorporated into religious practices. Ritual specialists blew smoke over ritual paraphernalia (such as images of *cemis*) during their ceremonies.[131] This practice can be observed across all Afro-Cuban creole religions today. This does not seem to be a ritual practice in the Kongo religion or

---

127. Robiou Lamarche, *Tainos and Caribs: The Aboriginal Cultures of the Antilles*, pp. 217 & 219.

128. Robiou Lamarche, *Tainos and Caribs: The Aboriginal Cultures of the Antilles*, pp. 217 & 219.

129. Robiou Lamarche, *Tainos and Caribs: The Aboriginal Cultures of the Antilles*, p. 217.

130. A. Cunha, 'Muerte, muertos y "llanto" palero', *Ateliers d'anthropologie*, 38 (2013) <https://journals.openedition.org/ateliers/9413>.

131. Edmonds, *Caribbean Religious History*, p. 18.

even the Yoruba religion, as the available literature demonstrates a conspicuous absence of this ritual practice.[132]

In Palo Mayombe, (the most traditional of the Kongo-derived religions in Cuba) and in Palo Monte in general (the Kongolese creole religious manifestation in Cuba), we see the use of tobacco smoke, named *nsunga*,[133] in various ritual forms. An example of *nsunga* being used in its ritual form includes the blowing of the smoke directly on the *nganga*, which can be observed in figure 4 of 'Making a Nganga, Begetting a God. Materiality and Belief in the Afro-Cuban Religion of Palo Monte' by K. Kerestetzi.[134] The nganga is also known as *la prenda* or *fundamento*. It is the foundation or fundament of Palo Monte, the magical cauldron where the *minkisi* and the *nfumbe* reside, achieved via the compilation of their material representations within the cauldron. Items such as the *kiyumba* of human beings, *palos*, the machete (the icon of the religion), and varied items from the animal, mineral, and vegetable kingdoms are utilized in order to construct a microcosm of the universe for the main *nkisi* (which can be any of the Kimpungulu), which provides the vital force by which the *nfumbe* manifest in the material plane, especially the *nfumbe* for which the *nganga* is built. It must be said that although there is a main *nfumbe* with which the *palero* or *palera* has made the pact and who acts as the chief or ruling *nfumbe* of the *nganga*, there are in fact many *nfumbe* inside the cauldron and not just one. Since the *nganga* represents a microcosm of the macrocosm (the universe), *paleros* or *paleras* need to provide a boundary or horizon which separates one from the other. This demarcation is achieved through the use of the iron chain around the cauldron.[135]

Also, in order for the *nfumbe* to be able to manifest in all types of material essences on the earth, the *palero* or *palera* tries to provide as

132. N. Lugo Aikulola Iwindara Fewehinmi, 'Diferencias entre Santeria Cubana y la practica de Nigeria', *Asociacion Cultural Yoruba de Canarias* (2014) <https://yorubacanarias.com/3/post/2014/07/diferencias-entre-santeria-cubana-y-la-practica-de-nigeria.html>.

133. Frisvold, *Palo Mayombe: The Garden of Blood and Bones*, p. 206.

134. K. Kerestetzi, 'Making a Nganga, Begetting a God. Materiality and Belief in the Afro-Cuban Religion of Palo Monte', *Ricerche di Storia Sociale e Religiosa*, 87 (2015) <https://www.academia.edu/22295918/Making_a_nganga_begetting_a_god_Materiality_and_Belief_in_the_Afro_Cuban_Religion_of_Palo_Monte>.

135. This summary is of my own making and was synthesized from the many years of audiovisual teachings offered up by Osvaldo Sesti at: *<https://www.youtube.com/user/OsvaldoSesti>*.

many of these essences as possible. Therefore, contrary to popular belief, the size of the *nganga* does not necessarily mean that it is more powerful because it is bigger, but that bigger *ngangas* are more powerful because they contain more of material items found in the universe which allows the *nfumbe* of the *nganga* to manifest in almost all aspects of this earth. Thus, the *minkisi* are more powerful and better equipped to complete any *nsara* required by the *palero* or *palera* and in a much shorter span of time. An example of this would be the introduction of a hollowed-out cane sugar *palo* or bamboo *palo* to the *nganga* that contains sea water inside of it and has been sealed at both ends. By providing this, the *palero* or *palera* is achieving the dual function of transmitting one of the main essences of the sea, that of perpetual motion (mercury ☿ is also used for this purpose in the *mpakas*) and allowing the *nfumbe* to travel and manifest over and on the sea and to travel to distant lands that are separated by the sea. Moreover, these *ngangas*, now built on three-legged iron cauldrons, used to often be built using terracotta or clay cauldrons, especially the Nsasi 7 Rayos cauldron, called a *kandango* (cooking pans or pots, used during the colonial times due to lack of utensils and proper religious paraphernalia), and even on turtle shells. Overall, the *nganga* is the lifeblood of the *palero* or *palera*, and the bloodline of the Ngueyo. It is the cardinal manifestation of the Palo Monte religion. It is also the name given to the medicine men of traditional Kongo belief.[136]

The *nganga* represents and fuses the composite body of the *nfumbe* (the disincarnate intelligences and spirits and the "unique material representation of cosmic and terrestrial powers adorning the resurrected dead")[137], the pure or ideal forms of *nkisi* (*minkisi* plural), and the Mpungo (Kimpungulu in plural). These are the forces behind the natural manifestations and powers that the *palero/palera* (*tata/yaya* that works the *nganga*) works with.[138] There is also the use of tobacco smoke in the ceremonial drink,[139] smoking it while performing works in order to help the *ngangulero* achieve the trance state that enables him to communicate with the spirits.[140] The *nganga* is also fed with tobacco and alcohol, and

136. This summary is of my own making and was synthesized from the many years of audiovisual teachings offered up by Osvaldo Sesti at: *<https://www.youtube.com/user/OsvaldoSesti>*.

137. Frisvold, *Palo Mayombe: The Garden of Blood and Bones*, pp. 44, 69, & 222.

138. Frisvold, *Palo Mayombe: The Garden of Blood and Bones*, pp. 44, 69, & 222.

139. Tukuenda, 'NSUNGA, TABACO'.

140. Frisvold, *Palo Mayombe: The Garden of Blood and Bones*, p. 157.

tobacco is also used when performing the pact with Cobayende in order buy the *nfumbe/nfuri*.[141]

The living dead of the Caribbean Amerindians were known for their particular liking for tobacco while they strolled about at night, while in Haitian Vodou a cigar or cigarette is the essential item of Ghede,[142] the spirit of the dead.[143] Moreover, in Santeria cigars are used by the *santeros* (Lucumi or Santeria Priests) to achieve a trance-like state, and are also used as offerings to the ancestors, known as Egun, as well as a tool in various Ashé-bringing rituals.[144] The use of tobacco is also present in Espiritismo Cruzado (Crossed Spiritism), where *santeros* or *paleros* place cigars on the Boveda Espiritual (spiritual vault) as an offering and way of contacting the dead.[145] Moreover, in Jamaica we see the practice by Obeah practitioners of interring the dead with tobacco pipes.[146] Therefore, the widespread acculturation and appropriation of tobacco for religious practices is significantly represented across the Afro-Caribbean religious diaspora, demonstrated by the imprint of Amerindian ritual forms on the African indigenous religions rooted there.

Ancestral Dead, Cult of the Dead, Cemis, Hanging Calabash, Gurunfinda, Cotton Idols and Ngangas

Perhaps beliefs and practices surrounding the dead represent the greatest point of contact of the African diaspora and the Amerindian religious habitus. The beliefs among the Arawaks (Taino) and Caribs was that the dead returned to a valley in their own country, in the Orinoco Guiana homeland, and would settle at the bottom of a lake.[147] This belief finds its mirror in both the Palo Monte and Haitian Vodou traditions.[148] The Palo

141. Frisvold, *Palo Mayombe: The Garden of Blood and Bones*, pp. 74 & 157.

142. Deren, *Divine Horsemen: The Living Gods of Haiti*, p. 282.

143. Deren, *Divine Horsemen: The Living Gods of Haiti*, pp. 102–14.

144. 'USOS DEL TABACO DENTRO DE LA SANTERÍA E IFA', *TuBrujo.com* (2014) <tubrujo.com/santeria/usos-del-tabaco-dentro-de-la-santeria-e-ifa>.

145. Ayorinde, *Afro-Cuban Religiosity, Revolution, and National Identity*, p. 21.

146. Jerome S. Handler, 'Slave Medicine and Obeah in Barbados, circa 1650 to 1834', *New West Indian Guide / Nieuwe West-Indische Gids*, 74.1–2 (2000), 57–90 (p. 70) <doi:10.1163/13822373–90002570>.

147. Deren, *Divine Horsemen: The Living Gods of Haiti*, p. 277.

148. It is also worth mentioning that in the East of Cuba there has been a long-standing presence of a Haitian diaspora. Their culture and influence has been increasingly poignant in the development of new forms of Afro-Caribbean practice in the

Monte tradition has the concept of Kalunga (the abysmal waters and the dead liquid of space, which itself is a Kongo belief) that comes to mean a multiplicity of things, but centrally, is the ocean, the passage to the king-dom of death and ancestry. Kalunga was both a metaphor for death and the fluid immanence of death itself, and since humans are composed of water, acting as carriers of this ancestral memory, this created the percep-tion of a shared materiality between the dead and the living under the collecting force of Nzambi (God).[149]

The Taino veneration of the ancestral dead through the *cemis* as well as the hanging of dried-out calabash or common fig with the bones of the ancestors, and the placement of the bones of *caciques* and great men in baskets or in plaited cotton fetishes are also particularly important among these trends of similitude between the two cultures.[150] An ex-ample of these Taino practices can be seen on page 180 of *Taino and Car-ibs: The Aboriginal Cultures of the Antilles*,[151] which depicts photographs and x-rays of a cotton idol with a human skull on its head. Nonetheless, this point of contact only reflects another avenue for the easy fusion of these cultures and not the factual absorption of these practices by the African diaspora. After all, we have seen that Africans came with similar ideas already ingrained in their beliefs and practices and therefore direct influence cannot be determined just from the scholarly record. Further ethnographical and empirical work may determine the level of influence these Taino practices had on the beliefs and practices of Palo Monte.

Moreover, like the Kongo Diaspora, the Taino respected their an-cestors, and their beliefs and practices were passed down orally from generation to generation, informing another aspect of the respect paid to the dead and the ancestors. The Taino believed that it was important to listen to elders and to venerate them after death in order to obtain their blessing, knowledge, and any wisdom the living may need. The practice

---

east. One such example of this is the new offspring of Palo Monte and Haitian Vodou called Palo Haitiano. This syncretism demonstrates the point made above about the similitudes in beliefs and practices observed in both traditions, which in turn derive many of their beliefs and practices from the Kongo diaspora. For a full exploration of this new East Cuba *rama* please refer to: *Palo Kimbiza: Brillumba Palo Kimbiza-Tumba Francesa Kikongo Piti Bantu Criollo Sanci and Palo Haitiano* by Reverend Baba Sabu Akoni Ifa Shola, described by the author as the book that presents the Haitian lineage of Congo worship transplanted to Cuba by Haitians.

149. Frisvold, *Palo Mayombe: The Garden of Blood and Bones*, pp. 2 &51.

150. Deren, Maya, *Divine Horsemen: The Living Gods of Haiti*, p. 278.

151. Robiou Lamarche, 2019.

of placing the bones of ancestors in dried calabash or dried vessels made from the common fig, which were then placed in a special location inside the *bohío* in order to pay them respect, was an important Taino tradition.[152] This practice of veneration resembles the Palo Monte practice of Gurunfinda. Gurunfinda is the power who provides the materials that make possible the animation of the corpse; there is not one *palero* who expects his corpse to work without the blessings of Gurunfinda. Gurunfinda is the power who sanctifies the herbs and sticks used in the practice of Palo Monte, which includes the construction of the *ngangas* itself. Gurunfinda is considered the lord or Mpungo of the forest and knows its secrets and mysteries, as well as those of Palo Monte, for that matter. This Mpungo is placed in a hanging dried-out *jicara* (calabash) in the middle of the *munanzo* which has been filled with bones (the provenance of which is unspecified as it is the most guarded secret of the religion) together with all sorts of things from the mineral and vegetal kingdoms.[153] This reflects a Taino influence.

The BaKongo, including the Angolan and Congolese people as well, had three ways of utilizing ancestral bones, together with the power of a specific *nkisi*. The three forms or manifestations involve the *ntende* (*cesto*—basket), the *nzungo* (*cazuela*—casserole) and the *makuku* (*caldero*—cauldron),[154] which are elements linked with Taino traditions of ancestral worship.[155] These parallels in the Taino and Palo practices in connection with the veneration of ancestors offer another example of the Taino influence on Palo Monte. Consequently, the Palo Monte ritual use of the *nganga* and the bones (including the skull called the *kiyumba*) of the ancestor or enslaved spirit bolsters my position.[156] As we have noted above, the inclusion of the skull in both the Palo Monte *nganga* and the cotton idol of the Taino formed and forms an integral part of these religious manifestations.

In the Kongo tradition there were wooden statues containing *nkisi* (in the case of beneficent spirits) or *ndoki* (in the case of maleficent spirits), which the *Yombe* people used to materialize the spirits in order to seek healing, protection, or revenge. These wooden statues, which were

---

152. Muñoz-Pando, *Creencias Mortuorias De Los Aborígenes Antillanos, Taínos Y Caribes*, 8.

153. Frisvold, *Palo Mayombe: The Garden of Blood and Bones*, pp. 117–18.

154. The translations into English are by the author.

155. Ferrer, *Raíces del Palo Monte en Cuba*, p. 45.

156. Deren, *Divine Horsemen: The Living Gods of Haiti*, p. 278.

anthropomorphic figures, charged by the *bilongos* (works, witchcraft, or potions) of the *nganga* (priest),[157] share much in terms of meaning and practice with the Taino *cemis*. The Taino *cemi* was made of stone or wood (hollowed out and containing speaking tubes when made of wood) and was said to be the receptacle of the spirit of the ancestral dead and the intermediary between the living and the divine. The *cemi* was addressed by the name of the father or other ancestral dead, and in return for their veneration would speak out oracles and advice, as is done in the Palo Monte practice of throwing the *chamalongos* for the purpose of directly addressing the dead found in the *nganga* in order to obtain their advice and wisdom.[158] My sense here is that this Palo practice demonstrates a strong Taino flavor.

The traditional Kongo power figure, *nkisi n'kondi*, did not include the skull in its entirety, but rather a medicine pouch in its belly composed of the magically charged bundle prepared by the *nganga*, the name for the Kongo indigenous priest in the African Kongolese practice. In Palo Monte, the cauldron, which I argue was an inheritance from Taino traditions, has assumed the identity, as well as the name *nganga*. This medicine bundle included varied compositions, depending on the needs of the individual or community. Generally, however, it contained various tree cuttings or plants without their barks, various types of earth, a horn with a mirror, some 'primitive' tools, money, cranial bones, as well as human phalanges and metacarpals. Animal bones were also included as symbolic representations of particular animals. The horn with the mirror was used for the purposes of divination, like its counterpart in Palo Monte, the *mpaka vititi menzo*.[159]

The addition of the cranial bones as well as the phalanges and metacarpals of humans and animals varied from *nkisi n'kondi* to *nkisi n'kondi*. Sometimes these bones were grounded into an *mpolo* (powder) and sometimes the bones as well as the cranium were added whole. The idea behind this practice (as in the construction of the *nganga* in Palo Monte) was to reconstruct a microcosm of the universe for the *nkisi* (the dead and the *bakisi banene*, the powers of nature empowering the dead, including the specific Mpungo working with that venerated dead) so that their power would be manifested in all the forces of the universe. This

---

157. Jo Tollebeek, *Mayombe: Ritual Statues from Congo* (Tielt, Belgium: Lannoo, 2011), p. 71.

158. Deren, Maya, *Divine Horsemen: The Living Gods of Haiti*, p. 278.

159. Ferrer, *Raíces del Palo Monte en Cuba*, pp. 45–46.

was achieved by providing the *minkisi* with material representations of the animal, mineral, and vegetal kingdoms.[160] The construction of the *nganga*, the foundation of Palo practice, is informed largely by Amerindian beliefs and practices in connection with the veneration of ancestors, especially the inclusion of the skull, cotton idols, and hanging gourds. The *nganga* as we find it in Palo as an object and practice is nothing but a performance of Kongo and Amerindian memory.

Although the *nganga* and the *fundamento* of Gurunfinda have their provenance in the performance of Kongo and Amerindian memory, the power and religious influence behind the construction of the first *nganga* and Gurunfinda *fundamento* seem to have been of Abakuá and Pygmy origin, a connection that Frisvold himself hints and connects with the founding legend of the Abakuá.[161] I base this on the origin story of the first Brillumba *fundamento* as detailed in *Palo Mayombe: The Garden of Blood and Bones*.[162] The Brillumba origin story tells us that the first *kiyumba* used for the construction of a *nganga* was that of an individual named Mambe who was sacrificed in order to keep the spirit of Ngó (leopard) strong. Mambe's *kiyumba*, together with an assortment of dismembered body parts and material from the animal and vegetable kingdoms, were then placed with Ngó inside a calabash veiled in wax. The purpose of this was to reanimate the spirit of Ngó who still aided Mambele and his lineage (including his grandson Mambe who was sacrificed), who dressed like leopards in combat, and who used the blood of Ngó to empower their *mpakas* and give them enhanced fighting senses.[163]

This cultural and religious syncretism was most likely precipitated by their geographical and cultural proximity in the Cross River region of Calabar, situated in what was the upper Kongo and lower Nigerian landscape.[164] This syncretic process seems to have been the catalyst for the creation of cultural and religious transculturations that not only took place in Africa, but also in Cuba's foreign lands, an observation which supports the Calabarí origin for the power and religious influence behind the construction of the first *nganga*. For example, see the use of the word Ngó (which is an Efik word), meaning leopard,[165] in the Palo

160. Ferrer, *Raíces del Palo Monte en Cuba*, pp. 45–46.
161. Frisvold, *Palo Mayombe: The Garden of Blood and Bones*, pp. 78–79.
162. Frisvold, *Palo Mayombe: The Garden of Blood and Bones*, pp. 75–79.
163. Frisvold, *Palo Mayombe: The Garden of Blood and Bones*, pp. 75–78.
164. Frisvold, *Palo Mayombe: The Garden of Blood and Bones*, pp. 75–78.
165. Diaz Fabelo, Teodoro, *Diccionario de la Lengua Conga Residual en Cuba* (Vista

Monte *mambo* at the at the end of this book (Postlude: Valediction) titled *Toque de Palo Monte-Buena Noche* (Palo Monte Ensemble, Good Night), where the following phrase *'Buena noche Ngó, saludando Ngó'* ('Good night Leopard, salutations Leopard') is recorded in the oral tradition of Palo Monte's liturgical cycle, used as a salutation call to the forces of Ngó and as a recognition for lending its power to the *ngangas* and the initiates. As for the power and religious influence behind the construction of the *fundamento* of Gurunfinda, please refer to the *'Excursus'* of this book.

Maboya, Ndoki, the Coribib Chemin and the Lechuza

Much like the idea of the *ndoki* in Palo Monte, the Caribs believed that there was a malevolent spirit/force named Maboya (as well as the less commonly used Mabouya and Mapoya). This spirit, they believed, caused upsets and disruptions in all aspects of their lives. The Maboya resided in the arms and, after the death of the individual in whom it had resided, moved into the woods to become the Spirit of the Forest. Caribs believed that Maboyas dwelled in the *guano* or balsa tree (*Ochroma pyramidale*). These spirits, they believed, were the third of the three spirits which inhabited the human body and constituted one of the three souls of humans that were transformed into the "evil spirits to which they attributed everything sinister and ill-fated."[166] To add to this similarity, the second spirit or 'soul' present in the human body, which was located in the head, was called Uméku and was also considered to be mischievous and somewhat malevolent after death. This spirit went, after the death of the individual in which it resided, to the edge of the sea to wreck boats. This second spirit also resonates with the idea of *ndoki*, which although found in the human psyche and can be seen to constitute the attributes of both spirits two and three, does resemble tremendously the idea of *ndoki* found in Palo Monte.

In Palo Monte, there is a specialized type of *nganga* called a nganga Judía (Jewish nganga), which is used solely for the purpose of *kindnoki* (the art or practice of *ndoki*), a specialized subsection of Palo Monte where practices such as *cambio de cabeza* (head exchange; see glossary)

Alegre, Santiago de Cuba: Casa del Caribe. Universidad de Alcalá. UNESCO ORCALC. Colección Africanía, 2007), p. 39; Cabrera, Lydia, and Isabel Castellanos, *Vocabulario Congo* (Miami, Florida: Ediciones Universal, 2001), p.247.

166. Robiou Lamarche, *Tainos and Caribs: The Aboriginal Cultures of the Antilles*, pp. 216–17.

and the complete submission of someone's free will, for their absolute subjugation, are commonplace. This *nganga*'s power, which has its own rituals and initiatory requirements as well as its own liturgy, falls under the domain of Lukankazi (see glossary), its ruling Mpungo, and the *nkisi* that provides the vital force to the malevolent or dark *nfumbe* called *nfuri*. However, *nfuri* should not be confused with *nfuiri*, the chamalongo sign of death. Rather, *nfuri* is the evil and tormented *nfumbe* with which the Palero made the pact, and which resides inside the nganga Judía. Although considered the fastest acting and most powerful of all the *ngangas*, it has a reputation among practitioners of ngangas Cristianas (Christian ngangas) of being ultimately harmful to the owner, whom the *nfumbe* slowly 'eats' (a Kongo preservation; see *ndoki* in the Glossary). This nganga is so powerful, however, that only a special *nganga* consisting of a hybrid of the Nsasi Siete Rayos and Zarabanda *ngangas* can fight against it.

The terms nganga Cristiana and nganga Judía refer to the addition of the Catholic crucifix or lack thereof, respectively, as a symbolic and factual spiritual force that either enacts Christian systems of values and ethics through the nganga (nganga Cristiana) or acts opposite or against these values and ethics when absent (nganga Judía). Also, the use of the word Judía here should not be taken as an anti-Semite sentiment, but rather should be understood from a perspective of the rich history of the Kingdom of Kongo as a Catholic country, and the enforced religious hegemony of Spanish Catholicism on the Congo diaspora, which understood the world through the lens of the Old and New Testaments and the messiah Jesus Christ. Thus, when referring to the maleficent *ngangas* as ngangas Judías, the Congo diaspora in Cuba and in particular Palo Monte practitioners refer here to the absence of the figure of Jesus Christ and all he represents as embodied through Christian values, rather than to a tarnishing anti-Semite sentiment against Judaism and its values and ethics. I also believe that this practice, being heavily influenced by the Christian tradition, may have dovetailed with the Western magical tradition.

I am particularly referring to the section in the pseudo-epigraphical *Testament of Solomon* where a reference is made to the destruction of Solomon's temple and the cataclysmic aftermath when the vessels containing the evil spirits which had been confined in them by King Solomon would be broken, resulting in their release, at which time they would be free to roam all over the world "until the Son of God is stretched upon the Cross, a King dominating all spirits, and conceived by his mother without contact with man. Him the first devil will tempt, but no prevail over and the number of his name 644, which is Emmanuel"[167], a millenarian prophesy imparted by the chthonic, two-headed female demon Ενέψιγος (*Enêpsigos*) who tells King Solomon that she is able to take on three different forms. The first, as described, is as a two-headed female demon called Ενέψιγος, the second as the Greek Titan Κρόνος (*Krónos* or Saturnus for the Romans; ♄), and the third as a triple-faced woman that has been associated with the Greek goddess Ἑκάτη (*Hekátē*, who in turn is associated with the three phases of the moon: ☽ ☿ ☾ [168]).[169]

Therefore, the concept of *ndoki* in Palo Monte is reserved in Cuba for something that is evil or bad. More importantly, this idea of *ndoki* is also an important part of the human psyche and is something that all humans have to varying degrees, or rather to various degrees of occultation. *Ndoki* is also used as a reference to the ancestors (*bakulu*), in which it is called *bakulu ndoki*, but this category of ancestors is considered bad or powerful (in the sense of a *brujo* or sorcerer). Overall, in Cuba, the concept of *ndoki* is seen also as the veiled aspects of ancestry, or what is termed 'the night of the ancestors'. Palo practitioners say that we all carry these elements within ourselves and that they form an integral part of our

---

167. Conybeare, *The Testament of Solomon*, p. 3

168. In the Lucumi tradition, Hekate's parallel divinity, the queen of the cult of witchcraft, is known as Ìyáàmi Òṣòròngá. However, although Ìyáàmi Òṣòròngá, can be considered Hekate's parallel divinity in Afro-Cuban traditions, as a warning, please refrain for uttering or writing this name. This name should only be spoken or written down by the Dignitaries or Elders of the Night; that is, Sorcerers, Sorceresses, and Witches and Warlocks. If the name is spoken, uttered or written down during the day (after sunrise and prior to sunset) by anybody else, this person should mark, with his index finger, an X in the ground where they stood when they wrote it or said. If the name is spoken, uttered written down during the night time (after sunset and prior to sunrise), then the person has to make the X on his body, starting from the back portion of the crown of their head (using the index finger), all the way to the end of his feet. These Xs are done with the index finger of the left hand. As for Dignitaries or Elders of the Night, the most propitious times to call on this energy/force/power/deity are (at a crossroads, liminal places, doors, etc.) at 12:00pm and 12:00am, for good works and bad works respectively. In the case that a person is not an Dignitary or Elder of the Night, but hears her name spoken in their presence, he/she should do either of two things: if he/she is sitting down when this occurs, then he/she needs to stand up as a sign of respect and recognition to the Grand Ancestral Mother and if he/she is standing up, then he/she needs to bow in veneration, respect and recognition to this primordial feminine energy/force/power and its role as generator of life. Information gathered from *Iyami Oshoronga (Los Ancianos de la Noche): El Culto a los Ancianos de la Noche* by Luis Diaz Castrillo.

169. Conybeare, *The Testament of Solomon*, pp. 2–4

unique composition, which defines our actions. Moreover, these night or dark forces are seen as the source of power from which acts of transgression, violence, and miracles are expressed. *Ndoki* then is the powerful part within humans that remains hidden from light and can be used for good or for evil depending on the context and wisdom of the individual.[170]

Furthermore, there are some Palo Monte lineages such as the Changani lineage, which segregates a place in the *nganga*, dedicated solely to the manifestation of *ndoki*. These lineages see this as a separate part of the nganga Cristiana and refer to it as Chicherichu or Chicherikú. These Chicherikú are usually wooden images or dolls which isolate the *ndoki* part of the nganga Cristiana. This isolated portion is enlisted when the *palero* desires to perform important and powerful rituals. Represented by maggots and termites and the decay of offerings which are left in the *munanzo* after sacrifice or offerings, this Chicherikú represents wickedness in humans. However, although the Chicherikú represents that which is aggressive and tense, it also, paradoxically, carries great protective potency and raw power, which can be used for good.[171]

The traditional Kongo beliefs regarding *ndoki* are a bit different than the current conceptualizations of the Cuban Palo Monte beliefs and related practices as explained above. The term *ndoki* was used often to refer to the underworld, as in Ku'mpemba (not Kalunga as some think), where the dead are living, and which is guarded by Luvemba (translated as threshold or door). However, Luvemba is also, sometimes, referred to as *nsila* (as we saw in the subsection 'Geometric Diagrams and Their Representations', which means a crossing or pathway. It is also worth mentioning that for the BaKongo, Kalunga means the vastness that is continuously moved by Nzambi, the creative and fertilizing agent of creation. Nzambi acts through its fire of creation as an active principle which comes into duality and dynamics with the cooling waters of Kalunga manifested in the interplay of degeneration and generation of the *minkisi*. *Ndoki* then is nothing more than knowledge from Ku'mpemba that humans bring with them into life. This is said to be strong in some and weak in others. It also leads to differences in the potential of these forces manifesting in the lives of humans. However, like the Palo practice of Chicherikú, the Bwiti practice from Gabon tries to remove the shadow aspect or the shadow portion of this knowledge that comes with us through the initiation rites

170. Frisvold, *Palo Mayombe: The Garden of Blood and Bones*, pp. 11 & 30.
171. Frisvold, *Palo Mayombe: The Garden of Blood and Bones*, p. 73.

of Iboga. The Iboga rite focuses on removing these shadows so that the raw protective potencies can be focused towards flourishing in a centered and benevolent manner, which can bring health to the community and to the individual.[172] This last point is in close connection with the Palo Monte belief in *ndoki* as some force that is powerful and capable of performing miracles for the good of the community, as noted above.

For the BaKongo, the term *ndoki* was reserved for those individuals who had become devoted to the dark arts of evil. These men were feared by the BaKongo and were considered assassins and devourers of souls. Moreover, these men did not make use of the *minkisi*, but rather sought the powers and fury of malevolent spirits of hate and vengeance called Nkonde or Nkose. The *ndoki* (the men) made use of these malevolent spirits through the use of conjures, which excited these restless spirits (resembling the idea of the *nfuri*, restless spirits in Palo Monte), which were charged with causing maladies and ailments of all kinds.[173] In comparison with the traditional Kongo view of *ndoki*, the aforementioned creole beliefs and practices, I believe, have been influenced by the Carib belief of the three souls found in the human body and their roles after the death of the individual.

Another important commonality observed, and one I have not found evidence of in the traditional Kongo belief system, is that of the owl as the messenger of death and the otherworld. More precisely, the Caribs believed that the *coribib chemin* (the *lechuza*, which is a type of owl endemic to Cuba, and which goes by the scientific name *Spéoyto cunincularia*), was the messenger bird of the afterlife and of the ancestral spirits. The Caribs believed that its song was a bad omen or a sign of death itself. On the other hand, the Caribs believed that the presence of bats, which they called *bulliri*, flying inside their homes was a good omen. They believed the bats were *cemis* that had come to protect them, and that anyone who did harm to the bats would become sick.[174]

The *coribib chemin* was also an important animal for the *boyez*, playing a significant role in the consecration ceremony of the young and aspiring newly volunteered *boyez*. During the ceremony of the consecration of the soon-to-be *boyez*, which was performed in the *carbet* (see page 218 of *Tainos and Caribs* for an artistic representation of the *coribib*

172. Frisvold, *Palo Mayombe: The Garden of Blood and Bones*, p. 73.

173. Ferrer, *Raíces del Palo Monte en Cuba*, pp. 37–38.

174. Robiou Lamarche, *Tainos and Caribs: The Aboriginal Cultures of the Antilles*, p. 217.

chemin and the *Boyez* initiatory ritual)[175], a small opening called the *tourar* was left intentionally so that the *coribib chemin* could be allowed to enter during the nocturnal stage of the ceremony due to its significance in the life of the newly consecrated *boyez*.[176] In Palo Monte, *nfuá* (death) is important and the *yimbe* (*brujo* or warlock) is its faithful ally, and for this reason *nfuá* compacts with the life of practitioners and protects them. *Nfuá* is believed in Palo Monte to translocate or move itself through the *lechuza* (the smaller owl known by the scientific name *Spéoyto cunincularia*), which lends its body to *nfuá* so that it may use it as its only mode of transportation on earth.[177] This Palo Monte belief, I conclude, was a direct borrowing from the Carib belief in the *coribib chemin* as the messenger of the death and the underworld.

Caracaracol, Kuballende, Babalú-Ayé and San Lázaro

In this subsection I will explore the nature of one of the twin brothers, Caracaracol and the Mpungo Kuballende. The reason for this is that there appears to be a point of commonality between the mythical Caribbean Amerindian Caracaracol and the Mpungo Kuballende, the Oricha Babalú-Ayé, and the Catholic saint, San Lázaro. According to the Caribbean Amerindian myth of the four twin brothers, the brother who was named Dimiuan and who was designated with the title of Caracaracol (which means scabby) was the first brother to be taken out of his mother (Gaia). Moreover, this brother, beyond the myth of creation, also played an important role in the myth cycles of the Caribbean Amerindians. The name Caracaracol was recorded previously, in the story of the re-creation of women among the Amerindians of the island of Hayti. According to this Taino myth, the Caracaracoli (the plural form) were sent to the island of Martinique, with the responsibility of grabbing the non-sexually differentiated 'women', who stood in the form of eagles. The myth tells us that these Caracaracoli were assigned with this task, because of the scabby and hard nature of their skin.[178]

175. Robiou Lamarche, 2019.

176. Robiou Lamarche, *Tainos and Caribs: The Aboriginal Cultures of the Antilles*, p. 217.

177. Rojas Calderon, *Palo Brakamundo*, p. 54.

178. Bourne, *Columbus, Ramon Pane, and the Beginnings of American Anthropology*, pp. 13–17.

The Taino myth informs us that (as mentioned above) that these Caracaracoli had rough hands which allowed them to hold tightly onto these sexually undeveloped women. Pané explains that these Caracaracoli derived their name from a disease which creates scabs that make the body very rough. The origin of this disease was derived from the myth of the four twin brothers who visit their grandfather in his *bohio* (recorded in Chapter 3). The genesis of this disease for the Taino was thus based on the encounter between the brothers' grandfather and Caracaracol, who was hit with his grandfather's bag of *cogioba* from which the disease sprang forth. Another story important to tracing the Caribbean Amerindian influence on the Afro-Cuban deities of Kuballende and Babalú-Ayé, and the Catholic saint, San Lázaro, is that of Guahagiona. The Taino mythical story of Guahagiona tells us of how this king was suffering from ailments from which he could get no respite. This king, who was very rich and respected, could not get rid of the disease ailing him. Only a woman he encountered on the ocean was able to help him, by washing his ailments with an unknown plant.[179]

Pané informs us that this mythical Guahagiona suffered from a body full of sores. He then observes that the most likely explanation for this mythical disease was an infection he saw among the Caribbean Amerindians when the Spanish arrived. Pané tells us that he believed the origin of both the myth and the infection to be the 'French disease'. Bourne notes that this was a translation by Ulloa of the Spanish *las bubas* (syphilis).[180] Therefore, I conclude that this disease was endemic to the Caribbean and had appeared there long before the Spanish arrived (with their own endemic illnesses). The prominent role of the Caracaracol (as well as the Caracaracoli) in the myth of the Caribbean Amerindians, together with the development of this myth before the arrival of the Spanish, raises the question of the influence of this mythological figure and his disease on the Afro-Caribbean religions in Cuba. My conclusion is that the figure of the saint San Lázaro, the Mpungo Kuballende, and Oricha Babalú-Ayé were directly influenced by this Taino myth and character.

The saint San Lazaro was viewed by the Catholic Church as not being Catholic in origin, but as a Caribbean colonial invention, arguing that San Lázaro had originated from the distortion and fusion of the two

179. Bourne, *Columbus, Ramon Pane, and the Beginnings of American Anthropology*, pp. 13–17.

180. Bourne, *Columbus, Ramon Pane, and the Beginnings of American Anthropology*, pp. 13–17.

Lazarus stories found in the Christian bible since it is only after the Spanish colonial period in the Caribbean and the Catholic encounter with Afro-Caribbean creole religious manifestations that we see the emergence of the image of San Lázaro venerated today. Ultimately, the Church concluded that this religious encounter led to the syncretization of both biblical individuals named Lazarus into one image, which was developed in close connection with the African imagery of the god Babalú-Ayé or Kuballende. My informed hypothesis is that this syncretic process may have had its origin from the Taino mythical figure of Caracaracol and its prominent position among the Caribbean Amerindians. This is especially evident in the fact that after the colonial expansion, and the syncretization of the Catholic and Afro-Caribbean religions in Cuba, we see the manifestation in Spain of the same saint with the same imagery in the church of San Nicolás in Bilbao, although, as the Catholic Church had decreed, this San Lázaro did not appear in the Bible. Likewise, San Lázaro plays a prominent role in the lives of the Afro-Caribbean believers and is seen as a particularly miraculous saint, with equally potent spiritual qualities.[181]

Although there is the equivalent god of diseases in the Yoruba pantheon (Babalú- Ayé) and the Congo pantheon (Koballende), the role they play in the traditional forms of these religions is as a minor god, although they are much feared and respected.[182] Even more interestingly, is the primacy (only second in devotion in Cuba to Oshún) with which Kuballende (the Cuban name of the god/force of nature) is venerated in Guanabacoa, La Habana, Cuba. This region of Cuba is considered one of the epicenters of the religion, which even declares Kuballende (San Lázaro) as the king of the religion. In Matanzas, the other epicenter of the religion, Nzasi Sasi or 7 Rayos is the supreme Mpungo.[183] Kuballende is considered to have absolute dominion over the dead, night, and the religion of Palo Monte, with its cult of the dead. Kuballende is also thought to be the inseparable friend of 7 Rayos, who is considered the father of the four human twins

181. 'Conozca Acerca De La Devoción A San Lázaro En Cuba', *DimeCuba* (2020) <https://www.dimecuba.com/revista/noticias-cuba/conozca-acerca-de-la-devocion-a-san-lazaro/>.

182. A. B. Ellis, *The Yoruba-Speaking Peoples of the Slave Coast of West Africa; Their Religion, Manners, Customs, Laws, Language, Etc. With an Appendix Containing a Comparison of the Tshi, Ga, Ewe, And Yoruba Languages* (London: Chipman and Hall, ltd., 1894), pp. 73–74.

183. 'Conozca Acerca De La Devoción A San Lázaro En Cuba' (2020).

who redeem humanity.[184] However, this is not the case in the Kongo traditional religion, where the origins of humanity can be traced back to three siblings named Kuiti Kuiti, Nkunda Mbaki Nranda and Mboze.[185] Therefore, it can be concluded that the Palo Monte belief in the four twins who redeem humanity is a direct Caribbean Amerindian influence.

The Mpungo Watariamba or Vence Bataya, Ochosi, Zarabanda and Ogun

By the way of conclusion, I would like to seal this chapter with a discussion of the *Mpungo* Watariamba and the Mpungo Zarabanda as formalizing the fusion of Caribbean Amerindian beliefs by the African diaspora in Cuba. The Mpungo, which is known in Palo Mayombe as Watariamba (*Wa tári a mbá* means 'stone of fire' in Kikongo) or as Vence Bataya, is syncretized in the Brillumba branch with the Oricha Ochosi. Both the Mpungo and the *Oricha* symbolize the spirit or power (in the case of Palo Monte) of the hunt, the hunter, and hunting in general. Watariamba is also considered the spirit or power that symbolizes war and justice. Other names of this Mpungo include Nkuyu Buenco, Saca Empeño, Lupokuyo, Santisi and Cabo Ronda. When Nkuyu is found in the name of the Mpungo, as in one of the examples above, it gives the added meaning of 'the errant spirit of the fiery stone' to the name.[186]

What is important to the thesis of this book, however, and what constitutes the most important aspect of this Mpungo in my investigation of the Caribbean Amerindian influence on the beliefs and practices of the Palo Monte religion, is the fact that the Mpungo Watariamba epitomizes the syncretic process of assimilation and integration explored so far. Watariamba then, is the Mpungo which exemplifies the Amerindian contributions to the Afro-Caribbean Congo-derived religion of Palo Monte. An important observation we must underline before we delve into the formalization of this syncretic process is the fact that the following information applies to the Brillumba branch of the religion and the Lucumi tradition in Cuba, but not the much older and traditional branch of Palo Mayombe. With this observation, supported by the fact that no similar

184. Rojas Calderon, *Palo Brakamundo*, pp. 39 & 43.
185. Ferrer, *Raíces del Palo Monte en Cuba*, pp. 31–33, 36 & 57.
186. Frisvold, *Palo Mayombe: The Garden of Blood and Bones*, pp. 91–93.

Mpungo is observed in the Kongo pantheon,[187] I conclude that beyond being the quintessential Caribbean Amerindian assimilation into the Congo diaspora in Cuba, the Mpungo Watariamba also holds the keys to understanding all of the aforementioned syncretic process. If we observe the mythology and legends associated with the Mpungo or the Oricha which were incorporated with it in the Afro-Cuban pantheon, then we can deduce a direct preservation epitomizing this syncretic process.

Although the Mpungo Watariamba and the Nigerian Orisha Oshoosi refer to the same spirit or power described above, their representations and myths vary from those of the Brillumba branch and the Lucumi tradition in Cuba.[188] Therefore, I will focus on the Brillumba and Lucumi explanation of this spirit or power, rather than the Palo Mayombe and traditional Nigerian Orisha worship and Ifá tradition.[189] This rationale will become apparent once the conceptions of the former creole manifestations are explored. Vence Bataya, or Palo Fuerte as he is also known (due to the main *palo*, stick or tree, used for his constructions) is conceived as the Mpungo or Oricha which gives the power or gift of astral

187. Ferrer, *Raíces del Palo Monte en Cuba*, pp. 25–57.

188. Frisvold, *Palo Mayombe: The Garden of Blood and Bones*, pp. 91–93. Also see Michael omo'Oshoosi, 'Study Notes for the Orisha Òshóòsi, *Oshoosi.com* (2015) <https://oshoosi.com/oshoosi-details.html>.

189. For those interested in a full investigation of the differences between the Lucumi tradition in Cuba, the traditional Nigerian *Orisha* worship, the Afro-Cuban Ifá and the traditional Nigerian Ifá, please refer to the following works: *Orí Eledá mí ó. . .Si mi Cabeza no me Vende*; *Obí Agbón: Lukumí Divination with Coconut*; *Adimú—Gbogbó Tén'unjé Lukumí: Revised and expanded English-Language Edition*; *Curamaguey: Enclave Lucumí en Matanzas*; *On the Orishas' Roads and Pathways: Oshun, Deity of Femininity*; *On the Orishas' Roads and Pathways: Yemojá, Mother of the World*; *On the Orishas' Roads and Pathways: Obatalá, Odúa, Oduduwá*; *Asé Omó Osayín.ewé Ayé* and *Oro Egungun.Las Honras de Egungun* by Míguel W. Ramos, Ilarí Obá; *Echu-Elegguá: Equilibrio dinámico de la existencia (religión yorubá)* and *Los Orichas en África: Una Aproximación a Nuestra Identidad* by Adrían de Souza Hernández; *Santeria: the Religion: Faith, Rites, Magic* by Migene González-Wippler; *Santeria: The Beliefs and Rituals of a Growing Religion in America* by Miguel A. De La Torre; *ORISA: Yoruba Gods and Spiritual Identity in Africa and the Diaspora* and *ÈŞÙ: Yoruba God, Power, and the Imaginative Frontiers* by Toyin Falola; *Òsun Sèègèsí: The Elegant Deity of Wealth, Power, and Femininity* by Diedre L. Badejo; *City of 201 Gods: Ilé-Ifè in Time, Space, and the Imagination* and *Ifá Divination, Knowledge, Power, and Performance* by Jacob K. Olupona; *Ilé Tüntun: La Nueva Tierra Sagrada* by Frank Cabrera Suárez, Òkàmbí; *Defendiendo Nuestras Tradiciones Tomos I-III*; *Teología en Ifá: Nuestra Visión de Olodumare y los Orishas*; *Comprendiendo Nuestras Tradiciones* and *Enseñanzas de un Amigo un Hermano, un Mastro* by Leonel Gámez Osheniwó y Águila de Ifá; *Ifá: A Forest of Mystery* by Nicholaj De Mattos Frisvold and *Ifá: The Book of Wisdom* by Chief Olayinka Babatunde Ogunsina Adewuyi.

travel. He also endows the hunter with the ability to merge with both the wild, and the soul of the animal he is hunting. This gift, given by Vence Bataya or Ochosi, allows the hunter to approach his prey in silence, so that he is not detected, ensuring success in the hunt. He also holds the secrets of Ntoto (the Earth) and the *mpolos* (powders) of the wilderness, since this is where his domain lies and where he is resurrected.[190]

This parallelism, of Gurunfinda and Vence Bataya, is a fact I briefly explore in the 'Excursus' of this book.[191] In the case of the Caribbean Amerindians, the Mpungo Vence Bataya (in Palo Brillumba and the Lucumi tradition) is conceived as having a pact with the Mpungo Zarabanda, who is believed to execute his potency. The Mpungo Zarabanda is the spirit or power of iron and fire and represents or symbolizes the force behind the blacksmith. Beyond being the *tronco mayor* (major trunk) of the Brillumba branch and the owner of the *mbele* (the machete; an icon of the religion) the Mpungo Zarabanda is also historically significant. The historical significance of the Mpungo Zarabanda lies in the fact that the histories of the BaKongo and Bantu-speaking people of West Central Africa are intimately tied with the practice of metallurgy. This practice, reflected in the name of their kingdom (*kongo* means iron in Kikongo)[192] and the wealth it brought them, would eventually make them important players on the African continent, while securing them a respected position as a technologically advanced and powerful kingdom.[193] Hence, on the basis of this understanding, we could take the Mpungo Zarabanda to represent or symbolize the BaKongo or Bantu-speaking people.

On the other hand, the creole attributes of Vence Bataya and the Orisha Ochosi paint him as an Amerindian, who lives in the woods and is a great hunter and fisherman. This force or spirit is believed to possess shamanistic powers, which allows him to induce powerful visions. He is also considered by Palo and Lucumi practitioners to be a warrior and a magician. Another important attribute of this spirit, force, or power, is the fact that he is believed to wear an intricately crafted headpiece with horns and feathers, while carrying a bow and arrow. He is also known as the protector of all wild animals and is seen as the patron of those

190. Frisvold, *Palo Mayombe: The Garden of Blood and Bones*, pp. 91–92.

191. See *Excursus* on this book.

192. Zeinab Badawi, 'Kongo and the Scramble for Africa—History of Africa with Zeinab Badawi', BBC News Africa, Episode 19 (2020), 3:58—9:18 <https://www.youtube.com/watch?v=Wov_SwObQns>.

193. Frisvold, *Palo Mayombe: The Garden of Blood and Bones*, pp. 91–92.

who work with dogs[194] (much like Zarabanda and Ogun).[195] From this information we can reconstruct Amerindian beliefs and practices as well as values, codified in the myth and representation of the Mpungo Vence Bataya and the Lucumi version of the Oricha Ochosi. Moreover, the fact that this spirit, force, or power is represented (most of the time) as an Amerindian conclusively supports the hypothesis that this Mpungo or Oricha denotes the formal absorption of Caribbean Amerindian beliefs and practices by the Afro-Cuban pantheon.

I see in the modern practice of placing the bow and arrow, representing Vence Bataya and Ochosi, inside the cauldron of Zarabanda and Ogun the culmination and formalization of the syncretic process arising from the Caribbean Amerindian and African diaspora religious encounters in the Caribbean wilderness. I support this by the *pataki* (Afro-Cuban Ifá sacred story; in traditional Ifá these stories are not called *pataki* and this particular one is not recorded)[196] which tells us that although Ogun and Ochosi are currently inseparable spirits within the

194. 'Ochosi', *AboutSanteria* (2021) <http://www.aboutsanteria.com/ochosi.html>.

195. 'The Orishas: Ochosi', *Original Botanica* (2021) <https://www.originalbotanica.com/blog/orishas-ochosi-santeria/>.

196. Even though it may seem counterintuitive to conclude with an Ifà story as the synthesis and formalization of the syncretic process arising out of the Amerindian and African encounter in the Caribbean, we must understand the role of Ifà in the Caribbean. I suggest that we must redraw Ifà's role as the repository of knowledge and wisdom of the Afro-Caribbean lived experience tied to the religious experience of the African diaspora in the New World. As noted above, the oracle of Ifà in the Afro-Cuban tradition and the Nigerian traditional are similar, but different. These differences and similitudes speak to the adaptive and utilitarian ἦθος (ethos) of the African habitus, which supports my theory of Ifà as the repository of knowledge and wisdom filtered through the utilitarian and pragmatic approach of the African habitus. Beyond the *patakis*, which are not included in the traditional form of Ifà, the Afro-Cuban Ifà oracle also forms an amalgam of all the various traditions discussed thus far, not present in the traditional form. It speaks to the Palo Monte, Orisha, Espiritismo, and Christian (and I propose Amerindian as well) spiritualities, and interweaves them in a wholly unique creole manifestation. When looking at the Odù (binary system of Ifà consisting of two columns of four units each of either zeros or ones, or I or II), which constitutes the wisdom of Ifà speaking through the *babalawo* (father of the secrets and priest of Ifà) and his *opele* (diving chain) or *ikin* Ifà (sacred palm nuts or kola nuts), the resulting analyses provide us with an easily discerned conclusion. The African and the Afro-Cuban Odduns (plural form) remain the same in nomenclature, but the knowledge found in them is very different. While the traditional Ifà Odù corpus speaks to the socio-religious experiences of the African individual, the Afro-Cuban ones speaks to those of the creole individual. Therefore, I postulate that although the *babalawos* made their presence in Cuba in the 19th century, their tradition constitutes the preserved folkloric history of the Caribbean.

Afro-Cuban pantheon, they originally were not on friendly terms with each other. However, the *pataki* tells us that soon after, both realized that they needed each other. This realization arose from the fact that, because although Ochosi was a great hunter who never missed his mark,[197] he had a hard time getting through the untamed forest of the newly formed earth (perhaps referring to the 'New World') to find his prey because there were no paths or clearings, which was somewhat similar to what Ogun experienced during his hunts.[198]

Although Ogun had a similar problem (he had no food to eat), his difficulty was that he was not able to trap or catch anything in his metal traps. In contrast to Ochosi, Ogun was able to set his traps in the wilderness, clearing it by making paths to hunt with his machete. Unfortunately, unlike Ochosi, Ogun was not able to catch any prey in this newly formed land. One day, while both of them were taking a sacrifice to the forest (following Òrúnmìlà's instructions), they encountered each other. After sharing their problems, they realized they could solve both of their difficulties if they worked together.[199] Together with the linguistic investigation of the name Zarabanda, detailed above as an amalgam of Taino and Bantu words (plus all of the other common themes investigated), we can observe how traces of the Caribbean Amerindian and African religious encounter and its indelible signs are located in the creole religion of Palo Monte.

197. 'Ochosi' (2021).

198. Frisvold, *Palo Mayombe: The Garden of Blood and Bones*, pp. 91–92.

199. 'Ochosi' (2021). Also see Frisvold, *Palo Mayombe: The Garden of Blood and Bones*, pp. 91–92.

5

Conclusion

"Kana kuyila, kya kukya"
"Por mucho que llegue la noche, se hará de día"[1]
"Does not matter how often night comes, it will always dawn"

—*PALO MONTE PROVERB*

IN THE TIME ALLOWED for the compilation, investigation, and synthesis of the scant amount of available material available (known to the author), I have discovered a well-spring of helpful sources. Popular beliefs seem to be well founded, but the influence of the Amerindian beliefs and practices on those of the Caribbean religious diaspora has only begun to be properly understood. Due to the large number of Kongolese slaves at the beginning of the 16th century, coupled with the rapid decimation of the Amerindian at about the same time, the Amerindian influence is traced through the Afro-Cuban Palo Monte religion as a creole manifestation. Although not apparent at first sight, the research into this religion elucidated the indelible signs left by the Amerindian religious habitus. Further research on other traditions, such as the Lucumi, also located the influence of the Amerindian beliefs and practices. However, these influences migrated from Palo Monte to the later creole manifestations, rather than directly from the Caribbean Amerindians. Moreover, viewed through the lens of the decolonial option, the silence of the Amerindian influence is

---

1. *Refranes de Palo.* n.d. p. 2

linked to the powerful influence of the Catholic hegemony on the religious habitus of the Afro-Caribbean descendants in Cuba.

This, coupled with the utilitarian emphasis of the African's religious habitus as explained by Maya Deren, gives us a hint for understanding the silence observed by Caribbean and African scholars. This silence most likely resulted from the need of the Afro-Caribbean diaspora to keep the Amerindian influence hidden from the religious hegemony. Also, due to the pressure felt by the established academic hegemony to continue the historical trope of Caribbean indigenous extinction, this influence was also lost to the Caribbean and Afro-Caribbean scholars. I attribute this unfortunate process to the gradual forgetting of the Caribbean Amerindian influence by the African diaspora in Cuba to it not being openly discussed. This most likely occurred through the passage of time, across generations of Afro-Caribbean religious practitioners. The result of this process can be observed in the ambivalent acknowledgement of the Caribbean Amerindian influence on the Caribbean religious diaspora today, with the popular belief that there is indeed a Caribbean Amerindian influence in the cultural and religious habitus of the Caribbean religious diaspora, juxtaposed with the complete negation by Afro-Caribbean religious practitioners of the Caribbean Amerindian influence on their creole religious traditions

Thus, Deren's insight into the African religious habitus of utility detailed in Chapter 2 leads to the conclusion that both the Amerindian and the African slaves had a similar mindset, which allowed them to cohabit and understand each other much more readily than the Spanish. This religious and cultural meeting ground would have constituted the foundation from which a steady exchange of ideas and religious powers would have occurred. Gaps in power or knowledge would have been filled by the incorporation of each other's belief systems, aiding in each other's survival. I believe that this phenomenon is the reason why, when we look at the creole religion of Palo Monte, we discern many beliefs and practices which have no Kongo origin, but rather demonstrate a multiplicity of voices (Amerindian beliefs, Spiritism, Lucumi tradition, Arará tradition, and Catholicism) which speak to us today through the religious manifestation of Palo Monte.

In this book I have focused on the Amerindian influence on Palo Monte. And, as we have seen in Chapter 4, this influence, although difficult to trace and difficult to proclaim with absolute certainty, is demonstrated by a proliferation of Amerindians beliefs and practices, and a bevy of other Amerindian influences quite distinct from the African origins of the religion. By compiling this information, I hope to provide leads for others with more knowledge about the religion to locate further plausible influences that may have escaped my limited awareness. After all, as the Lucumi proverb at the beginning of my book states, I am not the only voice in the field, and only through the extensive collaboration of all the voices will we be able to plant the seeds of a future discourse on the subject.

I hope that by completing this study I have contributed not only to the decolonial project, but to Latin American and Caribbean indigenous studies as well. I also hope that this project serves as an invitation to all Africanist and Afro-Caribbean scholars to start a dialogue about this much understudied and undervalued area of research which is in need of resuscitation. Lastly, I also challenge ethnographers to pursue fieldwork on these observations, utilizing my research project as a rough guide. The leads I have provided can be properly and empirically explored. I also encourage all Africanist and Afro-Caribbean scholars of other traditions to pursue similar scholarship in their religions of expertise. Only then will the true extent of the Caribbean Amerindian influence as it survives in the cultural and religious ethos of the Afro-Caribbean diaspora be understood, and the yoke of coloniality with its matrix of power will be lifted. This then would mean the first steps in approaching the goal of border-thinking for a creation of a pluriversal world that forces the trope of indigenous extinction to make room for a multiplicity of voices, which would speak something new. This last point, I believe, is an important factor in the future of Caribbean scholarship, since the cultural and religious landscape of the Caribbean with its dynamic and multicultural populations can only be properly comprehended through the decolonial lens of pluriversality and multiplicity of truths.

Postlude
Valediction

Dice-¡Nsala Malekum!
(¡Malekum Nsala!) (1x)
Dice-¿Somos o no somos?
(¡Somos!) (1x)
¡Santo Tomás!
(¡Ver para creer!) (1x)
¿Entre tres personas distintas?
(¡Un solo Dios verdadero!) (1x)
¡Munan Congo!
(¡Kwa!) (1x)

¡BUENA NOCHE MI LEMBA! *¡Buena noche mi Lemba! ¡Mundo Nuevo Carire! ¡Mundo Nuevo Carire! (Buena noche mi Lemba. Buena noche mi Lemba. Mundo Nuevo Carire. Mundo Nuevo Carire). ¡Hay la buena noche mi Lemba¡ [¡Siá carajo!] [¡Brrrrr!] ¡Á, eh saludando mi Lemba! [É, é, é, é, é] ¡Mundo Nuevo Carire! ¡Mundo Nuevo Carire! (Buena noche mi Lemba. Buena noche mi Lemba. Mundo Nuevo Carire. Mundo Nuevo Carire). ¡Hay la buena noche mi Lemba¡ [¡Siá muchacho carajo!] Saludando a todo los Congos, buenas noches mi Lemba. [é, é] [¡Hmmmm!]. Mundo Nuevo Carire. ¡Mundo Nuevo Carire! (Buena noche mi Lemba. Buena noche mi Lemba. Mundo Nuevo Carire. Mundo Nuevo Carire). ¡Mambe! (¡Dio!)*

Buena noche Ngó, saludando Ngó. ¡Buena noche! Saludando Ngó.
(Buena noche Ngó, saludando Ngó) Buena noche Ngó, saludando Ngó.
(Buena noche Ngó, saludando Ngó) É, saludando a todo los Congos, buena
noche Ngó. (Buena noche Ngó, saludando Ngó). ¡É, Saludando! ¡Saludando
Ngó! (Buena noche Ngó, saludando Ngó). É, buena noche Ngó, saludando
Ngó. (Buena noche Ngó, saludando Ngó). É, vuesta noche Centellita, salu-
dando Ngó. (Buena noche Ngó, saludando Ngó). É, buena noche a Lucero,
saludando Ngó. (Buena noche Ngó, saludando Ngó). Buena noche Tiembla
Tierra, saludando Ngó. (Buena noche Ngó, saludando Ngó). Buena noche a
todo los Congos, saludando Ngó. (Buena noche Ngó, saludando Ngó). ¡Sa-
ludando Ngó, saludando Ngó! (Buena noche Ngó, saludando Ngó). Buena
noche Zarabanda, saludando Ngó. (Buena noche Ngó, saludando Ngó). Bue-
na noche Siete Rayos, saludando Ngó. (Buena noche Ngó, saludando Ngó).

¡É-e, buena noche Te'Lemele, buena noche Te'Lemele! (Buena noche
Te'Lemele. Buena noche Te'Lemele). ¡Abre Nkuto! Buena noche Te'Lemele,
buena noche Te'Lemele. (Buena noche Te'Lemele. Buena noche Te'Lemele)
¡Ée, má yo saluda a lo Ta'Francisco! Buena noche Te'Lemele. (Buena noche
Te'Lemele. Buena noche Te'Lemele). ¡Ée, má yo saluda a tó lo Tata! Buena
noche Te'Lemele. (Buena noche Te'Lemele. Buena noche Te'Lemele). ¡Éeee,
buena noche Te'Lemele, buena noche Te'Lemele! (Buena noche Te'Lemele.
Buena noche Te'Lemele). É, buena noche, buena noche. Buena noche, la
Santa Noche. (Buena noche, buena noche). Buena noche a tó los Congos.
(Buena noche, buena noche). Buena noche, la Santa Noche. (Buena noche,
buena noche). Buena noche a Lucerito. (Buena noche, buena noche). Buena
noche a Madre Agua. (Buena noche, buena noche). É, buena noche a Chola
Wengue. (Buena noche, buena noche). ¡É, buena noche mi Congo, buena
noche! (Buena noche, buena noche). ¡Saludando, buena noche! (Buena
noche, buena noche).

¡É, llegué llegué, saludando! ¡Llegué llegué, saludando! (Llegué llegué,
saludando. Llegué llegué, saludando). Llegué llegué, saludando. Llegué
llegué, saludando. (Llegué llegué, saludando. Llegué llegué, saludando).
Llegué llegué, saludando. Llegué llegué, saludando a'wee. (Llegué llegué,
saludando. Llegué llegué, saludando). Má yo saluda a los Siete Rayos, má
yo saludo los Lucerito a'wee. (Llegué llegué, saludando. Llegué llegué, salu-
dando). ¡Má yo saluda a tó los Tata! Llegué llegué, saludando a'wee. (Llegué
llegué, saludando. Llegué llegué, saludando). É-e, llegué llegué, saludando
llegué. (Llegué llegué). Saludando llegué. (Llegué llegué). Paso a paso yo
llegué. (Llegué llegué). Caminando llegué. (Llegué llegué). Saludando yo

llegué. (Llegué llegué). ¡Llegué llegué! (Llegué llegué). Saludando llegué.
(Llegué llegué). Brillumba llegué. (Llegué llegué).

É-ee, buena noche aquí, buena noche allá. Buena noche aquí, buena
noche allá. Saludando aquí, saludando allá. (Buena noche aquí, buena
noche allá. Buena noche aquí, buena noche allá. Saludando aquí, sa-
ludando allá). Buena noche aquí, buena noche allá. Buena noche aquí,
buena noche allá. Saludando aquí, saludando allá. (Buena noche aquí,
buena noche allá. Buena noche aquí, buena noche allá. Saludando aquí,
saludando allá) (1x). {Saludando aquí. (Saludando allá) (14x)}

¡Éeeee! Andabia con sún dabia. {Éee, palo nganga. (Andabia con sún
dabia) (4x).} ¡Congo! ¡Palo nganga!. (Andabia con sún dabia). Arriba el
sube, palo nganga. (Andabia con sún dabia). Abajo suena, palo nganga.
(Andabia con sún dabia). Éee, palo nganga. (Andabia con sún dabia).
Abre Nkuto, palo nganga. (Andabia con sún dabia). Ya son las horas palo
nganga. (Andabia con sún dabia). {¡Congo! Palo nganga. (Andabia con sún
dabia) (4x).}

¡É-eeeeee! Buena noche pá usted, saludándolo a usted. ¡Buena noche!
Saludándolo a usted. (Buena noche pá usted, saludándolo a usted). Buena
noche pá usted, saludándolo a usted. (Buena noche pá usted, saludándolo a
usted). Saludando a todo los Congos, saludándolo a usted. (Buena noche pá
usted, saludándolo a usted). Buenas noches, saludándolo a usted. (Buena
noche pá usted, saludándolo a usted). ¡Saludando, saludándolo a usted!
(Buena noche pá usted, saludándolo a usted). ¡Mambe! (¡Dio!)

—From: *Toque de Palo Monte, Buena Noche*[1]

1. Transcribed from: "Toque De Palo Monte Mayombe- Buena Noche", *Youtube.*
Com, 2022 <https://www.youtube.com/watch?v=dSv1OwwqhJ4> [Accessed 6 February 2022]

Coda

S	A	T	O	R
A	R	E	P	O
T	E	N	E	T
O	P	E	R	A
R	O	T	A	S

Figure 4: Sator Square
SATOR=The Creator's, AREPO=Sickle, TENET=Maintains,
OPERA=His Creations, ROTAS=As Vortices; TENET forms the cardinal Cross.

☿
+
0
I
I
0

Baba Iwori Meji

À
R
Í
W
Á

+   +

0   I

♄   0   ÌLÀ-OÒRÙN   ⊕   ÌWỌ-OÒRÙN   I

0   I

0   I

Baba Oyeku Meji   G   Baba Ejiogbe

Ù
Ù
S
Ù
+
I
0
0
I

Baba Odi Meji
♄

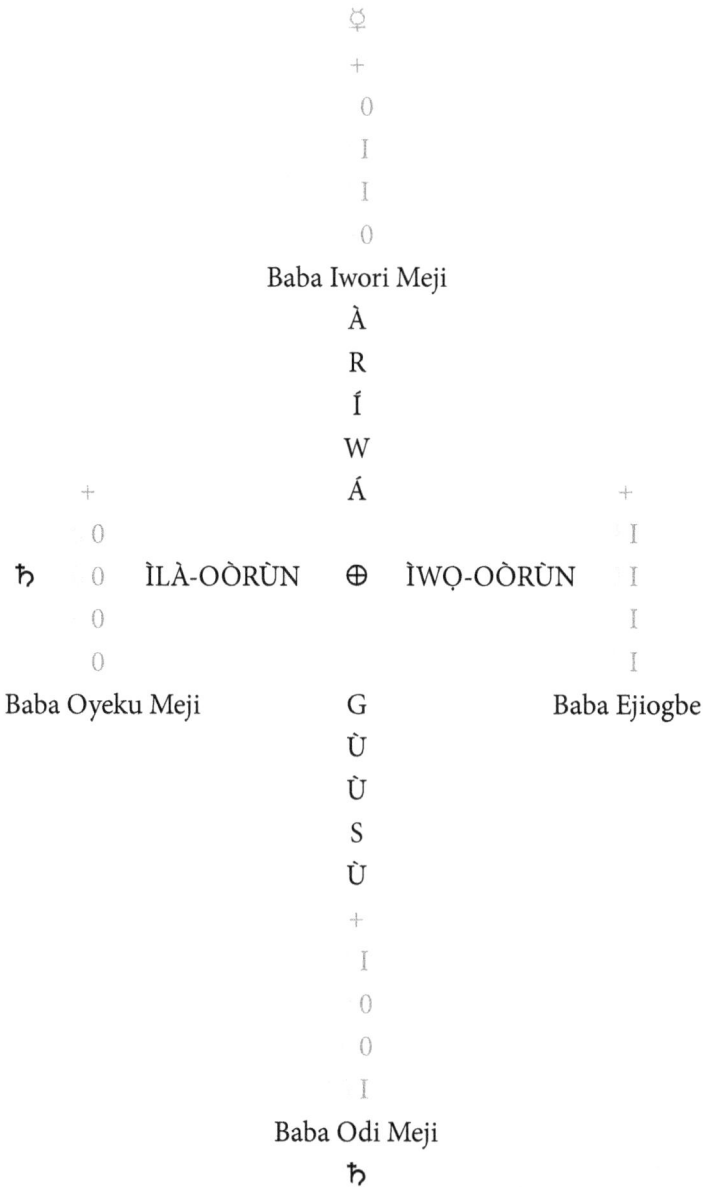

Figure 5: The Four Cardinal Gates

Egun Merinlaye: The four chief Eguns standing at the gates of the four cardinal points of the world. Àríwá is the chief Egun standing at the North gate; Gùùsù is the chief Egun standing at the South Gate; Ìlà-oòrùn is the chief Egun standing at the East Gate & Ìwọ-oòrùn is the chief Egun standing at the West Gate

"Awo Iku lele Awo losi itula belele ni lo Awo. Awo Iku leleo iwana Ashe lawao lawa Egun leleo. Egun Awo belele umba okurero Egun Awo Iku Egun otun oyorumbo balele beleleo bo bolele Egun".

—EGUN BABALAWO, SECRET INCANTATION

Malekum Nsala

Appendix

Excursus
Pygmy Contributions to the Kongo-Derived Creole Religion of Palo Monte
A survival of Aka, Baka, Mbuti and Batwa Spiritualities in the Mpungo Gurunfinda

"Otata kadianga ngulu za fioti ko kadiyeno awana kesanga omu mpasi"
"Si el padre no come cerdo vosotros los pequeños
van sufrir de no comerlo tampoco"[1]
"If the father does not eat pork, you the children,
will also suffer of not being able to eat it"

—*PALO MONTE PROVERB*

IN THIS SECTION I briefly trace the genesis of Palo Monte's Mpungo Gurunfinda to the primordial societies or cultures of the West Central African Pygmies. Much like my argument regarding the absorption of Caribbean Amerindian beliefs and practice as a tool of survival in the wilderness of the Caribbean lands, the Bantu-speaking people seem to have depended on the Pygmies because of their perceived supernatural powers over the untamed and unknown wilderness of the lands of West Central Africa. I take this point of convergence to denote that the Kongo belief system was based on a sort of cultural/religious model which saw the primacy of the first-comers (to the lands which they eventually

1. *Refranes de Palo.* n.d. p. 2

137

inhabited; as described by Igor Kopytoff)[2] as primordial beings, who had a privileged position as experts of the religious sphere. This was based on an understanding that they had mastered these lands through their supernatural powers and thus needed to be respected. In this vein, these spirit forces or powers can be interpreted as representing the much older and much respected cultures of the first-comers, which they eventually integrated into their pantheon.

The Africans brought to the Caribbean during the slave trade had a pragmatic and utilitarian mindset which is in fact based on the religious foundation of African societies, which emphasize the survival needs and quotidian worries of its adherents. I propose that due to the pragmatic orientation of African spiritualities, the migratory Bantu population to West Central Africa must have necessarily appropriated symbols of spiritual power from the native Pygmy populations to augment their own indigenous sources as they battled the immediate demands of an un-known and untamed land. My conclusion, that there was an amalgam of Bantu and Pygmy ritual practices and religious discourses, led me to the theoretical insights of Igor Kopytoff. In particular, I will focus on Kairn A. Klieman's re-purposing of Kopytoff's sociocultural/religious model, which she applies to the Bantu-Pygmy existential encounter and which explains the observed Bantu belief of the primacy of the first-comers as primordial beings, who had a privileged position as experts of the reli-gious sphere. Since the religious hegemony (today) of the Bantu-speaking people of Africa is Catholicism, Afro-Caribbean religious discourses and practices then offer the appropriate contexts for studying the survival or continuity of appropriated (by the Bantu) Pygmy religious beliefs and practices prior to and during the Transatlantic Slave Trade. Therefore, for the purposes of tracing this Pygmy contribution to the Bantu belief system, I will focus on the Congo-derived creole religion of Palo Monte.

Serendipitously, I stumbled upon Klieman's work while researching data for the project which became this book. Her work confirmed my semi-crystallized conclusions about Kopytoff's work as a possible source of explanation for theorizing Bantu models of syncretization with first-comer peoples. Moreover, her mature and well-structured modification of Igor Kopytoff's theory inevitably replaced my original intention of utilizing his insights for developing the project with her rather oppor-tune investigations of the Bantu and Batwa interactions. Central to her

2. Igor Kopytoff, *The African Frontier: The Reproduction of Traditional African Soci-eties* (Bloomington, Indiana: Indiana University Press, 1989).

revisionary theory is the premise that the social distinctions between im-
migrant Bantu populations and Pygmy autochthons communities have
been of vital importance ever since the early Bantu-speakers settled in
the western equatorial rainforest of Africa. Nonetheless, Klieman theo-
rizes that documented in the myths, rituals, and cosmologies of the Bantu
there is evidence of the idealization of the Pygmy as legitimizing agents
in the politico-religious systems of the Atlantic Age. This is especially so
in the myths, rituals, and cosmologies recorded in the last five hundred
years, which came with the advent of Bantu agriculture (especially banana plantations) and increased technological advances in metallurgy.[3]

During this time, the Bantu-speaking people reconstructed their relationship with the Pygmy in a new light; myths, rituals, and cosmologies
of the Bantu-speaking people started to reflect an understanding of the
Pygmy as both mythical and real first-comers whose legitimizing power
was cast in their politico-religious systems of belief as primordial and
mythical people whose domain of power was transferred to this sphere,
away from real world political power. This transfer was quietly moved to
the embodied character of the Bantu territorial chief and his agricultural
lands. In this new politico-religious landscape, the Pygmy was elevated
to the realm of myth and ritual, while simultaneously demoted to servi-
tude to their new agricultural Bantu chiefs. Curiously, Klieman reports
that this Bantu view of the Pygmy as religious experts is found all across
central Africa. Moreover, she claims that this social demarcation between
the two groups attests to some sort of deep ideological construct of social distinction between the two groups that may point to a confirmation
of the oral history of the Pygmy as stretching back in time. She claims
this by concluding that this deep ideological construction of the social
distinction between the Bantu and autochthon communities in the western equatorial rainforest of Africa is evidence that these hunter-gatherer
communities have been present in these regions prior to the migration of
the early Bantu-speaking settlers.[4]

Another clue that supports her reasoning is the etymology of the
term *Batwa* discovered by Thilo Schadeberg. According to Schadeberg,
the term Batwa was invented in the equatorial rainforest of Africa to refer to, in the majority of cases, non-Bantu-speaking autochthons whose

3. Kairn A. Klieman, *The Pygmies Were Our Compass: Bantu and Batwa in the History of West Central Africa, Early Times to C. 1900 C.E.*, Social History Of Africa Series
(Portsmouth, New Hampshire: Heinemann, 2003), p. xix.

4. Klieman, *The Pygmies Were Our Compass*, p. xix.

lifestyle is usually (but not necessarily always) non-agriculturalist. This connotation of the term is found across the Bantu-speaking world and originally made no reference to physical characteristics or a lower social status, which it unfortunately does today. Therefore, it was only used as social distinction between the two groups, based on their economic specialization. Here, Klieman shines with her insight by claiming that this social distinction can be understood in simple terms of 'agriculturalist' and 'forest specialist'. She gives a well traced and supported path from which I construct my own discourse of the Pygmy spiritualities codified in the Palo Monte Mpungo Gurunfinda.[5] This distinction, I claim, remains to this day and is of extreme importance to my argument (as we will see).

Klieman traces this economic specialization of these two groups to the Neolithic period. During the late Stone Age, new technologies had developed, such as the use of polished stone axes and iron.[6] As aforementioned, the advanced practice of metallurgy in the Kingdom of Kongo ('*kongo*' in Kikongo means iron)[7] made the Bantu-speaking people a powerhouse of unrivaled technological advancement during this period, which together with their success with banana plantations, catapulted them to primordial players in the African political and religious field. Klieman concludes that during the Neolithic period there was a widespread shift among most communities and tribes from hunter-gatherer economies to fully agricultural ones, which engendered the observed Pygmy adaptation towards a forest-oriented lifestyle, brought about by the increasing pressures manifested in their relationship with the Bantu. During this time, agricultural lifestyles started to prevail, and groups of people started to move away from the hunter-gatherer lifestyle. Moreover, due to the increasing success and pivotal role agricultural and Neolithic technologies played on the development of Bantu-speaking people, Klieman concludes that the Pygmy ancestors must have felt the pressure to specialize in forest-oriented economies, away from the agricultural hegemony of their neighbors. Therefore, by being pigeonholed into this role, the Pygmy (after the introduction of banana and iron) became forest specialists whose entire subsistence strategies and economic practices lay in their participation in the Bantu regional systems of trade as suppliers of

5. Klieman, *The Pygmies Were Our Compass*, pp. xviii-xix.

6. Klieman, *The Pygmies Were Our Compass*, pp. xviii-xix.

7. Badawi, 'Kongo and the Scramble for Africa—History of Africa with Zeinab Badawi', 3:58—9:18.

forest goods. An important distinction Klieman marks is that the reason she terms the Pygmy 'forest specialist' and not 'hunter-gatherers' is for this same reason. Their codependence and submission to the Bantu and their regional systems of trade, which differed greatly from the economic efforts of nomadic hunter-gatherers, situates the Pygmy lifestyle in a unique mode of economic specialization worthy of being differentiated.[8]

Starting from the premises of the African habitus and Klieman's exposition of the unique position of the Pygmy as forest specialist and first-comer, mythologized and idealized as legitimizing agents of the politico-religious field, I postulate that the Palo Monte Mpungo Gurunfinda presents a preservation of the survival of Aka, Baka, Mbuti, and Batwa spiritualities. As aforementioned, a proper study of this Afro-Caribbean creole Mpungo will yield an accurate picture of the systematization and appropriation of Pygmy beliefs and practices by the Bantu during the Atlantic Age. In short, I claim that the migrating Bantu-speaking people invaded Pygmy religious fields and appropriated their religious discourses and praxis prior to their forced migration to the Caribbean, and that studying the creole religion of Palo Monte is the most appropriate way of unearthing this long forgotten syncretic process.

So, what is the evidence in the Afro-Caribbean religion of Palo Monte regarding this appropriation of Pygmy's forest-oriented economic specialization and their idealization as primordial first-comer religious experts whose role in the Central African politico-religious field of the systems of the Atlantic Age is as legitimizing agents? In order to answer this long-winded question, I delved into Nicholaj de Mattos Frisvold's *Palo Mayombe: The Garden of Blood and Bones*. In this excellent and groundbreaking manuscript, Frisvold provides one of the most thorough explanations of the Kimpungulu (plural of Mpungo) available in print and expounds on the Mpungo Gurunfinda like no other available source. Here, the author tells us that in Palo Monte, Gurunfinda is venerated as the supreme power and master of the wilderness. The Mpungo is viewed as "the sap and blood of every tree, leaf and twig, and he is the buzzing and humming of all insects."[9] Gurunfinda is said, by Palo practitioners, to be the Lord of the Greenwood, which is the secret resting in the sorcerous forest hills of Mayombe. He is the "life-soaked matter, which penetrates all parts of nature."[10] Gurunfinda is the representation of the most

---

8. Klieman, *The Pygmies Were Our Compass*, pp. xviii-xix.

9. Frisvold, *Palo Mayombe: The Garden of Blood and Bones*, p. 117.

10. Frisvold, *Palo Mayombe: The Garden of Blood and Bones*, p. 117.

dense and untamed essence of all flora and fauna. Moreover, he is also the power of the birds (nocturnal birds in particular) and in his totality represents the essential nature of the wilderness.[11]

Palo Monte practitioners in Cuba call him simply Gurunfinda, which derives its name from the Kikongo word Ngúlumfinda. The word Ngúlumfinda in turn is composed of the Kikongo words *ngúlu* and *mfinda*,[12] which mean wild hog and wild forest, respectively. Gurunfinda depicted as a wild hog tells us that the spirit or force of nature is wild like nature itself, and like a hog it is extremely sensitive to smells, sounds, and changes in its environment. I also extrapolate that it raises connotations of a short stature, but stacked (with muscles and power), and of a ferocious warrior of the forest who is not afraid to go against much bigger adversaries. However, this is not his full name, only its short nomenclature. His full name in Kikongo is Sindaula Ndundu Yambaka Butan Seke. Within this name, as we will shortly see, lies the secret of the formal process of syncretization of Pygmy religious fields and praxis by the Bantu. Firstly, it is worth paying attention to the first name, that of Sindaula. *Sindaula* means 'to extract' or 'to dry up', which I interpret to be the actual process by which the Bantu extracted the essential power or mastery over the wilderness by the Pygmy as codified in the *Mpungo* Gurunfinda. The names Ndundu Yambaka mean 'albino Pygmy' and Butá Nseke means 'little man who is the master of the mountain'. Especially important to this formal recording of the Pygmy contributions to Bantu religious fields is the understanding that in Cuba all the various parts of the Kikongo name of Gurunfinda point to his qualities or attendant spirits.[13]

Frisvold also makes a remarkable insight about the Mpungo, claiming that "The image generated is one of a spirit defying the social order, it is the wilderness that speaks through this short, white dried-up figure".[14] This, as we have seen, is the essence of Pygmy societies. As Klieman has demonstrated, although they participated in the regional Bantu systems of trade as forest specialist whose entire subsistence depended on this economic specialization, their lifestyle defies the traditional agricultural and hunter-gatherer societies of the past and of the present. They are

11. Frisvold, *Palo Mayombe: The Garden of Blood and Bones*, p. 117.

12. However, in Palo Monte the word for wild forest or forest became Nfinda, which is evidenced in the name Gurunfinda and the name for the traditional *rama* of Palo Monte, Nkunia Nfinda Malongo. The word *nkunia* means *palo* (stick).

13. Frisvold, *Palo Mayombe: The Garden of Blood and Bones*, p. 117.

14. Frisvold, *Palo Mayombe: The Garden of Blood and Bones*, p. 117.

located in a unique position in the strata of human society, which defies the *status quo* of western social orders. As for the qualities of religious experts and legitimizing agents, the power and central role of Gurunfinda in Palo Monte cannot be accurately stated. The reason for this is that his role and power is so central to the religion, that without his presence and power, there is no Palo Monte religion.

Gurunfinda, beyond being the Lord of Greenwood and the essence of wilderness itself, is also the power that provides the necessary materials required for the resuscitation or the animation ritual of the corpse[15] performed in the *nkimba* (*rayamiento*, scratching initiatory ceremony) ceremony of Palo Monte and its preparatory procedures in the cemetery (of buying the dead from Centella and Kuballende). He is also the power that helps you find the plants found in the wild, which are necessary for the correct preparation of *macutos*[16] (amulets), *bilongos* (magical medicines) and *mpolos* (magical powders), which are primordial and essential tools of the *ngangulero* (priest of the religion). Frisvold tells us that "No Palero can expect to be able to make his *mumia* [dead] work if his blessings are not attained as he is the one who sanctifies the collection of sticks and herbs so precious and necessary for creating the nkisi [spirit of force of nature]".[17] Osvaldo Sesti, a respected Tata Tatandi (rank reserved for *paleros* considered to be among the highest experts in the religion), makes many mentions of Pigmeos (Pygmies) across multiple occasions in his videos. Sesti has shown the Pygmy depicted in many of his works as part of the liturgy of Palo Monte as particular *patimpembas* (chalk drawings) that provide power and instruction to the *nsara* (magical work).[18]

15. Frisvold, *Palo Mayombe: The Garden of Blood and Bones*, p. 117.

16. A word which was unequivocally borrowed from the Taino vocabulary. *Macuto* in Arawak means 'a deep basket made of vines'. From *El Diccionario del Lenguaje Taino* <https://www.taino-tribe.org/tsdict.html>.

17. Frisvold, *Palo Mayombe: The Garden of Blood and Bones*, p. 117–18.

18. This information was not obtained directly from any book but rather forms my synthesis of many videos by Osvaldo Sesti, Tata Iraka, who has delved into this topic many times throughout his ten-year project towards preserving the traditional Palo Mayombe religion via audiovisual teachings. These teachings are aimed at showing initiated and non-initiated individuals the way to perform *nsaras* or *bilongos* while providing a vast amount of knowledge on all things Palo Monte. As a side note, his contributions to the preservation of the religion and his openness (to an allowed degree that does not reveal the mysteries of the religion) in showing the practice of the religion within the confines of his *munanzo* are unparalleled and should be nominated as representative of Palo Monte practice for the UNESCO list of Intangible Cultural Heritage of Humanity. You can find his YouTube Channel at: <*https://www.youtube.com/user/ OsvaldoSesti*>.

These instances also support the inclusion and syncretization of Pygmy religious fields and praxis into the Bantu indigenous practices. If we take these beliefs and practices as proof of Pygmy borrowings by the Bantu-speaking people and their Kongo descendants in Cuba, then it will support the hypothesis that through the African pragmatic and utilitarian habitus, the Pygmy autochthon communities were syncretized and formally incorporated into the Bantu religious fields. Hence, the Pygmies were syncretized and idealized as primordial first-comer people that were seen as religious experts and legitimizing agents of the religious field, and as forest specialists whose domain and mastery over the untamed African equatorial rainforest is to be respected.

Conclusion

In this brief excursion, I have discovered that indeed there is a Pygmy contribution to the Kongo indigenous beliefs and practices. Fortunately, this creole religion represents the surviving beliefs and practices of the Bantu-speaking people during the Atlantic Age, which were forcibly brought to the Caribbean and the Americas during the Transatlantic Slave Trade. After some research, I conclude that the survival of Pygmy spiritualities was codified and preserve in the Mpungo Gurunfinda. This conclusion is supported by the fact that it is even preserved and acknowledged in the Kikongo name for the Mpungo Gurunfinda in the Palo Monte religion. The name, as explained above, refers to the qualities of the Mpungo as that of an albino Pygmy and a little man who is the master of the mountain.

Klieman's reinterpretation of Igor Kopytoff's theory applied to the Pygmies also provides us with some insights as to how their spiritualities and praxis were borrowed by the Bantu-speaking migrants. Underscoring the African habitus so beautifully described by Maya Deren is Klieman's reinvigorating theory of the Pygmy as forest specialists whose power and role for the Bantu was as legitimizing agents of the politico-religious field, due to their idealized religious expertise and mastery over the untamed land of the African equatorial rainforest. This ideology by the Bantu, Klieman explains, can be understood through the lens of a Bantu model or paradigm of belief, which places the Pygmy as primordial beings whose role and position as first-comers (to the West Central African lands) is mythologized and respected. Much the like the Caribbean process of fusing the Amerindian first-comers (codified in the Mpungo Watariamba), the Bantu migrants codified the Pygmy first-comers in the Mpungo Gurunfinda and maintained the Atlantic Age belief of these religious fields and praxis as legitimizing agents, hence fortifying my findings of the formal syncretization of Amerindian beliefs and practices as codified in the Mpungo Watariamba.

I conclude this from the facts explored above, and that without Gurunfinda's power to legitimize all religious paraphernalia of the religion and the animation of the dead itself, there would not be a Palo Monte religion. Overall, my research led me to conclude that there is indeed a direct survival of Pygmy spiritualities in the Mpungo Gurunfinda and that studying this codified syncretic process will lead researchers to a better understanding of the history and sociology of these two deeply interrelated cultures, and by extension to the Amerindian and Congo in Cuba. These may seem like trivial discoveries, but if we take into consideration the exoticized status of the Pygmy and the Amerindian in the western world, and the lack of proper understanding of these cultures in the African stage and world stage as legitimate and legitimizing players, then the magnitude and momentous importance of this book can be properly understood.

Glossary

7 Rayos: Seven Lightning bolts. Alternative name for Nsasi Siete Rayos or Nsasi 7 Rayos. See *Nsasi Siete Rayos*.

Ab origine: Latin term that means from the beginning.

Abakuá: Afro-Cuban fraternity or secret society also known as Ñañigos, which originated from the fraternal associations of the leopard men also known as Ekpe, Egbo, Ngbe or Ugbe from the Cross River region of Southeastern Nigeria and Southwestern Cameroon. Some scholars have termed it the Afro-Cuban version of Freemasonry. It is a highly insular fraternity and protective of its secrets. See *Ñañigos*.

Aborigines: Latin term meaning the first inhabitants, which in turn derives from the amalgamation of the words *ab origine*. See *Ab origine*.

Acáyouma: Carib term that means Cayman and from which the name of Acáyouman comes from. See *Caribs*.

Acáyouman: The Carib term for the Celestial Cayman and the Spirit of the Old Father, which represented the Milky Way and which was seen in the sky during the months of September and October. Also, a mythic character from which the anthropophagic rite was developed. Carib mythology seems to point to an actual historical character whose deeds passed first into legend and then mythology. It was the Kalinago naval captain who first sailed from the South American mainland to the Lesser Antilles and who exterminated all the Tainos living there. A mythical character that became Akeuman after being poisoned by his children and grandchildren. *See Caribs, Barbacoa, Tainos/Taino*, and *Akeuman*.

Agouti: Several types of rodent species related to guinea pigs, which are native to the Americas and the Caribbean. Although they are very similar to guinea pigs, they are larger and have longer legs, and vary in color among brown, reddish, dull-orange, greyish and blackish, but always with lighter underparts. They are covered in coarse hair, which is raised when alarmed, and weigh between 2.4–6.0 kg. They are 40.5 to 76.0 cm in length, with short hair and hairless tails. See *Jutia*.

Aiba: Ramón Pané's spelling variation of Baidrama. See *Baidrama*.

Akambue: Carib men's term for the soul. See *Caribs*.

Akeuman: Carib term for the celestial monstrous fish who, despite being celestial, lives in a river full of life. See *Caribs*.

Aldeas: Alternative name for *palenques*, which speaks more to a small and humble settlement of inhabitants who depend on a bigger city relatively nearby. Also has a connotation of a small Amerindian settlement structured around a few *bohíos*. See *Amerindian, Bohíos,* and *Palenques*.

Amaiuua: One of the two caves located on the mountain Canta. See *Caanau, Canta* and *Cacibagiagua*.

Amerindian(s): Academic term for a member or members of the indigenous peoples of the Americas, including the Caribbean. It is used primarily in anthropological and linguistic contexts as tool of demarcation, separating the indigenous people of the Caribbean territories, which were archaically called las Indias Orientales (the East Indies), from the peoples of the Indian Subcontinent. This modern confusion is the historical result of Christopher Columbus voyages to the uncharted waters west of Europe, which he initially pursued as new route to las Indias (the Indies). Hence the term Indias Occidentales (West Indies) from which the Spanish named their inhabitants as *indios* (Indians).

Anacri: Carib term for cassava. See *Caribs*.

Angel de la Guarda: Guardian Angel. A Lucumi creation in Cuba that derives from the Catholic belief of the guardian angels assigned to protect and guide a particular person, group, or nation. Although there is a somewhat similar belief and ceremony—the Esentaye ceremony—in traditional Ifá regarding a tutelary Oricha, this ceremony is done for children in Nigeria a week after they are born. This ceremony is performed with the twofold purpose of revealing the Odduns of Ifá that will inform the architectonic spiritual matrix of the child being divined for as well as the Orisha Alagbatorí, or head Oricha, that will rule and provide the baseline state frequency and his/her force or vitality to the Odduns of Ifá. In Cuba, due to the hegemony and concealed nature of the religion, Afro-Cuban practitioners had to find a workaround solution to this issue, which they resolved by assimilating the similar ancient belief and practice of assigning a tutelary spirit known in Spanish Catholicism as Angel de la Guarda. This way, individuals who are initiated into Ifá much later in the course of their lives could still be given an Orisha Alagbatorí that serves as an essential manual or guide for the proper moral and behavioral model they should strive for in life. Each Orisha has a set of moral and conduct-based compulsory prescriptions as well as proscriptions or taboos that inform the performative aspect of the individual within the religion. This Angel de la Guarda does not have anything to do with the Western tradition Holy Guardian Angel as found in *The Book of Abramelin* by Abraham von Worms and is not to be confused with it. For the closest equivalent to the Holy Guardian Angel in Afro-Caribbean religions please refer to *Ori: The Ifa Concept of Consciousness (The Metaphysical Foundations of Ifa)*, Volume 4, by Awo Fa'lokun Fatumbi.

Anima sola: Literally, 'lonely soul'. A Catholic tradition popular in some parts of Iberia, Italy, and Latin America, where an artist's depiction of a soul suffering in purgatory (in Spanish these images are called Ánimas del Purgatorio, Souls of Purgatory) is shown with the purpose of reminding good Catholics about the realities beyond death, and thus, ultimately instilling in the believers a desire to assist (usually through prayer or the purchase of indulgences) and to intercede on the behalf of it. I use it here in the sense of Souls of Purgatory, not the original Roman Catholic intention.

Anthropophagy: Human cannibalism; the act of cannibalism by human beings. From the Greek αvθρωποφάγος (*anthrōpophágos*), which means man-eating or human-eating, which in turn derives from and is an amalgam of άvθρωπος (*anthrōpos*), which means human being and φάγος (*phágos*), which means glutton.

Apito: One of the five names ascribed to the god who had no beginning and who was mother to the Taino creator god Iocahuuague Maorocon. See *Iermaoguacar, Atabei, Zuimaco*, and *Iella*.

Arará: Afro-Cuban ethnoreligious group that descends from the Kingdom of Dahomey in West Africa. This group preserved their own religion, culture, language, and identity, which are separate from the other extant Afro-Cuban peoples.

Arawak: A term describing a vast conglomeration of peoples of which the Taino are a subgroup. Used as a term for the Tainos. See *Tainos/Taino*.

Areito: Modern spelling of *areyto*. See *Areyto*.

Areyto: Taino religious songs and dance performed for the purpose of remembrance. These areytos were full of fables and recitations about their laws.

Arriba en lo alto: Up there in the heights.

Ashé: A Yoruba term that encapsulates a central, but highly complex philosophical concept of the state of the universe, and the way that Orisha and Ifá devotees understand power dynamics and how it leads to movement and change. It is a power, force, spirit, or blessing that can only be given or taken away by Olodumare, and which is bestowed to gods, ancestors, spirits, humans, animals, plants, rocks, rivers, and even to the manifestation of these things by descent of Ashé. It is the essence of essences; it is existence itself that serves as the ground from which all the essences of the universe (including gods) manifest, if Olodumare wills it and if Eshu does not interfere. It is the breath of Olodumare, which has often been syncretized with the Holy Ghost of Christianity. See *Orisha, Ifá, Olodumare*, and *Eshu*.

Ashiakuabú: The name of Eshu Ashikuelú's staff, which is made out of wood from the ceiba tree. Ashiakuabú is considered its own entity and requires its own veneration and sacrifices when these are propitiated to Eshu Ashikuelú. It is the receptacle of Eshu Ashikuelú's magical powers and the symbol that grants him rightful sovereignty over the dead and the kingdoms of the dead. *Information gathered from ashepamicuba.com/en/eshu-ashikuelu/*. See *Eshu Ashikuelú*, and *Orun*.

Atabei: One of the five names ascribed to the god who had no beginning and who was mother to the Taino creator god Iocahuuague Maorocon. See *Iermaoguacar, Apito, Zuimaco* and *Iella.*

Atabex: De las Casas' variation of one of the five names ascribed to the god who had no beginning and who was mother to the Taino creator god Iocahuuague Maorocon. See *Guaca.*

Atabey: Robiou Lamarche's spelling variation of Atabei. See *Atabei.*

Attabeira: Peter Martyr's variation of one of the five names ascribed to the god who had no beginning and who was mother to the Taino creator god Iocahuuague Maorocon. See *Mamona, Guacarapita, Iella,* and *Guimasoa.*

Autochthon: Literally, 'from the land itself'. It means aborigines or primitive inhabitants. From the Greek αυτοχθον (autochthon), which is an amalgam of αυτος (*autos*), meaning self, and χθών (*chthōn*), meaning land, earth, or soil. *Autochthon* was a word used by Athenians and other Greeks who claimed descent from the Pelasgians.

Axatse: Ghanaian term for the West African *shekere.* See *Shekere.*

Axis mundi: Literally, 'the axis of the world'; the cosmic axis, or center of the world. Also used as a symbol representing the center of the world where the heaven or sky connects with earth.

Ayé: The visible realm, which here specifically refers to Earth.

Aztecs: A Mesoamerican culture that flourished in central Mexico in the post-classical period from 1300–1521, made up of distinct ethnic groups of Central Mexico who spoke the Nahualt language.

Babalawos: The father of the mysteries of the cult of Ifá. The priest of Ifá. See *Ifá.*

Babalú-Ayé: Oricha of death, resurrection, patron of the dead, night, healing, illness, and Ayé. Among his symbols of power are a whip, a palm frond, and a branch with a piece of rough sack tied to it and which is adorned with beads and shells. His color is bishop purple. See *Ayé.*

Baidrama: Taino *cemi,* which was burnt down during times of war and washed with the juice of the cassava after war's end so that its limbs would regrow. See *Cemi.*

Bakámo: Carib constellation where the celestial Great Serpent was found. It included the astrological constellations of Scorpio, Sagittarius, and Capricorn. See *Caribs*.

Bakisi banene: The powers of nature.

BaKongo: Plural form of Kongo. See *Kongo*.

Bakulu ndoki: Ancestors of evil, who practiced *ndoki* while alive and who were malevolent and wicked. See *Ndoki*.

Bakulu: Venerated ancestors.

Baluande Madre Agua: Mpungo of the oceans and of maternity, and the universal mother. Its dwelling is in the oceans. Also presides over the equilibrium of the world and constitutes human stability and plays an important role in human health. Among her symbols of power are a fan made from the plumes of a duck or peacock and decorated with mother pearls and conchs, and an *iruke* (a duster of sorts used for the same function in Santeria and Ifá) made of horsehair and adorned with marine blue and white beads and a blue bell. Its color is marine blue. See *Mpungo, Santeria,* and *Ifá*.

Banda: The Spanish word for band or the Bantu word *banda*, meaning 'to go up' or 'goes up'. See *Bantu languages*.

Bantu languages: A large family of languages spoken by the Bantu people of Central and South Africa, derived from a proto-Bantu language thought to have been spoken in the area of what is modern-day Cameroon. See *Bantu people*.

Bantu people: The speakers of Bantu languages, which are comprised of several hundred indigenous ethnic groups whose territory extends from central to southern Africa. The name derives from Wilhelm Bleek's 19th century reconstruction of a proto-Bantu language of the area as a word that meant 'people' or 'humans'. People who started the great Bantu Expansion: an eastward and southward migration to the Central and South African continent from modern day Cameroon around 1000–500 B.C.E. See *Bantu languages*.

Baobab: *Adansonia digitata.* The axis mundi for the Yoruba and the Fon of Dahomey of Africa. It plays an important role in the socioreligious experience of these communities.

Barbacoa: Arawak term used by the Caribs for their annual anthropophagic rite as the zenith of their religious calendar, which was based on the cosmological myth of the Celestial Barbecue. Also used by the Taino to mean a wooden structure for the storage of meat and fish. The word barbecue derives from this Arawak term. See *Caribs* and *Tainos/Taino*.

Bassamanaco: Grandfather of the four twin brothers, progenitors of humankind, and god that enters into conflict with them over a trade of cassava bread for tobacco.

Bateys: Taino courts for playing ball. The batey was the central plaza in the village, where ceremonial practices such as the ceremonial ball game, called by the same name, and *areitos* took place. It is also a name used in Palo Monte for *munanzos*. See *Munanzos* and *Tainos/Taino*.

Behique: De las Casas' spelling of the word for a Taino medicine man or shaman. It has become the accepted standard form.

Bilongo: Alternative term used for *nsara* by some Palo Monte practitioners that occurs due to the different Bantu dialects that arrived in Cuba and coalesced into the Palo Monte religion. Yet others use *bilongo* for the magical infusions and potions concocted in Palo Monte. See *Nsara, Palo Monte,* and *Bantu*.

Bilongos: Magical works, witchcraft, or potions.

Binthaitel: Peter Martyr's spelling variation of Boinaiel. See *Boinaiel*.

Black Magic: The left-hand path. Magic traditionally used for evil, selfish, malicious purposes. The usage of supernatural powers for antisocial means.

Bohío: Taino house. It was also the name used by Caribs for their houses, perhaps a Taino influence through their kidnapped wives. See *Tainos/Taino* and *Caribs*.

Bohuti: Ramón Pané's spelling variation of *behique*. See *Behique*.

Boinaiel: One of the two *cemis* found inside Giououaua, which the Taino greatly venerated for purposes of rain, agriculture, and child-bearing pains. See *Giououaua* and *Maroio*.

Boitius: Peter Martyr's spelling variation of Behique. See *Behique*.

Border gnosis: The movement or remapping of the cartography of knowledge beyond the horizon of western education, which constitutes the reshaping of the border of epistemology, hermeneutics, and any other colonial institutionalized field or subject of education.

Border-thinking: Alternative name of border gnosis, and usually the preferred form. See *Border gnosis.*

Boveda Espiritual: Spiritual vault. Used in Spiritism and Espiritismo as an altar or shrine in which several (numbers differ, but usually 7, 9, or 21) plain or crystal glasses are used, with a lone crucifix at the center or one in each glass, as well as incense, flowers, perfumes, and books of prayers (usually Catholic prayer books or a series of Allan Kardec's selected prayers). Candles are arranged (there are variations in arrangement, like the cards of Tarot, and also variations of the altar set-up, for example *de escalera*, a ladder or step-like shrine) in various forms in front of photos and items depicting and belonging, respectively, to the ancestors of the owner of the Boveda Espiritual. This altar or shrine is used as a means of veneration and propitiation of the dead in Cuba, serving as an alternative to Palo Monte for those not wishing to involve themselves with this Afro-Cuban creole religion. This phenomenon occurs in Cuba in all forms of creole religions due to the loss of the cult of Egungun brought about by the abrupt uprooting of the transatlantic slave trade. The reason for this is because in Ifá, for a person to be able to venerate and propitiate their ancestors through the cult of Egungun, they need to know and call upon the names of at least seven generations of both patrilineal and matrilineal bloodlines. This became impossible due to the deliberate obliteration of the African extended family (which is focused on the communal) and enforced exile by the hegemony of the Spanish, causing these ancestries and the tradition to be lost to oblivion. Please refer to *Egun: The Ifa Concept of Ancestor Reverence* by Awo Fa'lokun Fatumbi for the most extensive treatment of this tradition. See *Egungun.*

Boye: Spelling variation of *boyez.* See *Boyez.*

Boyez: Carib shaman or medicine man. See *Carib.*

Bóyez: Spelling variation of *boyez.* See *Boyez.*

Brujería: Witchcraft.

Brujo: Sorcerer, warlock.

Bugia: Ramón Pané's spelling variation of Baidrama. See *Baidrama.*

Bukulu (cardinal point): East.

Bulliri: Carib term for bats. See *Caribs.*

Butá Nseke: Little man who is the master of the mountain.

Bwiti: Spiritual discipline of the Punu and Mitsogo peoples of Gabon, and the Fang peoples of Gabon and Cameroon.

Caanau: Taino mythological province on which the mountain Canta is situated. See *Caunana* and *Canta*.

Cabo Ronda: Alternative name of the *mpungo* Watariamba. See *Watariamba*.

Cacibagiagua: One of the two caves located on the mountain Canta from which the Taino people originated. See *Amaiuua, Caanau* and *Canta*.

Cacique Guarionex: Chieftain who reigned over a large part of the Caribbean and whose language was used in vast areas of the Caribbean.

Cacique: Taino chieftain or king.

Caizzihu: The great *cacique* of the Taino heaven, who performed a celestial fast. See *Cacique*.

Caldero: Spanish term for cauldron.

Cambio de cabeza: Literally means head exchange. The praxis of the *cambio de cabeza* lies in the knowledge that the Ori (being among other things, one's personal destiny) of the person is found within the crown of the head. This destiny includes the life span or predetermined duration of the person here on Earth. Although it may seem that such destiny and its duration would be a hard, predetermined one, Palo Monte shows us how this destiny can be affected and changed by internal and external forces, either by a negative polarization brought about by an intentional change in consciousness of the person towards lower or base emotions and ideas, or by the attachment of negative entities and emotional parasites. Based on this understanding, the *palero* or *palera* of a nganga Judía seeks to exchange the Ori of a person whose destiny marks the potential and real possibility of a long, successful, and healthy life with the Ori of a person who is dying and has come to the finality of their destiny. Hence, the *cambio de cabeza* is performed by the *ngangulero* or *ngangulera* with the purpose of exchanging the life of a doomed person with the life of an innocent one who in turn is doomed in the process. Nonetheless, it should be said that this practice has become increasingly more commonplace in the praxis of *paleros* and *paleras* of ngangas Cristianas. See *Palero, Palera, Ngangulero, Ngangulera, Palo Monte, Ori, Nganga Judía,* and *Nganga Cristiana.*

Canibales: According to de las Casas the original name given to the Caribs by the Taino. It is now the word used for those who eat other human beings. The English word cannibal derives from the Spanish, which in turn derives from *canibales.*

Canta: Mountain located in the mythological province of Caanau on which there were two caves. These caves are Cacibagiagua and Amaiuua. See *Caanau, Cacibagiagua,* and *Amaiuua.*

Caouynage: Carib ritual festivity similar to the *areito.* It also served as a platform on which to resolve conflicts and discord among the Carib. See *Areito* and *Carib.*

Caouynages: Plural of Caouynage. See *Caouynage.*

Capataz: Spanish term for the chieftains of the *palenques.* Can also be translated as foreman, overseer, or taskmaster; carries colonial connotations. See *Palenques.*

Capital: In Pierre Bourdieu's theoretical framework, *capital* equals resources, but these resources are not only material (as in Marx), they are also symbolic. This symbolism is used as a source of power in the *field* in which agents move. See *Field.*

Carabalí: Spanish term for the Afro-Cuban ethnoreligious group that descends from the Calabar capital found on the coast of the Cross River State of Nigeria. Also known for their religious institutions as secret societies that are considered fraternities or brotherhoods which preserved their own identity, language, culture, and religious manifestation. See *Abakuá.*

Caracaracol: One of the four twin brothers, progenitors of humankind, who suffers from swollen scabs and pain due to a confrontation with Bassamanaco after he was hit with a bag of *guanguaio.* See *Bassamanaco* and *Guanguaio.*

Caracaracoli: Amerindians who suffered from the same scabby and painful disease as the mythological Caracaracol, which condition they believed resembled the skin of a turtle. See *Caracaracol.*

Caracolis: Adornments made of shell used by the Caribs during the *Caouynage.* See *Caribs* and *Caouynage.*

Carbet: A big hut used as a sacred space where the Caribs would meet when they decided to celebrate festivities or rites, and which also served as a neutral space, dedicated to diplomacy with non-Carib representatives of other villages and European nations. See *Caribs*.

Caribes: Spanish spelling of Caribs.

Caribs: Also known as Kalinago; the people after whom the Caribbean Sea was named, who lived in the Lesser Antilles and constituted, with the Taino, the Amerindian presence in the Caribbean when Cristopher Columbus 'discovered' the 'New World'. They are chiefly remembered for their anthropophagic practices and for their sea-faring culture. See *Kalinago, Tainos/Taino*, and *Amerindian*.

Carire: Palo Monte term for Caribs and the Caribbean. See *Caribs*.

Cariré: Spelling variation of Carire. See *Carire*.

Casibaragua: Spelling variation of Cacibagiagua. See *Cacibagiagua*.

Catáluyuman: The Carib Celestial Turtle that gave its essence or spawning ability to the sea turtles. See *Caribs*.

Cauauaniouaua: *Cacique* who owned the *cemi* Opigielguoiran. See *cemi* & *Opigielguoiran*.

Caunabo: chieftain who explained to Columbus the eschatological destiny of the *Caciques*. See *Cacique*.

Caunana: Spelling variation of Caanau. See *Caanau*.

Cauta: Spelling variation of Canta. See *Canta*.

Cazuela: Spanish term for casserole.

Cazziuaquel: *Cacique* who spoke to his people while in a trance and prophesied that after his death those ruling after him would only do so for a short while, because a clothed people would come to their lands and would slay and rule over them. See *Cacique*.

Ceiba: *Ceiba pentandra*. A Taino word meaning the giant silk-cotton or kapok tree. A word completely transferred to other languages today. It was also the tree of life for the Maya of the Yucatan peninsula and the region of Guatemala. This plant and its role as a ritual object was completely taken up by the African-derived traditions of Cuba. For example, the Carabalí and their descendants in Cuba incorporated the *ceiba* and the royal palm into the ritual praxis of Abakuá; these sacred trees have become fundamental for their religion. The axis mundi for the Taino, Caribs, and all Afro-Caribbean religions. See *Tainos, Maya, Axis mundi, Carabalí, Abakuá*, and *Caribs*.

Cemi: A deity or ancestral spirit, and sculptural object housing the spirit in the Taino religious habitus.

Centella: Literally the lightning spark of low intensity that occurs during storms and which illuminates the clouds, or incandescent sparks or particles (referring here to the will-o'-the-wisp or jack-o'-lantern). The Mpungo of storms, hurricanes, tornados, derechos, and all atmospheric phenomena. Also the patron Mpungo of the cemetery or graveyard, which is believed to be dangerously wrathful. Centella is often represented as la Santa Muerte (Lady Death). Among her symbols of power are the *iruke*, a duster-like object that has a similar function in Santeria and Ifá, and nine copper bracelets. Colors are all colors except black. See *Mpungo*.

Cesto: Spanish term for basket.

Cima: Spanish term for the peak of a mountain. Also a Hispanicized Taino expression that meant undomesticated plants and animals, which is no longer in use. See *Tainos/Taino*.

Cimarrón: Spanish word for Maroon. See *Maroons*.

Cimarronaje: Spanish word for marronage. See *Marronage*.

Cimarrones: Spanish word for Maroons. See *Maroons*.

Ciruela: *Spondias purpura*. A species of flowering plant in the cashew family *Anacardiaceae* native to South America and the Caribbean. A type of plum. See *Iobi*.

Civilizing Process: Norbert Elias' theoretical stance to describe the way that individual's impulses interweave, informing their culture which in turn moderates the drives, immediate desires, affects and aesthetics of the agents vying for power in the Field. See *Field*.

Coaibai: Taino underworld or place where the dead would go after death. This place was on an island called Soraia. See *Soraia*.

Coatrischie: One of the two *cemis* which accompanied Guabancex. Its role was as a governor or gatherer of the waters rained by Guabancex. It gathered these waters into the valleys and between mountains, which it then would let loose. See *Guabancex, Guatauua*, and *Cemis*.

Coaybay: Robiou Lamarche's spelling variation of Coaibai. See *Coaibai*.

Cobayende: The Mpungo of death, resurrection, patron of the dead, night, illness (especially incurable illnesses and venereal diseases) and Ntoto. Among his symbols of power are the plumes of the *lechuza* whip, a palm frond, and a branch with a piece of rough sack tied to it and which is adorned with beads and shells. His color is bishop purple. See *Mpungo, Ntoto* and *Lechuza*.

Cogioba: Amerindian term for what is called tobacco today. See *Tabaco* and *Guanguaio*.

Cohoba: De las Casas' spelling variation of *cogioba*. See *Cogioba*.

Colonial matrix of power: An institutionalized and autonomous function put in place by European countries of power during the colonial expansion to the 'New World' which functions through a set of logical heterogenous historico-structural nodes interconnected by the logic of coloniality and capitalism for the purpose of the control of the world economy in favor of those colonizing. This includes the exploitation of labor of those deemed uncivilized by Western standards, the subjectivity of knowledge at all levels of society in order to secure a homogenous epistemology, the control of authority in order to maintain the hegemony over these colonies, and the control of gender and sexuality. See *Heterogeneous historico-structural nodes*.

Coloniality: The patterns of power that emerged as a result of colonialism and its managerial matrix of power. See *Colonial matrix of power* and *Heterogeneous historico-structural nodes*.

Comparative methodology: The methodology put in place during the 19th century in academia, which epitomizes the hubris of zero point epistemology. It is a method that ensured the observer remained uncontaminated by non-Western epistemologies, thus ensuring their privileged status at the stop of the social matrix. This, of course, was with the aim of controlling all forms of knowledge and of assigning arbitrary designations to those epistemologies deemed dangerous and undesirable to modernity and coloniality. It privileged dialectic and argumentative reasoning. See *modernity* and *Zero point epistemology*.

Congo: Umbrella term used in the Cuban colonial period which designated a vast region of culturally and ethnically diverse people originating from South and Central Africa.

Conucos: A Taino term that means a plot of cultivated land or farming field, which is generally small and consists of small mounds of interred agricultural goods and staves protruding from inside them. See *Tainos/Taino*.

Cordón espiritual: Literally 'spiritual cord' or 'spiritual chain'. It refers to the belief that each individual person is born with a set or chain of highly illuminated or beneficent spiritual entities that accompany, guide, and protect them for the duration of their life. Also known as *cuadro espiritual*. See *Cuadro espiritual*.

Coribib Chemin: Carib term for the *lechuza*, which was the symbol of the Carib *boyez* and was essential to the consecration of the *boyez*. See *Lechuza, Caribs*, and *Boyez*.

Corocote: Taino *cemi* which they placed on top of the house of Guamorete. This *cemi* would always have sexual relations with the women of the house on which it was placed. Its defining feature was that it grew two crowns on its head. See *Guamorete* and *Cemi*.

Corpus: From the Latin for 'body'. A collection of written texts, assembled for the purpose of studying and preserving it.

Coulouras: Carib flutes made of either bone or wood used for summoning and during the Caouynage. See *Carib* and *Caouynage*.

Cristóbal Colón: Christopher Columbus's name in its Spanish form.

Cuadro espiritual: Alternative name for *cordón espiritual*. Literally 'spiritual quadrant', or more appropriately, 'spiritual cadre'. See *Cordón espiritual*.

Cuatro vientos: Literally 'four winds'. The Spanish name given to the *dikenga* in Palo Monte and to the Ifá cardinal cross (of the four cardinal points) encircled halfway through the length of the x-axis and the y-axis by four equal quadrants; much like the *dikenga*. See *Dikenga, Palo Monte*, and *Ifá*.

Chamalongos: Religious paraphernalia of Palo Monte used for divination with the *nganga*. Four round pieces of coconut shell that have been consecrated by a Tata, which are used for necromancy with the *nfumbe* of the *nganga*. Each shell consists of a concave side and a convex side that gives the combinations from which the signs are obtained. These signs range in answer and messages in a spectrum from positive or resounding yes to negative or resounding no, with possibilities in between. See *Nfume, Nganga, and Tata*.

Changani: Rama of Palo Monte prevalent in the provinces of Pinar del Río, La Habana, Ciudad Habana, and Matanzas, distinguishable for its use of the Chicherikú to separate the *ndoki* part of the nganga Cristiana. See *Rama, Palo Monte, Nganga Cristiana*, and *Chicherikú*.

Chemíjn: Spelling variation of Chemyn. See *Chemyn*.

Chemyn: Term used for the spirit of Carib women who performed good deeds. See *dfCaribs*.

Chicherichu: Alternative spelling of Chicherikú. See *Chicherikú*.

Chicherikú: Wooden images or dolls that isolate the *ndoki* part of the nganga Cristiana. These Chicherikú are usually images or dolls depicting infants, which in this case since it is for *ndoki* purposes, uses the dead spirit of unbaptized infants. The symbolic meaning of these wooden images or dolls is the undifferentiated and raw wicked power of humanity before the development of conscious reflection. Therefore, it stands for the aggressive and tense drives of the cerebellum (Eshu's domain), prior to the organization and myelination of neurons in the cerebral cortex and the development of the pre-frontal cortex. This is the raw manifestation of *nkisi* before it is defined by the forces of the galaxies, filtered through the celestial bodies of this solar system and manifested here on Earth through the first year of life and the four seasons (marked by the solstices and equinoxes). This force or vitality of nature is represented by maggots, termites, and the decay of offerings that are left in *munanzo*. See *Eshu, Nganga Cristiana, Nkisi, Ndoki*, and *Munanzo*.

Chthonic: From the Greek χθόνιος (*chthónios*) meaning in, under, or beneath the earth, but which usually refers to things under the earth. Also, referring to the spirits of the underworld.

Decolonial Option: The scholarly project of delinking from the colonial matrix of power underlying western modernity in order to build a global and pluriversal future in harmony with the natural world. See *Delinking, Coloniality, Pluriverse*, and *Colonial matrix of power*.

Decolonial Project: Another name for Decolonial Option. See *Decolonial Option.*

Decoloniality: A sphere of beliefs and actions which orient our thinking from a new ground of understanding outside the cartography of Western history of ideas and development. See *Decolonial Option.*

Delinking: A process de-Westernization or re-Westernization by which those that had been the victims of modernity, coloniality, and its logic of coloniality start to forcibly separate themselves through the decolonial project, with the aim of achieving a transmodern world. See *Modernity, Logic of coloniality*, and *Decolonial Project.*

Deminán Caracaracol: Robiou Lamarche's spelling variation of Caracaracol and considered the full name of the mythological figure. See *Caracaracol.*

Diasporic marronage: Term used by Jorge L. Chinea that describes the colonial era phenomenon of marronage, by which both Amerindian and African Slaves sought to free themselves from the bonds of slavery and which also served as a form of resistance against the religious and political hegemony of the Spanish. See *Amerindian* and *Marronage.*

Dikenga: Kongo cosmogram almost imperceptibly different from the *yowa*, but which is used in the religious context of the Bantu and the Congo in Cuba. The *dikenga* emphasizes the religious and spiritual aspects of the *yowa* and forms an integral part of the *nganga's* (person) and the *palero's/palera's* religious toolkit. Has much in common with the Western magickal tradition's use of magic circles, but instead of being used for the protection of the magician or esotericist as in Western magick, serves to locate the object or body as the center of the universe and to manifest and manipulate the forces, powers, or spirits of the universe via the utilization of the cosmogram in specific *patimpemba* forms that lead to specific outcomes in the waves of potentialities being amplified over others. Believed in Cuba to be the domain of Lucero, and one of the patimpemba that represents him. This is why, in Cuba, Lucero is the first Mpungo called upon, and the first with whom the Palo Monte practitioners try to curry favor, because without his consent as the divine messenger and the *mpungo* of the crossroads and doors, nothing can be accomplished. See *Kongo, Bantu, Congo, Yowa, Nganga (person),*

Palero, Palera, Western Magick, Magic circles, Patimpemba, Lucero, Mpungo, and *Palo Monte.*

Dimiuan: Original name of Caracaracol, before he was inflicted with the scabby ailment from which took on the latter name. See *Caracaracol.*

Egáno: Term for the center of the *dikenga* in Palo Monte.

Egun: Lucumi term for the spirits of the dead who are venerated and propitiated in Nigeria through the Egungun.

Egungun: Traditional Orisha cult of the dead, through which they venerate and propitiate their ancestors. The ritualistic aspects of the cult have very public ceremonies where the whole community is involved, but which is led by a small group of Egungun priests who masquerade in very colorful (colors of the Egun) masked costumes by means of which they venerate, revere, and propitiate their ancestors as a collective force through ecstasies brought about by altered states of consciousness. See *Orisha* and *Egun.*

El Caribe: The Caribbean.

El Mundo Nuevo Carire: A Palo Monte term that refers to the Carib sub-nation within Palo Monte that seems to have preserved the entire Carib religious habitus under a highly veiled side of Palo Monte. This sub-nation preserves its own liturgy, Kimpungulu, as well as its own *patimpemba.* Literally, 'The Carib New World'. See *Palo Monte, Caribs,* and *Habitus.*

El Oriente de Cuba: Literally, 'the Orient of Cuba'. Cuban folk term used by Cubans hailing from the Western and Central provinces to indicate the easternmost provinces of Cuba.

Elegba: Alternative name, used in Ifá for Eshu and Eleguá. See *Ifá, Eshu* and *Eleguá.*

Eleguá: The Oricha of crossroads, doors, and paths, and the divine messenger of Santeria. It is considered by some the positive and childish aspect of the Eleguá-Eshu dichotomy that is represented by the red color in the red and black colors of Eleguá-Eshu. It is a dual or two-faced Orisha that has much in common with the Olympian Greek god Ἑρμῆς (Hermes) and the Roman god Mercurius (Mercury). His symbol of power is the *garabato,* which is a wooden staff with a curved end made from the guava tree that serves both as a grabbing extension as well as handle. His colors are red and black. See *Oricha*, *Santeria*, and *Eshu*.

Eshu Ashikuelú: This path of Eshu presides over the infernal (underworld) and celestial kingdoms of the dead. He is the Oricha who guides the Eguns to their corresponding land of the dead and is their chief and Lord. He is the genius of the earth and owner of the minerals and the properties derived from them, and of all the wealth deep inside the earth. Thus, he is the only one who knows the secrets hidden within the bowels of the earth. Eshu Ashikuelú is associated with the absence of sunlight and his ceremonies should be performed after the sun sets in the sky or during a solar eclipse. He was also blessed with the role of being a participant in the creation of the universe with Olodumare, and he was the Oricha that ended the great deluge. Eshu Ashikuelú is spiritual and is linked to the spirituality and the energy released by souls when they leave their material prisons (bodies); hence, this Oricha preserves and institutes the pact made with ancestral spirits to allow for their incarnation here on earth and also the return, from beyond, of the souls that seek to settle pending accounts with the living. He is also the Oricha who presides over the Ituto ceremony and his presence and blessing is sought before starting it. Moreover, this Oricha is the cause and origin of the four seasons, for when he came here on Earth for the first time and was walking through mother nature, he saw her (Mother Nature's) daughter Afokoyeri who was walking among the endless fields of flowers and vegetation that she created when she stepped on the bare earth. Upon descending to his kingdom and being overtaken by her beauty and sweetness, he decided to win her for himself. After six months had passed and he was still obsessing over Afokoyeri, he decided to act on his well-devised strategies to win her heart. He then ascended from his kingdom, returning to the same field in which he had seen her, and began using his vast magical knowledge to enchant her with the purpose of unleashing the passion buried within her. After this failed and he stumbled on a sloped road and lost consciousness, Afokoyeri took care of him, which led to both falling in love with each other over time. However, every time Eshu Ashikuelú would come to earth the sun would hide behind the clouds and the fields and vegetation would start to wilt and die. Hence, Eshu Ashikuelú soon realized that mother nature would oppose their union (with her only descendant). For this reason, he took Afokoyeri to the bowels of the earth, to his kingdom, where they lived and loved each other. However, after a while Afokoyeri started to miss her mother and the flora and fauna and longed to return to her side. She then decided to ascend to Earth without Eshu Ashikuelú's knowledge, where she found that the earth had become devastated and withered due to her mother's sadness at her separation from her daughter. The enraged Eshu Ashikuelú ascended to Earth searching for his beloved, who he encountered with her saddened and enraged mother. At this point, Afokoyeri decided to draw up a pact that would allow for her coexistence with her mother and with Eshu Ashikuelú, which would also calm the circumstances between them. This pact established that Afokoyeri would live six months on earth and six months in the kingdom of Eshu Ashikuelú, which resulted in the four seasons of the year being born. Information gathered from *ashepamicuba.com/en/eshu-ashikuelu/* and *ashepamicuba.com/en/ashikuelu-y-afokoyeri/*. See *Eshu Ashikuelú, Oricha, Ituto, Olodumare,* and *Egun.*

Eshu: Divine messenger of Ifá and the Orisha of the crossroads, doors, and paths. It is sometimes considered the dark aspect of Eleguá or Elegba and it is therefore depicted as the black aspect of the red and black colors of Eleguá or Elegba. In Ifá cosmology, it is considered the primordial substrate darkness from which the fire or spirit (Ashé) of Olodumare condenses spirit into matter. See *Ifá, Orisha, Ashé, Olodumare, Eleguá,* and *Elegba.*

Española: Spanish term for Hispaniola.

Espiritismo Cruzado: Spanish term used in Cuba for the Spiritism that has borrowed significantly from the Afro-Caribbean religions, used to distinguish it from Kardecian Spiritism. I have simplified and achieved this aim in English by using Spiritism for the European Scientific Kardecian sort and Espiritismo for the Cuban folk Spiritism that has integrated itself into the Afro-Caribbean Spiritual Ladder. See *Spiritism* and *Espiritismo.*

Espiritismo del Cordón: A form of Spiritism which derives its name from its central ritual, where participants move in a circle or chain called the *cordón.* See *Spiritism.*

Espiritismo: Creolized version of Kardecian Spiritism. Although similar to the original Kardecian Spiritism, Espiritismo has been highly syncretized and fused with the liturgy of Afro-Caribbean religions. The spirits communicating in this creolized form also include novel creole archetypes such as colonial Africans, Roma, and other diasporic ethnic groups which were not present in the traditional Kardecian scientific Spiritism, but which speak to the creole socio-religious experience. See *Spiritism*.

Espiritista: Individual who practices Espiritismo and who communicates which the dead by means of the technologies provided by Espritismo. See *Espiritismo*.

Ethos (ἦθος): Literally, 'character'. It refers to the guiding beliefs and ideals that characterize a community, nation, ideology, or individual.

Excursus: From the Latin *excurrere*, 'to run out of'. An appendix or digression that contains further exposition of some point or topic. In academia it is a section applied to a piece of writing in order to provide digressive information that does not contribute directly to the main argument being discussed, but that nonetheless can still be connected and applied to the overall topic being discussed in the text. It is also used in order to provide a backstory to the matter being discussed in the main narrative.

Faraguuaol: A mythical *cemi* owned by an unnamed *cacique* of the island of Hispaniola. This *cemi* was said to predate the Taino and was found by them on the island; however, the myth of the *cemi* indicates that its origin is most likely mythical, outside the realm of mortal space-time. It was created from a log or beam found in a ditch by two hunters after they lost track of their prey. See *Hispaniola*, *Cemi*, and *Cacique*.

Field: A space of action and struggle over the different forms of capital, the actions taken towards producing that capital, the consumption of that capital, and the jockeying for position among agents and institutions within the field, competing for this structured place of social force. See *Capital*.

Firmas: Literally, 'signature'. Alternative name of the *patimpembas*, especially when they are penciled into a book or other type of media (though not drawn in chalk) either for educational purposes or for the preservation of the Ngueyo's *patimpemba* when it is first given by the godfather *palero*, so that he may memorize and study it. There is a *firma* or *patimpemba* known as *fondo canasta*, which contains and synthesizes the codified karmic language and history of the *nganga*, and the *nfumbe* with which they made the pact as well as the Ngueyo's conjunct spiritual path. See *Patimpemba, Ngueyo, Palero, Fondo Canasta,* and *Nfumbe.*

Fondo Canasta: Literally a basket's bottom or a basket's base. Refers to a *firma* or *patimpemba* which contains and synthesizes the codified karmic language and history of the *nganga*, and the *nfumbe* with which they made the pact as well as the Ngueyo's conjunct spiritual path. Ultimately, this *patimpemba* or *firma* becomes the representation of the soul of these three forces of nature, now unified, which is why traditionalists vehemently declare that the ceremony of *jubilacion* does not exist. See *Firma, Patimpemba, Nganga, Nfumbe, Jubilacion,* and *Ngueyo.*

Freemasonry: Secret societies built around Masonic lodges, where the initiates congregate and impart wisdom and esoteric knowledge according to rank and hierarchy. It is a fraternal organization that traces its origins to the European guilds of stonemasons, but which in the 14th century started to evolve into what it is today. It became a very popular and influential secret society in both the Americas and the European continent, due to which they became embroiled in many conspiracy theories and were scrutinized by the authorities.

Fula: Gunpowder. Used as a catalyst in magical works.

Fundamento: Alternative name for *nganga*. Literally, 'fundament'. See *Nganga.*

Gaia: God who created the oceans and the fish and sealed them off inside herself (the gourd) until *Itiba Tahuuaua* broke them out by accident. See *Itiba Tahuuaua.*

Gamanacoel: Spelling variation offered by Ramón Pané of the *cacique* Cazziuaquel. See *Cazziuaquel* and *Cacique.*

Gangá: Afro-Cuban ethnoreligious group that descends from the Sierra Leone, Libya, and Côte d'Ivoire in West Africa. This group preserved its own religion, culture, language, and identity, which are separate from those of the other extant Afro-Cuban peoples.

Ghede nanchon: Nation of Haitian Vodou which preserves the beliefs and practices relating to the dead. See *Haitian Vodou.*

Ghede: Haitian Vodou spirits of the dead who have their own nanchon. See *Haitian Vodou* and *Nanchon.*

Giououaua: Cave located in the land of Maucia Tiuuel which was held in high regard by the Taino. This is the cave out of which the sun and moon originated, according to the Taino mythology. See *Maucia Tiuuel.*

Giuca: Amerindian term for yucca. See *yucca.*

Guabancex: Taino *cemi* found in the lands of *cacique* Aumatex, thought to be a woman made of stone. It was accompanied by two other *cemis* called Guatauua and Coatrischie. Guabancex's power was over the winds and rain that could destroy houses and topple trees.

Guabazza: Amerindian term for *guanábana.* See *Guanábana.*

Guaca: De las Casas' variation of one of the five names ascribed to the god who had no beginning and who was mother to the Taino creator god Iocahuuague Maorocon. See *Atabex.*

Guacarapita: Peter Martyr's variation of one of the five names ascribed to the god who had no beginning and who was mother to the Taino creator god Iocahuuague Maorocon. See *Attabeira, Mamona, Iella,* and *Guimasoa.*

Guahagiona: Amerindian king who is the protagonist of one of their legends. This legend revolves around the ailment known to the Spanish as *las bubas.* Contrary to previous belief, based on this legend this ailment seems to have been endemic to the Caribbean prior to the arrival of the Spanish.

Guamorete: Important Taino individual who owned Corocote at one time. See *Corocote.*

Guanábana: *Annona muricata.* A broadleaf, flowering, and evergreen tree native to the Americas and the Caribbean.

Guanahatabey: Hunter-gatherer people who lived in caves in the westernmost part of Cuba and spoke a distinct language from the Arawak Taino.

Guanguaio: tobacco pouch. See *Cogioba* and *Tabaco.*

Guannaba: Peter Martyr's spelling variation of Guabazza. See *Guabazza.*

Guano: Excrement of seabirds and bats, which is used as a fertilizer.

Guaraguao: Carib term for the solar or diurnal red-tailed hawk *Buteo jamaicensis*, which was associated with life. See *Caribs* and *Yeretté*.

Guaraionel: Individual mentioned by Ramón Pané in the mythical creation story of the *cemi* Faraguuaol. See *Cemi* and *Faraguuaol*.

Guataba: Taino god or spirit of lightning. See *Tainos/Taino*.

Guatauua: One of the two *cemis* which accompanied Guabancex. Its role was as a screamer. By the order of Guabancex, this *cemi* would cry out to all other *cemis* of the land so that together they could raise a high wind and bring heavy rain. See *Guabancex, Coatrischie,* and *Cemi*.

Güeya: Amerindian name for an unknown plant they made use of, which has been speculated to be either a type of freshwater algae or the coca plant. See *Amerindian*.

Güeyo: Substance used by the Taino that was either the coca plant *Erythroxylum coca*, or a substance consumed by some Arawak-speaking communities which consisted of tobacco and ashes and a salty freshwater algae (*Mourera fluvialitis*). See *Tainos/Taino*.

Guimasoa: Peter Martyr's variation of one of the five names ascribed to the god who had no beginning and who was mother to the Taino creator god Iocahuuague Maorocon. See *Attabeira, Mamona, Guacarapita,* and *Iella*.

Gurunfinda: The Mpungo of the wilderness and the divine power of the flora. See *Mpungo*.

Habiti: Plural of Habitus. See *Habitus*.

Habitus: Theoretical term used by Norbert Elias and Pierre Bourdieu that encapsulates complex psycho-social dynamics. It is the seat of an individual's dispositions and filter of all that is perceived by them. It is a constituent of the field, rendering it a world of meanings, while reciprocally being informed by the field. Habitus informs the individual's thoughts, actions, and feelings throughout the course of his or her social development. See *Field*.

Habla bozal: Muzzled speech. Palo Monte Spanish term for the creolized liturgical language used in Palo Monte. The word *bozal* (the verb 'muzzled') here demonstrates the scars left by the colonial wound. The term *bozal* refers to the apparatus that is fastened around the nose and mouth (the noun 'muzzle') of an animal so that it may not bite, a word which in Spanish and English also refers to the process by which a person or a group is prevented from expressing themselves and their opinions freely. The word *habla* means speech, to speak, or language. See *Palo Monte*.

Hades (Ἅιδης): Ancient Greek god of the underworld and the lord of the dead. Also the name for the underworld of the ancient Greek world. Among his symbols are the cornucopia that represents the riches of the underworld, serpents, and dogs. See *Pluto*.

Haitian Vodou: Highly creole and syncretic African diasporic religion of Haiti.

Hamaca: Hammock.

Hayti: Taino name for the Island of Hispaniola. See *Tainos/Taino*.

Hegemony: From the Greek ἡγεμονία (*hegemonía*), which means rule, leadership, authority, sovereignty, and reign. A word that has entered the repertoire of academic scholarship, but which is seldom rightly attributed to its inventor Antonio Gramsci, a Marxist philosopher who first coined it to describe the "dominance of a culturally diverse society by the ruling class who manipulate the culture of that society—the beliefs and explanations, perceptions, values, and mores—so that the worldview of the ruling class becomes the accepted cultural norm. As the universal dominant ideology, the ruling-class worldview misrepresents the social, political, and economic *status quo* as natural, inevitable, and perpetual social conditions that benefit every social class, rather than as artificial social constructs that benefit only the ruling class" <https://en.wikipedia. org/wiki/Cultural_hegemony>. Hence my desire to use its original meaning instead of its current one, which is similar in character to that of this study.

Hekátē (Ἑκάτη): The triple-formed goddess of crossroads, entranceways, light and night, magic, witchcraft, the knowledge of the healing and poisonous essences of plants, ghosts, sorcery, and necromancy.

Henotheism: Friedrich Schelling's term, used by the renowned philologist Max Müller to describe religions such as Hinduism which venerate and worship many deities, because they are seen as intermediaries between a supreme god and humankind.

Hermano: brother.

Heterogenous historico-structural nodes: The nodes of logical structure that anchor the colonial matrix of power and which underlie the totality of Western civilization. Simultaneously, these nodes serve as the system of managerial logic which controls the actions and borders of the actors/agents within the colonial matrix of power. See *Colonial matrix of power.*

Hiali: The incestuous daughter of Luna and her brother brought to the sky after Luna ascended by the *yeretté.* See *Luna* and *Yeretté.*

Higüero: *Crescentia cujete.* The calabash tree. Also the Taino funerary basket, which derives from the myth of Yayael's parricidal intentions. It was hung at the centermost position of the *bohío.* See *Tainos/Taino, Yayael,* and *Bohío.*

Historical trope of indigenous extinction: The process of elimination or of scriptural genocide performed by European historians and scholars, which aligned with the discourse and progress of Modernity. This consists of the systematization of the trope in the Western educational system, where individuals are routinely taught that the indigenous people of the Caribbean were wiped out during the 16th century and have been extinct for the past five centuries for the benefit of the logic of coloniality. See *Modernity* and *Logic of coloniality.*

Hobo: Spelling Variation of Iobi. See *Iobi* and *Ciruela.*

Huracán (lower case): Taino term that means 'storm'. It became the Spanish word used for the natural phenomena of hurricanes. The English term hurricane was borrowed in turn from the Spanish.

Huracán: Maya god of wind, storm, and fire. See *Maya.*

Huricán: Taino term for the Carib god of evil. See *Tainos/Taino* and *Caribs.*

Ia: Arawak superlative that means spirit, cause, and essence of life. See *Arawak.*

Iboga rite: Ritual ceremony led by the *nganga* (Bwiti medicine men are called by the same name as the Kongo and Palo Monte medicine men) where the iboga plant (*Tabernanthe iboga*) was first used by the Aka, Baka, Mbuti, and Batwa peoples of West Central Africa. This ceremony is highly important in the context of these communities. This crucial rite is an initiation ceremony into Bwiti in which young Gabonese (and Cameroonian) men and women partake in

the drinking of a potion made of the iboga plant. This highly ritual-
ized and ceremonial rite is conducted in the privacy of huts that
separate women and men while they participate in it. Once these
young individuals have drunk from the *iboga* brew, they officially
become members of the spiritual practice of Bwiti. Moreover, during this ceremony these youngsters are instructed in various mysteries and legends that pertain to the sociocultural history of these
communities. One such mystery is the origin story of the iboga
plant itself.

Icheíri: Term used for the spirit of Carib men who performed good
deeds. See *Caribs.*

Ichetriku: Namesake of the Carib men's personal god. See *Caribs.*

Iella: One of the five names ascribed to the god who had no beginning
and who was mother to the Taino creator god Iocahuuague Maorocon. See *Iermaoguacar, Apito, Zuimaco,* and *Atabei.*

Iermaoguacar: One of the five names ascribed to the god who had no beginning and who was mother to the Taino creator god Iocahuuague
Maorocon. See *Atabei, Apito, Zuimaco,* and *Iella.*

Ifá: Nigerian and Afro-Cuban religion of the cult of Òrúnmìlà headed by
priests called *babalawos.* Concerned primarily with bringing wisdom, healing, good character, and fortune to the devotees by means
of divination which re-traces or re-connects them with their original planned karmic or spiritual mission here on earth, re-balancing
(bringing to harmony) the energies and consciousness of the individual with their destiny. A holistic type of religious worship whose
priests are considered the highest and most respected members of
the Lucumi tradition in Cuba. Although in Nigeria the Iyanifa are
allowed, in Cuba only men are allowed as *babalawos.* See *Iyanifa.*

IFA: Spelling Variation of Ifá. See *Ifá.*

Ikin Ifá: Sacred palm nuts or kola nuts of Ifá. See *Ifá.*

Ikú: Lucumi term for Death or the Grim Reaper. See *Nfuá.*

Ile-Ife: The old capital city of Yorubaland. It is considered a sacred city
by the Yoruba practitioners of indigenous Orisha worship. The locus of power of the Oòni, who has become more of a figurehead in
modern Nigerian politics and whose role has increasingly become
ceremonial. See *Oòni.*

Imperative methodology: Alternative methodology to comparative methodology proposed by Mignolo. It focuses on dialogue, praxis, and existential encounters, reasoning from the senses, and knowledge produced from the locations of bodies within the colonial matrix of power. See *Comparative methodology* and *Colonial matrix of power.*

Indio de nganga: Amerindian who dwells in the *nganga*. See *Nganga.*

Inriri: Taino term for the Caribbean woodpecker (*Melanerpes superciliaris*). See *Tainos/Taino.*

Iobi: Name given in the mythological story of the Taino to the men who are turned into *ciruela* trees after they had gone fishing and not returned before the sun was carried off due to Marocael's irresponsibility. See *Ciruela* and *Marocael.*

Iocahuuague Maorocon: The Taino creator god. See *Tainos/Taino.*

Iounaboina: Peter Martyr's spelling variation of Giououaua. See *Giououaua.*

Irunmole: The semi-divine entities sent down by Olorun to complete some unfinished task here on earth and who later started to serve as intermediaries between Orún and Ayé. See *Olorun, Orún,* and *Ayé.*

Isúla: Celestial constellation in the Carib religious habitus that marked the beginning of the Celestial Barbecue when present in the sky and allowed for the felling of the *ceiba* for building canoes when absent. See *Caribs, Barbacoa,* and *Habitus.*

Itiba Tahuuaua: God that released the oceans and the fish inside them after he destroyed Gaia by accident. Father of the four twin brothers, progenitors of humankind. See *Gaia* and *Caracaracol.*

Itutu: Funerary rite or ceremony of the Lucumi tradition reserved for a *santera/santero* or *babalawo*. See *Santera, Santero, Lucumi,* and *Babalawo.*

Iyanifa: Traditional Ifá female priest. See *Ifá.*

Jicara: *Lagenaria siceraria*. Spanish term for calabash.

Jobo tree: The term jobo was a Taino word that has been borrowed and has remained one of the names of *Spondias mombin*, the hobo tree or hog plum.

Jobo: Spelling Variation of Iobi. See *Iobi* and *Ciruela.*

Jubilacion: Literally 'retirement'. Highly controversial and recent development in Palo Monte where the taboo of initiating someone in Palo Monte after being initiated in the Regla de Ocha is performed. The crowning of the Oricha that serves as Angel de la Guarda (Guardian Angel) is retired or reversed, which is performed by some modern *paleros* or *paleras* in order to initiate someone crowned with an Oricha into the Palo Monte religion. See *Angel de la Guarda, Palo Monte, Regla de Ocha, Palero, Palera,* and *Oricha.*

Juegos: Literally, 'games'. Abakuá religious institutions or secret societies, also considered brotherhoods or fraternities, where they preserved their own identity, language, culture, and religious manifestation. See *Abakuá.*

Juluca: Carib term for the rainbow. See *Caribs.*

Jutia: Spanish name used for the native type of agouti found in Cuba. See *Agouti.*

Kala: Kongo term for the black sun. See *Kongo.*

Kalinago: Modern alternative word for Caribs. See *Caribs.*

Kalunga: The underworld of Palo Monte; the Palo Monte and BaKongo abysmal waters to which the dead return. Also, the ocean and the means for the middle passage to the kingdom of death and ancestry, represented as a metaphor for death and the fluid immanence of death itself. See *Palo Monte* and *BaKongo.*

Kandango: Term reserved in Palo Monte for the Nsasi Siete Rayos *ngangas* made out of terracotta or clay. See *Nganga, Palo Monte,* and *Nsasi Siete Rayos.*

Kikongo: A Bantu language spoken by the Kongo people. It was the official language of the Kingdom of Kongo. See *Kongo, Kingdom of Kongo,* and *Bantu.*

Kilisu: Alternative name used by some Bantu tribes for the *yowa.* See *Yowa.*

Kilos: Cuban coin with an equivalent pecuniary value to that of seven American pennies and seven British pence in U.S.A. and U.K. respectively.

Kimbundo (cardinal point): South.

Kimpungulu: Plural form of Mpungo. See *Mpungo.*

Kimpúngulu: Spelling variation of Kimpungulu. See *Kimpungulu*.

Kindnoki: The art or practice of *ndoki*. See *Ndoki*.

Kinganga: Term used in traditional Kongo belief to describe the art or praxis of their medicine man, which they called *nganga*. See *Kongo and Nganga*.

Kingdom of Dahomey: West African Kingdom that was located in what is today Benin. Its history spanned from around 1600 to 1904 until the French conquest. It was a highly influential kingdom in the history of West Africa due to its role in the transatlantic slave trade after it conquered the coastal kingdoms of Allada and Whydah on the African Gold Coast, which ultimately became major ports and centers of the slave trade. Its highly adaptable religion Vodun became influential in the region due to its tendency to absorb and integrate the gods and socioreligious customs of the people they conquered, but which they always managed to relegate to lower positions than those of their native religion. The Afro-Caribbean religion of Haitian Vodou takes its name and much of its theory and praxis from Vodun and this old African Kingdom. See *Haitian Vodou*.

Kingdom of Kongo: *Kongo dia Ntolila* or *Wene wa Kongo*. A kingdom located in west central Africa ruled by the *manikongo* from its capital of Mbanza-Kongo, and which lasted as a sovereign kingdom from 1390 to 1857. See *Manikongo*.

Kinkimba: Kongo preparatory school for future *ngangas*. See *Kongo* and *Nganga (person)*.

Kiyekwa: Power or potencies.

Kiyumba: Term in Palo Monte for the human bones that reside within the *nganga*. It is the skeletal remains of the *nfumbe* with which the *palero* or *palera* has made the pact during the *nkimba* initiation. The bones used and how the bones are used varies between each *rama* and each *munanzo* within the *ramas*, but the spectrum goes from the usage of the skull, the clavicles, the femur and tibia and the humerus, to the ulna and radius. See *Palo Monte, Nganga, Palero, Palera, Nkimba, Munanzo, Rama*, and *Mpolo*.

Kizimbi (cardinal point): North.

Kongo (lowercase): Means iron in Kikongo. See *Kikongo*.

Kongo Diaspora: The forcefully dispersed people of the Kingdom of Kongo brought as slaves to the Americas and the Caribbean. See *Kingdom of Kongo*.

Kongo nanchon: Nation of Haitian Vodou which preserves the beliefs and practices of the Kongo brought to Haiti. See *Haitian Vodou*.

Kongo: An individual or citizen of the old Kingdom of Kongo. See *Kingdom of Kongo*.

Krónos (Κρόνος): The king of the Titans and father of the first generation of Olympian gods, who was exiled to Latium after his son Zeus dethroned him. In Latium he lived in prosperity and became the supreme god of the pantheon whose reign was considered by the Romans as the Golden Age of plenty and peace. The Titan god of time, harvest, fate, justice, evil, and death. Among his symbols are the scythe and/or sickle. See *Saturnus*.

Ku'mpemba: The Kongo underworld.

Kuballende: Alternative spelling of Cobayende. See *Cobayende*.

Kuiti Kuiti, Nkunda Mbaki Nranda, and Mboze: Three siblings of the Kongo religion, who were the progenitors of humanity. See *Kongo*.

La misa de coronación del muerto: Literally, 'coronation' or 'crowning mass of the dead'. Coronation ceremony where the chief spiritual entity of the *cordón espiritual* of the individual being initiated into Spiritism is crowned or acknowledged. Ceremony where the spiritual gap between the individual and the chief spiritual entity of his *cuadro espiritual* is bridged. See *Cordón espiritual, Spiritism,* and *Cuadro espiritual*.

La misa de investigación: Literally 'investigation mass'. Ceremony where a Spiritist investigates an individual through means of a medium or psychic abilities in order to unveil or investigate the *cordón espiritual* of the person. See *Spiritist* and *Cordon espiritual*.

Lacuna: A missing portion of a book or manuscript (plural: *lacunae*).

Las Bubas: Old Spanish term for syphilis, which was also known as the French disease during the Spanish conquest.

Latium: The region of central western Italy in which the city of Rome was founded and the sociocultural foundation from which the Roman Empire expanded.

Lechuza: *Spéoyto cunincularia*. A species of small owl found in the Caribbean.

Licencia: Palo Monte salutatory process which initiates communication, performed by the *ngangulero* or *ngangulera* when establishing communication with their *nganga*, the *nfumbe*, and the Kimpungulu. Consists of the individuals and powers that have granted him permission to work with and communicate with the powers of nature and the *nfumbes*. Simultaneously, it is also used as a request for permission in working with the *nfumbes*, *paleros* or *paleras* who initiated them, and the Kimpungulu. See *Palo Monte, Ngangulero, Ngangulera, Nganga, Nfumbe, Kimpungulu, Paleros*, and *Paleras*.

Locus of enunciation: The place from which codified power relations are established, but with the caveat that it is done from an unequal stance. Those at the center control the knowledge and the power of decision-making across all socio-political lines. Hence, those who stand at the epicenter of the locus of enunciation can include everyone, but do not allow everyone to be included, thus systematizing the codified power relations that lead to oppression.

Logic of coloniality: The rhetoric of modernity hidden behind the rhetoric of Christian salvation, which blesses and sanctifies destruction, war, racism, genocide, colonialism, and rampant capitalism geared towards the support of the colonial matrix of power that in turn supports the Eurocentric model of the world with its Christian Universal spirituality based on the two pillars of modernity and coloniality. See *Modernity* and *Colonial matrix of power*.

Low Magic: Magic performed for the aim of pursuing base things, such as money and other material gains. Magic that concerns itself with the pursuit of wealth and comfort.

Lucero: Literally, the 'morning star' or 'light-bringer'; it is for this reason this Mpungo has often been syncretized with Lucifer, erroneously believed to be the proper name of Satan. This misunderstanding arose out of a Christian interpretation of Isaiah 14.4, where the Greek Φωσφόρος (Phōsphoros, the morning star) was rendered from the Hebrew word הֵילֵל (*hêylêl*, the morning star), which in the King James bible was translated via the Latin Vulgate as lucifer (lowercase: the morning star) thought to be a reference to Satan, but which instead refers to the King of Babylon. However, Lucero's name actually refers to the spark that allows for communication between the world of the living, the world of the dead, and the world of the Kimpungulu. It is the Mpungo of doors, crossroads, voyages, fortunes, and paths. It is sometimes considered a tricky, fickle, and mischievous *mpungo* who behaves like a child. An alternative name for Lucero that is often used is Nkuyu, which is simultaneously used for the *dikenga* or *los cuatro vientos* over which he presides. His symbol of power is the *garabato*, which is a wooden staff made from the guava tree that has a curved end that serves both as a grabbing extension as well as handle. Its colors are red and black. See *Kimpungulu, Mpungo, Nkuyu, Cuatro vientos*, and *Dikenga*.

Lucumi tradition: Another name for the religion Santeria, and the most appropriate due to its highly syncretic nature with all other Lucumi religions. See *Santeria* and *Lucumi*.

Lucumi: A term which describes the diaspora from West Africa and which includes people from Yorubaland, but also the Kingdom of Oyo, the Ebo, the Fulani and many more.

Lukankazi: The Mpungo often syncretized with the Devil, a word that comes from διάβολος (*diábolos*, meaning a slanderer, defamer, false accuser, and maligner), or Satan, that was in turn taken from the Hebrew term שָׂטָן (*śāṭān*, meaning adversary, accuser, and obstructor or opponent), due to its characteristics as the Mpungo of the dark arts, the forces of antagonism against life, and the fire that is animated from the material world, inside the earth instead of in the heavens. Among his symbols of power are the scythe, horns, and black cats. His color is black or the absence of color. See *Mpungo*.

Lukúni-yáruba: Carib term for the Big Dipper, which meant the Celestial Canoe. It marked the beginning of the Carib warring and seafaring season. See *Caribs*.

Luna: Carib term for the moon and its mythological character. See *Caribs* and *Hiali*.

Lupokuyo: Alternative name of the Mpungo Watariamba. See *Watariamba*.

Luvemba: Guardian of Ku'mpemba. It translates to 'threshold' or 'door'. See *Ku'mpemba*.

Luvemba: Kongo term for the gray/white sun. See *Kongo*.

Lwas: The intermediary spirits, forces of nature, or energy between the supreme god and humanity of Haitian Vodou. See *Haitian Vodou*.

Llanto: Funerary rite or ceremony of Palo Monte reserved for a *palero* or *palera*. See *Palo Monte, Palero,* and *Palera*.

Mabouya: Spelling variation of Maboya. See *Maboya*.

Maboya: Mischievous and malevolent spirit for both male and female Caribs, whose deeds caused disruptions and upset. Also considered the third soul found in the arms of the human body and which was said to flee it after death, at which point it became the evil and sinister spirit of everything ill-fated. See *Caribs, Uméku,* and *Yuanni*.

Macana: A wooden weapon or agricultural tool used by the Taino, which was usually made like a flattened club or sword and was sometimes edged or headed with a stone or stones. See *Tainos/Taino*.

Macuto: Taino word that means a deep bag made of vines. See *Tainos/Taino*.

Macutos: Amulets.

Machoehael: Peter Martyr's spelling variation of Marocael. Considered the appropriate spelling in modern scholarship. See *Marocael*.

Magic circles: A circled space made by a Western Magick practitioner for the purposes of creating a sacred space that will provide them with magical protection, often drawn out in salt or chalk. See *Western Magick*.

Maiohauau: A sort of drum of about 45 inches long and 22.5 inches in breadth that was played by the Taino, which in part resembled "the shape of the pincers of a farrier" and had at its opposite end a club-shaped form. See *Tainos/Taino*.

Maiouauan: Brasseur de Bourbourg's spelling variation of *maiohauau*. See *Maiohauau*.

Makuku: Cauldron.

Malekum Nsala: Kikongo salutation used by Palo Monte practitioners which was borrowed from the Arabic وَعَلَيْكُمُ ٱلسَّلَامُ (*wa ʿalaykumu s-salam*), meaning, 'May peace be upon you', said in response to the religious salutation as-*salāmu ʿalaykum* used by Muslims when greeting one another. Other less reliable sources have placed the origin of this Palo Monte salutation on a BaKongo misinterpretation of the Muslim salutation, meaning, 'And I wave my hand back at you in greeting'. See *Nsala Malekum, Kikongo, Palo Monte*, and *BaKongo*.

Malongo Kisonga Kia: Palo Monte festivity performed with the aim of dedicating a collective party to the *bakulu* and the current of forces presiding over the magical world of Palo Mayombe. See *Palo Monte, Palo Mayombe*, and *Bakulu*.

Malongo: Used interchangeably as an alternative name for the Palo Mayombe *rama* and as shorter name for the Malongo Kisonga Kia ceremony. Malongo also means *arriba en lo alto*, Barbacoa, and *remolino*. See *Rama, Malongo Kisonga Kia, Arriba en lo alto, Barbacoa, and Remolino*.

Mama Chola Wengue: The Mpungo of fertility, femininity, sexuality, rivers, brooks, gold, and honey. Among her symbols of power are a sandalwood fan painted yellow or made of the plumes of the peacock, five gold bracelets, and a half moon. Her color is gold or golden yellow. See *Mpungo*.

Mambos: Liturgical songs of Palo Monte. See *Palo Monte*.

Mamona: Peter Martyr's variation of one of the five names ascribed to the god who had no beginning and who was mother to the Taino creator god Iocahuuague Maorocon. See *Attabeira, Guacarapita, Iella*, and *Guimasoa*.

Manaia Tiunel: Considered the proper spelling of Maucia Tiuuel according to modern scholarship. See *Maucia Tiuuel*.

Mancenillier: Carib term for the extremely poisonous plant *Hippomane mancinella*, which they saw as the manifestation of evil on earth. See *Caribs*.

Manchineel: Another name for *mancenillier*. See *Mancenillier*.

Mandinga: Umbrella term for Afro-Cuban ethnoreligious groups that descend from the Mandinka or Mendé people of Niger, Senegal, and Gambia in West Africa. It also included other neighboring ethnic groups such as the Bambara, Diola, and Yola. These peoples were highly influenced by Islam and the Arabic habitus, which they brought to Cuba during the colonial period. See *Habitus*.

Manikongo: lord ruler of the Kingdom of Kongo; literally, 'the lord of iron'. See *Kingdom of Kongo*.

Manioc: *Manihot esculenta.* Cassava.

Mapoya: Spelling variation of Maboya. See *Maboya.*

Maracas: A gourd rattle with a long skinny neck and seeds inside, used by the Taino, which appears in many genres of Caribbean and Latin music and is much louder than the African *shekere.* More importantly to this book, this Taino religious item has become a staple of Afro-Cuban religions and forms an essential part of the ritual paraphernalia and process of *santeros* and *babalawos* in Cuba when calling and working directly with the Kimpungulu and the Orichas. See *Tainos/Taino, Palo Monte, Santero, Babalawo, Kimpungulu, Shekere,* and *Orichas.*

Marocael: Mythological character who was given the responsibility of keeping watch over Cacibagiagua. See *Canta* and *Cacibagiagua.*

Marohu: Peter Martyr's spelling variation of Maroio. See *Maroio.*

Maroio: One of the two *cemis* found inside Giououaua, which the Taino greatly venerated for purposes of rain, agriculture, and relief of child-bearing pains. See *Giououaua* and *Maroio.*

Maroons: Runaway slaves.

Marronage: An act carried out by Maroons by means of which they extricated themselves from the bonds of slavery and escaped to the *palenques.* See *Maroons* and *Palenques.*

Matanza: Spanish term that means massacre or slaughter.

Matutu: A table used by the Caribs inside the Carbet on which offerings of cassava and *uicú* were placed. See *Caribs, Carbet,* and *Uicú.*

Maucia Tiuuel: *Cacique* in whose land was situated the cave Giououaua, out of which the sun and the moon originated. See *Giououaua.*

Maya: One of the greatest civilizations of the Western Hemisphere, which occupied a continuous territory from modern southern Mexico through Guatemala to Northern Belize prior to the Spanish conquest. They had a long tradition (settlements extend back in time to 1500 BCE) of agriculture, stone building (including pyramid temples), metallurgy, hieroglyphic writings (Yucatc Maya) and maritime exploration that took them from the Yucantan Peninsula to Caribbean. Information gathered from: Amy McKenna, 'Maya |

People, Language, & Civilization', *Encyclopedia Britannica* <https://www.britannica.com/topic/Maya-people>.

Mayombo: Carib word that means a stick which could magically beat any other stick.

Mbele: Machete

Mbozos: Incised signs or scarification marks of the *nkimba* ceremony. See *Nkimba*.

Menga: Blood.

Mestizos: A term used in the Caribbean and Latin America to describe men of mixed race, and especially those of Spanish and Amerindian descent. See *Amerindian*.

Mfinda: Wild forest.

Milieu: Person's environment or the physical or social setting in which something occurs or develops.

Minkisi: plural of *nkisi*. See *Nkisi*.

Mirabolans: Spelling variation of Iobi. See *Iobi* and *Ciruela*.

Miscegenation: The interbreeding of people or the mixture of different races through marriage, cohabitation, or sexual intercourse.

Modernity: The historical period considered the modern era, which typically is believed to have started in either the 17th or the 18th century. It also refers to the socio-cultural norms, values, attitudes and practices fomented by the Renaissance that led to the Age of Reason of the 17th century and the Enlightenment of the 18th century.

Mpaka vititi menzo: This *mpaka* is used for divinatory purposes and contains a mirror which allows the spirit inside the *mpaka* to see into the world and thus provide the *ngangulero* or *ngangulera* with divinatory forewarnings. See *Nganga, Palero, Palera, Ngangulero,* and *Ngangulera*.

Mpaka: A smaller and portable version of the *nganga*, constructed of the same on a horn. The *mpaka* represents a microcosm of the *nganga* on the top of which it was constructed, and by extension the *nganga* itself. See *Nganga*.

Mpolo: Powder.

Mpungo: The *nkisi*, spirit, elemental or raw force of nature of the Palo Monte religion. The vital force presiding over specific elements and phenomena of nature that give life to the *nfumbe* and the *nganga*. Celestial force that represents the manifestation of Nzambi on the celestial spheres and on earth. It is the pure manifestation from the creative fire of Nzambi that coalesces with the cooling waters of Kalunga (as darkness) and manifests into an elemental force or natural spiritual entity of the universe. The pure or ideal form of *nkisi*. Also the heavenly spheres and the principal gods and goddesses of veneration and worship in Palo Monte. They serve as intermediaries between Nzambi and human beings. See *Nkisi, Palo Monte, Nfumbe, Nkisi, Nganga, Nzambi,* and *Kalunga.*

Mubé: Carib name for month that includes the Gregorian months of September and October. Also the name they gave to the jobo tree because it bore fruit during this month. See *Caribs* and *Jobo tree.*

Mumia: Medieval Latin term that means 'dead', or more appropriately, 'mummy'. A term used in medieval medicine.

Munanzo: The sacred space housing the *ngangas* and the Palo Monte paraphernalia of the head *palero*. A religious house made up of a multitude of individuals, both male and female, who have been initiated by the head *palero* on one of his *ngangas* and who belong to the hierarchical structure of the *rama* which the *munanzo* represents. See *Palo Monte, Palero,* and *Rama.*

Musoni: Kongo term for the yellow sun. See *Kongo.*

Naborías: Taino term for the common man or woman. See *Tainos/Taino.*

Nanchon: Haitian Vodou nation or family of *lwas*. See *Lwas* and *Haitian Vodou.*

Nativist movement: A political movement that seeks to mandate political policies directed at promoting the interests of native inhabitants, even if it goes against those of immigrants.

Nchufla: Blade.

Ndoki: Reserved in Paolo Monte for something that is wicked, evil, or bad. More importantly, this idea of *ndoki* is also an important part of the human psyche and is something that all humans have to varying degrees, or rather to various degrees of occultation. *Ndoki* is also used as a reference to the *bakulu*, in which it is called *bakulu ndoki*, but this category of ancestors is considered bad or powerful (in the sense of a *brujo* or sorcerer). Overall, in Cuba, the concept of *ndoki* is also seen as the veiled aspects of ancestry, or what is termed the 'night of the ancestors'. Palo practitioners say that we all carry these elements within ourselves and that they form an integral part of our unique composition, which defines our actions. Moreover, these night or dark forces are seen as the source of power from which acts of transgression, violence, and miracles are expressed. *Ndoki*, then, is the powerful part within humans that remains hidden from light and can be used for good or for evil depending on the context and wisdom of the individual. In Kongo belief *ndoki* referred to the men who practice *kindnoki*: evil and malevolent individuals who would spiritually 'eat' bit-by-bit another individual, usually within the family, until that person would pass away. They would also consort and meet and plan attacks on individuals within the community. They would work with the Nkose and would get into the practice of *ndoki* just to protect some family members from other *ndoki* in the villages. The Kongo practice and practitioners of witchcraft that was highly secretive and highly veiled even to other Kongo members and *ngangas* (persons). They were afraid of the leaves of the pineapple tree. See *Kongo, Ngangas (person), Bakulu, Bakulu Ndoki, Brujo, Nkose,* and *Kindnoki.*

Ndundu Yambaka: Albino pygmy.

Necromancer: A person who practices necromancy. See *Necromancy.*

Necromancy: The practice of magic that involves communication with the dead for the purposes of divination, foretelling the future, unveiling esoteric knowledge, to bring someone back from the dead, or to use them as weapon in magical warfare. An amalgam of the Greek νεκρός (*nekrós*), which means dead body or corpse and μαντεία (*manteía*), which means divination.

Nechemeraku: Namesake of Carib women's personal god. See *Carib.*

Nfinda: Wild forest, or forest.

Nfuá: Palo Monte term for Death, as in the Grim Reaper, not Lord Death or Lord of the Underworld, which is Cobayende. Similar in concept to the Lucumi Ikú. See *Cobayende* and *Ikú.*

Nfuiri: Chamalongo interpretative sign that speaks of death, endings, blockages, darkness, and pessimism. See *Chamalongo.*

Nfumbe: The dead. Usually referring to those found inside the Palo Monte cauldron used in their necromantic beliefs and practices. See *Palo Monte*.

Nfuri: Malevolent or wicked spirit of the dead that perturbs and seeks to endanger living beings. Used in ngangas Judías and in bad *nsaras*. See *Nganga Judía* and *Nsara*.

Nganga (Cardinal point): West.

Nganga (person): Refers to the Bantu medicine men. These priests of the Bantu indigenous religion took on the role of receptacle, much like the Indigenous shamans. Rather than the locus of power being found outside the priest like in Palo Monte, these figures were magically charged receptacles who embodied the powers of nature. Nonetheless, they made use of *nkisi n'kondi* and other religious paraphernalia to aid them in their divinatory and judicial responsibilities. See *Nkisi n'kondi, Bantu,* and *Palo Monte*.

Nganga Cristiana: Literally 'Christian nganga'. *Nganga* that adds the Catholic crucifix as a symbolic and factual spiritual force which enacts Christian systems of values and ethics through the *nganga* and the *nfumbe* aligned with these spiritual values and ethics. See *Nganga*.

Nganga Judía: Literally 'Jewish *nganga*'. A specialized type of *nganga* which is used solely for the purposes of *kindnoki* (the art or practice of *ndoki*). This *nganga*'s power, which has its own rituals and initiatory requirements as well as its own liturgy, falls under the domain of Lukankazi, who is its ruling Mpungo and the *nkisi* that provides the vital force to the malevolent or dark *nfumbe* called *nfuri* (not to be confused with *nfuiri*, the *chamalongo* sign of death) with which the *palero* made the pact and which resides inside the nganga Judía. Considered the fastest acting and most powerful of all the *ngangas*. See *Nganga, Lukankazi, Ndoki, Mpungo, Chamalongo, Nfuiri, Nfuri, Nkisi, Nfumbe* and *Palero*.

Nganga padre: Father *nganga*. A *nganga* from which three generations of *nganguleros* have been born. See *Ngangulero*.

Nganga: Also known as *la prenda* or *fundamento*. It is the foundation or fundament of Palo Monte. The magical cauldron where the *minkisi* and the *nfumbe* reside. This is achieved via the compilation of the material representations of these within the cauldron. Items such as the *kiyumba* of human beings, *palos*, the machete (the icon of the religion) and varied items from the animal, mineral, and vegetable kingdoms are utilized in order to construct a microcosm of the universe for the main *nkisi* (which can be any of the Kimpungulu), which provides the vital force on which the *nfumbe* manifest in the material plane, and especially the *nfumbe* for which the *nganga* is built. See *Palo Monte, Nsara, Kandango, Nsasi Siete Rayos, Palera, Palero, Palos, Mpolo, Kiyumba, Fundamento, Prenda, Minkisi, Nkisi, Nfumbe, Kongo, Kimpungulu,* and *Ngueyo.*

Ngangulera: Alternative name used instead of *palera*, and by some considered the most appropriate, for the female priest or medicine woman of Palo Monte. See *Palera* and *Palo Monte.*

Ngangulero: Alternative name used instead of *palero*, and by some considered the most appropriate, for the male priest or medicine man of Palo Monte. See *Palero* and *Palo Monte.*

Ngó: Leopard.

Ngueyo: Initiate of Palo Monte who does not own a *nganga* either due to time constraints, because they need to wait a year, or because the *nfumbe* divines through the Tata's skill as a necromancer (using the *chamalongos*). See *Palo Monte, Tata, Necromancer,* and *Chamalongos.*

Ngúlu: Wild hog.

Ngúlumfinda: Kikongo name for Gurunfinda. See *Gurunfinda* and *Kikongo.*

Ngunda: Moon.

Ngwâwanu: Union.

Nitaínos: Taino term for a sort of royal or noble class of warriors, much like the medieval knights of Europe. See *Tainos/Taino.*

Nkandu: Contract.

Nkimba: Highly arduous initiatory ceremony or rite of the Palo Monte religion also known as *rayamiento* in which a lay person becomes a Ngueyo and *pino nuevo.* See *Palo Monte, Rayamiento, Pino nuevo,* and *Ngueyo.*

Nkisi Malongo: The spirits, powers, or forces of nature of Palo Mayombe. See *Palo Mayombe.*

Nkisi n'kondi: Bantu and especially Kongo power figurines that were charged with *nkisi* and all types of items from the three kingdoms of nature. Famous for having their bodies full of nails and mirrors in their stomachs. See *Bantu, Kongo,* and *Nkisi.*

Nkisi: Spirit, force, energy, or power of nature. Also an object which a spirit, *nfumbe,* or force of nature inhabits. See *Nfumbe.*

Nkonde: Kongo term for the malevolent spirits of hate and vengeance. See *Kongo.*

Nkose: Alternative name for Nkonde. See *Nkonde.*

Nkunia Nfinda Malongo: Original Palo Monte branch. This should not be confused with the modern usage as an umbrella term for all the branches of Palo.

Nkunia: Stick.

Nkuyu Buenco: Alternative name of the *mpungo* Watariamba. See *Watariamba.*

Nkuyu: Name given in Cuba to the Dikenga, which is also used sometimes as the name for Lucero. *Nkuyu* means bringer of light or the spirit of light, which in Spanish is Lucero. It is also used for the forest spirits of light that reside on the top branches of trees, which sometimes consist of good ancestors that are waiting before integrating back into the Kalunga, when they finally become part of the *bakulu.* See *Dikenga, Kalunga, Bakulu,* and *Lucero.*

Nota bene: Literally, 'note well'; take notice of.

Nsala Malekum: Kikongo salutation used by Palo Monte practitioners which was borrowed from the Arabic اَلسَّلَامُ عَلَيْكُمْ (*as-salāmu ʿalaykum*) that means 'peace be upon you' and is used as a religious salutation by Muslims when greeting one another. See *Malekum Nsala, BaKongo, Kikongo,* and *Palo Monte.*

Nsara: Magical work.

Nsasi Nzasi: Bantu name of Nsasi Siete Rayos. Means Seven Lightning Bolts. See *Bantu* and *Nsasi Siete Rayos.*

Nsasi Siete Rayos: Translates as Seven Lightning Bolts. Mpungo of lightning and the celestial fire, and of tactical warfare. Brought civilization and fire to humanity. Among his symbols of power are the λάβρυς (*lábrus* or *labrys*), the πέλεκυς (*pélekus*) which is the double-bitted axe, a cup, and a long sword. His colors are red and white. See *Mpungo*.

Nsila: Crossing or pathway. It is also used as an alternative name for Luvemba. *See Luvemba*.

Nsunga: Tobacco smoke.

Ntala y Nzamba: Progenitor twins of humankind. They preside over good and evil, day and night, and all emanated dualities manifested by Nzambi. The symbols of these powers are the umbilical cord and two infant dolls. Their colors are black and white. See *Nzambi*.

Ntango: Sun.

Ntende: Basket.

Ntoto: Earth.

Nzambi: Supreme god of the Bantu and of Palo Monte. See *Bantu* and *Palo Monte*.

Nzungo: Casserole.

Ñañigos: Alternative term for the Abakuá. See *Abakuá*.

Obàtálá: Variant spelling of Obbatalá. See *Obbatalá*.

Obbatalá: Oricha of the white cloth, and the sky father. The Oricha owner of all human heads and the creator of human bodies brought to life by the breath of Olodumare. Father of all Orichas and the Oricha of purity and morals. Obàtálá is Olodumare's creative light (white; life) and the shadow (black; death) that comes with it. The shadow side of Obàtálá is represented in the Lucumi tradition of Cuba as Odùduwà, who for traditional Orisha worshipers and Ifá practitioners is the primordial man who descended to earth prior to Obàtálá. Obàtálá's color is white. Among his symbols are the white scepter, a bracelet made of silver, an *iruke* (a sort of duster used for the same function in Santeria and Ifá), a silver bell (called *agogó*), and the sickle. Maferefun Obbatalá (praise be Obbatalá)! See *Oricha, Odùduwà*, and *Olodumare*.

Ochosi: The Oricha of the hunt, hunters, and divine justice. An Oricha who was infused with many Amerindian attributes, and who came to symbolize the syncretic process of the African and Caribbean Indigenous encounter. This was preserved in the practice of placing Zarabanda and Watariamba in Palo Monte and Ogun and Ochosi in Santeria together inside the iron cauldron of Ogun. Among his symbols of powers are the bow and arrow as well as an iron cage. His colors are azure and yellow. See *Oricha, Amerindian, Ogun, Watariamba, Zarabanda,* and *Palo Monte.*

Odduns: Plural of Odù. See *Odù.*

Odù: Binary sign of Ifá consisting of two columns of four units each of either zeros or ones, or I or II. Constitutes the wisdom of Ifá speaking through the *babalawo* and his *opele* or *ikin Ifá.* They encapsulate the wisdom and experience of the African and Afro-Caribbean socioreligious experience of previous generations that is remembered for the sake of the client for whom the *babalawo* is performing divination so that the current architectonic spiritual matrix that the client is living and its concomitant problematics and blessings could be analyzed and resolved. It speaks to the lived experience of the initiate and adept alike and offers solutions or guidance based on this preserved wisdom. Also the architectonic spiritual matrix of the initiate's entire life. See *Ifá, Babalawo, Opele,* and *Ikin Ifá.*

Odùduwà: Primordial man and progenitor of all the successive Oòni of Ile-Ife. In Cuba this Orunmole has taken on the role of the shadow side of Obbatalá and is crowned some Ifá lineages of Matanzas. In Cuba he is the Oricha that presides over the secrets of the Egun and Ikú. Among his symbols of power are a black staff, a coffin made of oak, a skeleton made of silver, a serpent, and male and female dolls. His colors are black, or rather the absence of color, and white. See *Oòni, Ile-Ife, Orunmole, Obbatalá, Oricha, Egun, Ikú,* and *Ifá.*

Ogun: Oricha of war, iron, metallurgy, and technology. Also symbolizes beginning, virility, force, violence, impulse, fire, and fire weapons. Among his symbols of power are the machete, iron chains, and all iron-casted tools and weapons. His colors are green and black, but also some paths require purple. See *Oricha.*

Olodumare:

$$+$$
$$I\,I$$
$$I\,0$$
$$0\,0$$
$$0\,I$$

Supreme God of the Yoruba and the Lucumi tradition. Olodumare is neither light nor darkness; rather, he is a singularity suspended in the primordial substrate darkness (Eshu). Neither is Olodumare the sound (or verb/word) or Holy Ghost, which I believe to be Olofin and Ashé, respectively. Rather, light, darkness and sound being the three manifestations emanated from him. See *Lucumi Tradition, Eshu, Obbatalá, Ifá, Orisha, Olofin,* and *Ashé.*

Olofin: One of the names of the Yoruba supreme god in traditional Orisha worship and Ifá, but which has taken on a meaning and role in itself in Afro-Cuban practices. In Cuba it is considered the third manifestation of the supreme god (which is not considered to be Olodumare; Olodumare becomes the creative god) who in this manifestation is the conduit between Orún and Ayé. His color is ivory white. See *Ifá, Olodumare, Olorun, Orún,* and *Ayé.*

Olorun: The ruler of or existing in the heavens or celestial spheres. In Cuba Olorun is considered one of the three manifestations of the supreme god, which is from a Catholic influence, the others being Olodumare and Olofin. See *Olodumare* and *Olofin.*

Olubera: Kalinago language variation of Bakámo in Dominica, demonstrating the multiplicity of dialects within the Caribs. See *Bakámo* and *Kalinago.*

Oòni: Divinely appointed king of Ile-Ife who is said to trace his lineage back to Odùduwà. His role is so important that even in religious ceremonies (in traditional Nigerian Ifá and Orisha worship) and the annual cycle of rituals, his presence and blessings are requested as an affirmative concession to what is being done. See *Ile-Ife, Odùduwà, Ifá,* and *Orisha.*

Opele: The *babalawo*'s divining chain. See *Babalawos.*

Operito: Taino term for the dead. See *Tainos/Taino.*

Opia: Taino term for the soul of the person after death. See *Tainos/Taino.*

Opigielguoiran: Taino *cemi* owned by Cauauaniouaua. This *cemi*'s recognizable attribute was that it was made of wood and had four legs like a dog. This *cemi* would escape every night and would need to be brought back, only for it to escape again. The last time it was seen was right before the arrival of the Spanish. See *Cemi* and *Cauauaniouaua.*

Opoyem: Carib women's term for the soul, which seems to have been closely related to the Taino Opia. See *Caribs* and *Opia.*

Orichas: The deities of Santeria that are the intermediaries between the supreme god Olodumare and human beings. These deities or in some cases semi-divine beings with some human negative and positive human traits are associated with elements of the natural world. Also known as *Santos* due to the Catholic influence on the religion, from which term the religion takes its folk name. See *Santeria* and *Olodumare.*

Orisha: Spelling used in the Anglo-Saxon world and in traditional Nigerian Orisha worship instead of the Afro-Cuban term Oricha. *See Orichas.*

Orun: Represents the first man and servant of the Orichas who became the King of the Dead. The Orun black jar with a cobo shell in the middle and nine cowrie shells in a spiral around the top of the cobo shell cemented in place also represents the lands or kingdoms (both the nine infernal and the nine celestial realms) of the dead or spirits, and the pact made with Ikú so that he may not take the initiate before his/her time as set in his Ori. See *Orichas, Cambio de cabeza,* and *Ikú.*

Orún: The heavens or the celestial spheres. Also the invisible realm.

Òrúnmìlà: The Oricha of divination; the oracle of Ifá, destiny, and wisdom. Among his symbols of power are the diving board of Ifá and the *iruke.* His colors are green and yellow in Cuba, and green and coca brown in Nigeria. Iború, Iboyá, Ibosheshé (religious salutation used by devotees of Ifá)! See *Ifá.*

Oshoosi: Traditional Orisha worship and Ifá spelling of Ochosi. This Orisha, instead of Amerindian attributes, has attributes more similar to the leopard warrior societies of Calabar, whose multilingual Ekpe, Egbo, Ngbe, or Ugbe groups comprised these secret warrior and hunting fraternal societies.

Oshún: Oricha of pleasures, sensuality, dance, love, fertility, gold, honey, streams, brooks, and rivers. Often depicted as a beautiful mulatta dressed in a yellow dress emerging from the river (which brings to mind the painting 'The Birth of Venus' by Sandro Botticelli). Patron Saint/Oricha of Cuba. She is considered one of the most powerful

Orichas and her darker side in the Lucumi tradition is tied to the untamed and dark feminine powers and witchcraft. Among her symbols of power are a sandalwood fan painted yellow or made of the plumes of the peacock, five gold bracelets, a half-moon, two oars, one star, and one sun. Her color is gold or golden yellow. See *Oricha*.

Osteophagy: The consumption of bones. From the Greek amalgam of ὀστέον (*osteon*), which means a bone, and φάγος (*phágos*), which means glutton: οστεοφαγία (*oesteophagía*): the act of eating bones.

Paganus: Latin term that means country dweller or rustic individual.

Palenque: A community of Maroons, which was usually hidden in the bowels of the most geographically isolated hinterlands and the most dense and dangerous corners of the wilderness. See *Maroons*.

Palera: Female priest or medicine woman of Palo Monte. See *Palo Monte*.

Palero: Male priest or medicine man of Palo Monte. See *Palo Monte*.

Palestino/Palestina: Term used in the Occident or western regions of Cuba as a derogatory term for male and female, respectively, natives of el Oriente de Cuba, or the eastern regions of Cuba. A term that derives from the complex demography and hegemony of Cuba that has its roots in the history of the three Abrahamic religions and Jerusalem. See *El Oriente de Cuba*.

Palo Brillumba: A *rama* of Palo Monte which has been syncretized with the Palo Mayombe *rama* and the Lucumi tradition. It is also one of the three main *ramas* of Palo Monte. See *Lucumi, Rama, Palo Monte, Palo Kimbisa,* and *Palo Mayombe*.

Palo Cruzado: A *rama* of Palo Monte that represents the most recent form. It is an amalgam of Palo Monte and Kardecian Spiritism. This latest innovation is distinct from other Palo Monte *ramas* in that the priest is both a *ngangulero/ngangulera* and an *espiritista*. Established communications are approached through the Spiritism lens and not through the traditional Palo Monte way. See *Rama, Palo Monte, Espiritismo, Ngangulero, Ngangulera,* and *Espiritista*.

Palo Haitiano: The most recent syncretic Afro-Caribbean religion manifested in Cuba. It is the offspring of Palo Monte oriental (eastern Cuba Palo Monte) and Haitian Vodou brought to the east of Cuba by Haitians. See *Palo Monte* and *Haitian Vodou*.

Palo Kimbisa: A highly syncretic *rama* and one of the three main *ramas* of Palo Monte, together with Palo Mayombe and Palo Brilumba, founded by Andres Petit. Includes Congo, Lucumi, Catholic, Freemasonry, Spiritism and Abakuá spiritualities. See *Rama, Palo Mayombe, Palo Monte, Palo Brillumba, Congo, Lucumi, Spiritism,* and *Abakuá.*

Palo Mayombe: Highly traditional *rama* of Palo Monte. Considered the most traditional of all the *ramas.* Also known as Malongo. It maintains many of the BaKongo indigenous beliefs and practices and focuses on the celestial sphere as a source of power and abode of the Kimpungulu, which the other *ramas* have lost through gradual transculturation. It is also considered the most powerful *rama* (sometimes the most evil) of the three main *ramas.* See *Palo Monte, Palo Brillumba, Palo Kimbisa, BaKongo,* and *Malongo.*

Palo Monte: Umbrella term for a multiplicity of *ramas* of an Afro-Cuban religion which has its origin in the Congo Basin among the BaKongo and their meeting with the Caribbean Amerindians in Cuba. Palo Monte's main three *ramas* are the Palo Mayombe, the Palo Brillumba, and the Palo Kimbisa. A henotheistic religion, like Santeria, whose primary point of veneration or worship is the Kimpungulu who gives life to the *nfumbe* found in the fundament of the religion, the *nganga.* The Kimpungulu, instead of being deities like the Orichas, are best understood as the raw forces of nature. Each Mpungo reigns or presides over a force of nature. A highly secretive, hierarchical, and magically complex religion based on the relationship of the priest known as Tata, Tata Nganga, or Tata Nkisi, and the Yayi, who run a *munanzo* of Ngueyos who are initiated through the *nkimba* on the *nganga padre* of the Tata and who belong to the rules of that *munanzo.* A religion primarily concerned with the *bakulu* and the *nfumbe* and of gaining insights and wisdom through the use of necromancy. See *BaKongo, Amerindian, Henotheism, Kimpungulu, Mpungo, Tata, Tata Nkisi, Tata Nganga, Yayi, Ngueyo, Nkimba, Nganga, Nganga padre, Munanzo, Necromancy,* and *Nfumbe.*

Palo: Spanish word for stick that can also be interpreted as tree.

Palos: Stick or trees.

Panacea: Latin term derived from the Greek goddess Πανάχεια (Panáke-ia) of universal remedy, for a supposed remedy or cure-all for diseases, ailments, or difficulties, and which prolongs life indefinitely.

Pángolas: Spanish term for the primordial peoples of the equatorial Guinea region.

Pataki: Afro-Cuban Ifá sacred story. See *Ifá*.

Patimpemba: Palo Monte graphic writing system drawn in chalk (colors vary depending on the type of *nsara*) that derives from the Kongo graphic writing system. This codified graphic system of language serves both as a beacon and as a representation of the Kimpungulu's frequencies as manifested in the universe. See *Kimpungulu, Nsara, Palo Monte,* and *Kongo*.

Petro nanchon: Nation of Haitian Vodou which preserves the beliefs and practices of the hottest *lwas* found in Haitian Vodou. Also, according to Maya Deren, it preserves many Amerindian, especially Carib, beliefs and practices. See *Haitian Vodou* and *Lwas*.

Pigmeos: Pygmies, in Spanish.

Pikinako Ofuma Ndoki: Palo Monte term used in el Oriente de Cuba for the *ceiba*. See *Ceiba*.

Pino nuevo: Literally 'new pine' or 'new wood'. However, I believe that this word was used intentionally as word play due to the second level of meaning the word *pino* holds, which is the first step a child takes when he/she wants to let go and walk. A term used in Palo Monte when referring to the newly initiated person. Serves as a sort of metaphor for the creation or the growth and development of a new *rama* in the living symbolic tree that is Palo Monte. See *Palo Monte* and *Rama*.

Pluriversal world: A world where there is no set universality, but a multiplicity of universes within the cartography of the world.

Pluriversality: Put forth by Walter Mignolo as a counter-narrative against the Eurocentric assumptions of what is universal (usually those values and things aligned with Christianity and capitalism).

Pluriverse: A world in which diverse hopes, multiple opportunities, and a plurality of meanings are allowed and potentially achieved.

Pluto: From the Greek Πλούτων (Ploútōn). The Roman equivalent of the ancient Greek god Hades. Also the name of the Roman underworld. Lord of the dead, although more positive than the ancient Greek god Hades. His symbols are the same as those of Hades. See *Hades*.

Polycentrism or Polycentric world: A term put forth by Mignolo to describe the ideal world, which the decolonial project is trying to approach. It refers an eventual movement from a world based on capitalism and Eurocentrism, towards a world organized on the principle of many-sidedness and a doctrine of leadership stemming from an independent center of equal value, power and ideology co-existing together. See *Decolonial Project*.

Postmodernism: A school of thought that separated itself from Modernism during the mid to late 20th century which criticizes the Enlightenment and its emphasis on rationality. Another inherent quality of postmodernism is the understanding that knowledge claims and value systems are socially conditioned. See *Zeitgeist* and *Modernism*.

Potencias: Literally, 'potencies'. Alternative name for the Abakuá *juegos*. See *Juegos* and *Abakuá*.

Prenda: Alternative name for *nganga*. Literally, 'jewel'. See *Nganga*.

Raison d'être: Literally means reason for being. More appropriately, the most important reason or purpose for someone or something's existence.

Rama: Branch of Palo Monte

Rancheador: Runaway slave hunter. A bit more literal, 'Maroon herder', which carries racist connotations of the Maroons as rogue animals.

Rayamiento: Spanish name for the Palo Monte *nkimba* ceremony. See *Nkimba* and *Palo Monte*.

Regla de Ocha: Properly recognized name of Santeria. See *Santeria*.

Reglas de Congo: Properly recognized name of Palo Monte. See *Palo Monte*.

Relegere: To re-trace or to-recollect.

Religare: To bind or tied again.

Religere: Spelling variation of *relegere*. See *Relegere*.

Religio licita: Latin term that means legal religion.

Religio: Latin origin of the word religion, which in turn derives from *religare* or *relegere*, according to Christian or pre-Christian writers respectively. See *Religare* and *Relegere*.

Remolino: Vortex, twister, spiral, tornado, eddies, and all rotating phenomena.

Ritz: The Maya sacred mountain that represented the middle realm which consists of the world in which we live. See *Maya*.

Saca Empeño: Alternative name of the *mpungo* Watariamba. See *Watariamba*.

San Lazaro: Saint Lazarus. Catholic Saint who is a syncretic creation of the Amerindian, Spanish, and African encounter. An amalgam of the two Lazaruses found in the Bible and Amerindian and African gods. His imagery depicts him as bedeviled with illnesses and scabby skin, surrounded by dogs while he walks with crutches.

Sanda Fumandanda: Palo Monte alternative term for *sanda naribe*. See *Sanda Naribe* and *Palo Monte*.

Sanda Naribe: Palo Monte term for the *ceiba*. See *Palo Monte* and *Ceiba*.

Santera: Female priest of Santeria. See *Santeria*.

Santeria: Folk term for *la Regla de Ocha*, which has become the standard name for the Afro-Cuban Lucumi tradition in Cuba. Afro-diasporic religion that developed during the colonial period in Cuba through a process of syncretism with various African, European, and Amerindian faiths, centered in the veneration and worship of the Oricha. See *Regla de Ocha, Lucumi tradition, Amerindian,* and *Oricha*.

Santero: Male priest of Santeria. See *Santeria*.

Santisi: Alternative name of the Mpungo Watariamba. See *Watariamba*.

Santo Cristo del Buen Viaje: Proper name given by Petit to his created *rama*, Palo Kimbisa. See *Palo Kimbisa* and *Rama*.

Santos: Saints. Also Spanish name for the Catholic saints and the Lucumi Oricha that are veiled in them. See *Lucumi* and *Oricha*.

Saturnus: Saturn. The Roman god of agriculture, generation, dissolution, wealth, poverty, periodic renewal, and liberation. Equated with Krónos and all that Krónos presided over, but seen as the father and creator god of the Roman pantheon rather than as a terrifying and evil figure. Among his symbols are the sickle or scythe. See Krónos.

Self-fashioning: The phenomenon described by David Waldstreicher that describes the colonial era survival trick used by the African Maroons in which they impersonated free Blacks, mestizos, and Amerindians. This phenomenon included, according to Rubén Silié, adopting the cultural markers of these individuals and hence integrated these cultural beliefs and practices through embodied cultural performance. See *Amerindians* and *Mestizos*.

Shekere: West African percussive instrument similar to the Amerindian maracas, used in a religious manner and in a similar fashion in music, which is made using a hollowed calabash. It is dressed with a latticework of Job's Tear seeds (or other seeds of similar composition; beads and cowrie shells are also sometimes used) and a thick and rather short handle is glued to the calabash. It is bigger and wider than the maracas due to the acoustic demand for a louder sound. See *Maracas*.

Sheol (שְׁאוֹל): The underworld of Judaism.

Siboney: A term used to differentiate the Taino of western and central Cuba from the Taino of eastern Cuba, Hispaniola, and Puerto Rico (known as Classical Taino). *See Tainos/Taino*.

Siete Rayos: Seven Lightning Bolts. Alternative name for Nsasi Siete Rayos or Nsasi 7 Rayos. See *Nsasi Siete Rayos*.

Simbi: The spirit of fresh bodies of water.

Sindaula Ndundu Yambaka Butan Seke: Gurunfinda's full name in Kikongo. See *Gurunfinda* and *Kikongo*.

Soraia: Island to the west of Hispaniola where the mythical Coaibai was found. See *Coaibai*.

Spiritism: Also known as Kardecian or scientific Spiritism, it is the doctrine developed by the late French medium and soothsayer Allan Kardec.

Spiritist: English term for *espiritista*. See *Espiritista*.

Status Quo: The existing state of affairs, the current situation, or the way things are now. This phrase is used especially regarding social, political, or religious matters.

Strata: Literally, 'a series of layers or coats of a substance'; however, I use it in its modern sociological context, which means the levels or classes to which people are assigned in a social matrix.

Sutamutokuni: Alternative name of Nkunia Nfinda Malongo. See *Nkunia Nfinda Malongo.*

Symbolic Capital: Term denoting the resources available to an individual on the basis of honor, prestige, social status, or recognition, which serves as value that one holds within a culture. It could also be described as the economic or cultural capital that is known or recognized as such when they are decidedly conceived as such by the agents of the field. See *Field.*

Symbolic Power: The term used for when institutionalized systems of societies implement arbitrary forms of symbolic capital that carry with them actions that have discriminatory or injurious meaning or implications leading to power dynamics within the agent in the field. Examples of this symbolic power would be racism and gender dominance, to name two. Ultimately, these forms of symbolic power are set up with the sole purpose of creating and maintaining a desired (by those in power) homeostasis of power relations, which maintains the social hierarchies of the status quo upon which the social matrix stands. See *Field, Symbolic Capital,* and *Status quo.*

Symbolic Violence: Refers to and describes a type of non-physical violence manifested in the field where agents jockey for power, where those with symbolic capital and symbolic power use these non-material assets as a weapon against those in a different social group, which usually refers to those on the lower strata of the social matrix. Such symbolic violence, however, stems not from actual manifested power, but from unconsciously agreed upon rules and regulations, by all parties of the social matrix, that ultimately lead to the imposition of these as beneficial to those in greater social standing and detrimental to those in a subordinate position. Therefore, those in the subordinate position are complicit in this arbitrarily exercised violence, which is based on some type of negotiation for the potential to participate in the field and resources available in said field. See *Field, Symbolic Capital,* and *Symbolic Power.*

Syncretism: The amalgamation or attempted amalgamation of different religions, cultures, or schools of thought. A term proposed by Melville J. Herskovits that encapsulates the idea of the blending of traits from two or more different cultures to form a new trait or culture, which he thought explained the cultural continuity of African cultures and spiritualities as expressed in Afro-American and Afro-Caribbean communities.

Tabaco: Spanish term for what the Amerindians called *cogioba* or *cohoba*. This misunderstanding and misinterpretation by the Spanish derives from their misappropriation of the word tabaco, which meant the bifurcated tube from which the hallucinatory *cogioba* powder was inhaled. See *Cogioba* and *Guanguaio*.

Tainos/Taino: The indigenous people of the Bahamas and the Greater Antilles, and some isolated areas of the Lesser Antilles. Also known as Arawak, although the Caribs spoke a dialect of the Arawak language, which is a member of the Maipurean linguistic family. Remembered for being peaceful and constantly accosted by the pugnacious and cannibalistic Caribs. See *Arawak* and *Caribs*.

Taínos: Spanish spelling of Tainos. See *Tainos/Taino*.

Taragabaol: Peter Martyr's spelling variation of Faraguuaol. Considered by modern scholars the correct spelling. See *Faraguuaol*.

Tata Nganga: Alternative name for Tata. See *Tata*.

Tata Nkisi: Alternative name for Tata. See *Tata*.

Tata: High male priest of Palo Monte. See *Palo Monte*.

Theo-politics: A term that describes the phenomenon of using Christian theology to critique national, civic, and political structures, which in turn are weaponized against all other forms of religions and indigenous spiritualities.

Tiembla Tierra Kengue: The Mpungo of the mountain top, of divination, and of divine interaction. He is also the Mpungo of peace, mercy, prophecy, and the sages. Considered the primogenitor of all the other Kimpungulu, he presides over the destiny of humanity and their communities. Father of all Kimpungulu and the Mpungo of purity and morals. His color is white. Among his symbols are the white scepter, a bracelet made of silver, an albino serpent, and the sickle. See *Mpungo* and *Kimpungulu*.

Toque de Palo: Alternative name of the Malongo Kisonga Kia ceremony. See *Malongo Kisonga Kia ceremony*.

Tornar: Spanish term which means to turn.

Toúlála: Carib term for *Maranta arundinacea*. The arrowroot; a small and edible tuber. See *Caribs*.

Tourar: Carib term for a small opening in the *carbet* that was left opened intentionally during the initiation of new *boyez*. This was done for the purpose of attracting and allowing the *coribib* chemin to enter and to participate in said ceremony. See *Caribs, Carbet, Boyez,* and *Coribib Chemin*.

Transculturation: Fernando Ortiz's term for the process by which a culture is transformed through the addition of new elements and the loss of existing elements.

Transmodernism: The school of thought that places an emphasis on the love and appreciation for foreign cultures, customs, and peoples. It also places emphasis on globalism and the promotion of different cultures and cultural appreciation as a necessary and important facet of cosmopolitan societies, which are increasingly common in a globalized world. This school of thought also aims at changing the current worldview on cultural affairs towards an anti-Eurocentric and anti-imperialist one, and which also aligns itself with environmentally sustainable and ecologically aware policies.

Tronado: Old Spanish term for thunderstorm.

Tukula: Kongo term for the red sun. See *Kongo*.

Ubutu: Carib village chief, not to be confused in power, influence, and socio-economic status with the privileged position of the *cacique* in the Taino social hierarchy. See *Carib, Cacique,* and *Tainos/Taino*.

Uicú: Carib intoxicating drink they prepared for festivities and rites. See *Caribs*.

Uméku: The second spirit found in the head of the human body in Carib mythology. This spirit was said to translocate to the edge of the sea after the death of a Carib individual, with the aim of wrecking boats. See *Caribs, Maboya,* and *Yuanni*.

Vaybrama: De las Casas' spelling variation of Baidrama. It remains the standard form. See *Baidrama*.

Vence Bataya: Alternative name for Watariamba. See *Watariamba*.

Vevè: Haitian Vodou graphic writing system (the color varies depending on the type of magical work) that derives from the Kongo graphic writing system. This codified graphic system of language serves both as a beacon and as a representation of the *Lwas'* frequencies as manifested in the Universe. See *Haitian Vodou, Kongo,* and *Lwas.*

Vili: Kikongo word which denotes a native of Angola, but also means works. See *Kikongo.*

Vis-à-vis: Literally means face-to-face. More appropriately, 'in relation to', or face-to-face with.

Vox populi: Literally, 'the voice of the people'. Also used in English to refer to the opinion of the majority of the people. I use the term at both levels of meaning.

Vriyumba: Alternative spelling used for Brillumba of the Palo Brillumba *rama.* See *Palo Brillumba* and *Rama.*

Wa tári a mbá: Means 'stone of fire' in Kikongo. See *Kikongo.*

Watariamba: The Mpungo of the hunt, hunter, and of divine justice. A Mpungo that was infused with many Amerindian attributes, and which came to symbolize the syncretic process of the African and Caribbean Indigenous encounter. This was preserved in the practice of placing Zarabanda and Watariamba in Palo Monte and Ogun and Ochosi in Santeria together inside the iron cauldron of Ogun. Among his symbols of powers are the bow and arrow as well as an iron cage. His colors are azure and yellow. See *Mpungo, Amerindian, Ogun, Ochosi, Zarabanda,* and *Palo Monte.*

Western Magick: Also known as Western Esotericism or the Western Mystery Tradition, consisting of an amalgam of a wide variety of indigenous (pagan, although I don't like this term) traditions, religions, philosophical schools, and occult esoteric teachings that encompass information and practices from sources such as Hermeticism, Qabalah, Enochian magic, Abramelin's ritual of calling upon the Holy Guardian Angel, Aleister Crowley's Thelema, grimoires, astrology, goetia, ceremonial magick, Gnosticism, and Neoplatonism, to name a few. A tradition undergoing a renaissance of its own and which recently has started to look at African and Afro-Caribbean indigenous religions as sources of wisdom and guidance.

Yaya: The first being or entity emanated from the origin and the beginning of the Universe in the Taino creation myth. Also considered the supreme spirit of the universe. See *Tainos/Taino.*

Yayael: Son of Yaya who wanted to kill her. Yaya banished him for four months, but eventually decided to kill him and to turn him into the first funerary basket called a *higüero.* See *Yaya* and *Higüero.*

Yayi: High female priest of Palo Monte. See *Palo Monte.*

Yeretté: Carib term for the solar or diurnal Caribbean hummingbird, of which there are four distinct species. This bird was also an important animal in the mythology of the Caribs due to its role in the myth of Luna and Hiali. See *Caribs, Luna,* and *Hiali.*

Yimbe: Warlock or sorcerer.

Yocahu Vagua Maorocoti: De las Casas' spelling of the Taino creator god. See *Iocahuuague Maorocon.*

Yocahú: Current scholarly alternative name for Yocahu Vagua Maorocoti. See *Yocahu Vagua Maorocoti.*

Yombe people: Peoples hailing from the Mayombe hills of the Kingdom of Kongo. See *Kingdom of Kongo.*

Yorubaland: Present-day southwestern Nigeria.

Yowa: Kongo cosmogram consisting of the cardinal cross and the four stations of the sun which serves as a metaphor for time and life cycles. It represents the sign of the cosmos and the continuity of human life, including the living and the dead aspects of the human soul. It encapsulates the entire Kongo system of beliefs under one image (including the world of Kalunga). See *Kongo* and *Kalunga.*

Yuanni: The first spirit found in the heart of the human body in Carib mythology. This spirit was said to translocate to the other world after the death of the individual in which it resided. See *Caribs, Uméku,* and *Maboya.*

Yúcahu Bagua Maórocoti: Practical name given by the Taino to the supreme being Yaya. It means, 'Being of the Yuca, Sea and Without Male Predecessor'. See *Yaya, Tainos/Taino,* and *Yuca.*

Yucayeque: The Taino term for their villages. See *Tainos/Taino.*

Yucca: *Manihot esculenta.* Cassava.

Yúmba: Kikongo word meaning spirit of the departed one. See *Kikongo*.

Zachon: Variation in spelling used only once by Ramón Pané instead of *cogioba*. See *Cogioba*.

Zara: Amerindian word meaning corn. See *Amerindian*.

Zarabanda: The Mpungo of war, iron, metallurgy, and technology. Among his symbols of power are the machete, iron chains, and all iron-casted tools and weapons. His colors are green and black, but also some paths require purple. See *Mpungo*.

Zeitgeist: Literally, 'spirit of the age'. More appropriately it is the general intellectual, moral, and cultural climate of the era.

Zero point epistemology: A term used by Mignolo, but created by Santiago Castro-Gómez, which describes the hubris of the Eurocentric belief that constructs knowledge from the perspective of an observer who observes without being observed or represented. In other words, as Mignolo describes it, it is the hubris of Eurocentrism and its adherents' perceived right to modernize and colonialize other lesser or less developed nations.

Zuimaco: One of the five names ascribed to the god who had no beginning and who was mother to the Taino creator god Iocahuuague Maorocon. See *Iermaoguacar, Apito, Atabei,* and *Iella*.

About the Author

ALEJANDRO CASAS WAS BORN and raised in the birthplace of Palo Monte-Matanzas, Cuba. There, he had the unique experience of growing up with unrestricted access to the 19th century Pharmaceutical Museum: *La Botica Francesa de Dr. Ernesto Triolet.* This was possible thanks to his mother, who was a researcher and a museum guide. The pharmacy preserves many traditional medicines that were used by the indigenous population, as well as a huge kitchen where the medicinal recipes were concocted for Dr. Ernesto Triolet's apothecary practice. Although, the place was a French pharmaceutical museum it also contained a personal library on the second floor, which was filled with a large gathering of books from all fields of study. Some of these books were of antiquarian and medieval origin with (what seemed at the time) very intriguing and strange drawings and languages. These encounters sparked his curiosity and lifelong passions for languages, history, anthropology, religion, science, pharmacopoeia, chemistry, and books in general.

At 14 years of age he immigrated to United States where he has lived since. He holds a M.A. in Religious studies, Graduate Certificates in Latin American and Caribbean Studies and African and African Diaspora Studies, a post-bachelor in pre-medicine, as well as B.A in Psychology with a second major in Philosophy. Alejandro Casas is also the recipient of the prestigious FLAS Fellowship-Haitian Creole, and the Interdisciplinary Writing Teaching Assistantship IWTA fellowship for Writing Across the Curriculum, as well as the Dunnick Scholarship and the Ronal E. McNair Scholarship. Beyond these accomplishments, Casas has published on a handful of academic journals and been inducted into The Scientific Research Honor Society (Sigma Xi), the National Honors

Society for Scholars of Religious Studies and Theology (TAK), the International Honors Society in Psychology (PSI CHI), and the International Honors Society in Philosophy (Phi Sigma Tau). An astrologer, initiate of the mysteries of Ifá and author of *Fugue* (Resource Publications-Wipf and Stock, 2019), a book of mystical poetry, he has also studied Classical Latin, Biblical Hebrew, and koine Greek. He is currently an Adjunct Lecturer in English and a Ph.D. student in the Department of Global and Sociocultural Studies at Florida International University.

Bibliography

"Axatse or Shekere", *Africa Heartwood Project*, 2015 <https://www.africaheartwoodproject.org/product/axatse-or-shekere/>

"Basenji Dog Breed Information", *American Kennel Club*, 2021 <https://www.akc.org/dog-breeds/basenji/>

"Conozca Acerca De La Devoción A San Lázaro En Cuba", *Dime Cuba*, 2020 <https://www.dimecuba.com/revista/noticias-cuba/conozca-acerca-de-la-devocion-a-san-lazaro/>

"El Diccionario del Lenguaje Taino", *Taino Tribe*, 1999 <https://www.taino-tribe.org/tsdict.html>

"Historia de IFA en Cuba: Testimonio de un Sacerdote", *Ile Yoruba Esoterica*, 2021 <https://ileyoruba.wixsite.com/ileyoruba/religion-yoruba-en-cuba>

"Ochosi", *AboutSanteria*, 2021 <http://www.aboutsanteria.com/ochosi.html>

"The Orishas: Ochosi", *Orignal Botanica*, 2021 <https://www.originalbotanica.com/blog/orishas-ochosi-santeria/>

"Toque De Palo Monte Mayombe- Buena Noche", online video recording, YouTube, 2022 <https://www.youtube.com/watch?v=dSv1OwwqhJ4>

"Usos Del Tabaco Dentro De La Santería E Ifa", *TuBrujo*, 2014 <https://tubrujo.com/santeria/usos-del-tabaco-dentro-de-la-santeria-e-ifa/>

"Voodoo Mysteries, the Initiated", *Culture—Planet Doc Full Documentaries*, online video recording, YouTube, 2014 <https://www.youtube.com/watch?v=MtQOxBezo7w>

7 Rayos, Tata Nkisy Malongo. *Tratado con 7 Rayos: Tratado de Nfumbe* (Centro Palero de Estudios 7 Rayos Vence Mundo, 2003)

Akoni Ifa Shola, Reverend Baba Sabu, *Palo Kimbiza: Brillumba Palo Kimbiza-Tumba Francesa Kikongo Piti Bantu Criollo Sanci and Palo Haitiano* (Ile Olofin Aiye, 2002)

Allen, Alexander, "Credibility and Incredulity: A Critique of Bartolomé de las Casas"s A Short Account of the Destruction of the Indies", *The Gettysburg Historical Journal*, 9 (2010) <https://cupola.gettysburg.edu/ghj/vol9/iss1/5, 2010>

Alpizar, Ralph, and Guillermo Gonzalo Calleja Leal *La Nfinda: La Concepción del Ser y del Conocimiento* (Madrid: R. Alpizar Valdés, 2019)

———. *Afroamérica y la Bantuidad en Cuba.* Ediciones Maiombe (Madrid: R. Alpizar Valdés, 2019)

———. *El Kimpúngulu: Corpus Santoral del Palo Monte Mayombe* (Madrid: R. Alpizar Valdés, 2019)

———. *El Lenguaje Ritual: En el Palo Monte Mayombe* (Madrid: R. Alpizar Valdés, 2019)

———. *Kuna Nkisi: Los Lugares de Culto en el Palo Congo Mayombe* (Madrid: R. Alpizar Valdés, 2019)

———. *Nfumbe: El Universo de los Espíritus Como Lenguaje Articulado.* Ediciones Maiombe (Madrid: R. Alpizar Valdés, 2019)

———. *Nganga: Él Caldero Mágico del Mayombero* (Madrid: R. Alpizar Valdés, 2019)

———. *Nkunia Ngunda: El Culto a la Ceiba.* Ediciones Maiombe (Madrid: R. Alpizar Valdés, 2019)

———. *Nsambia Mpungo: Dios en la Creencia Cubana del Palo Monte Mayombe* (Madrid: R. Alpizar Valdés, 2019)

———. *Nsó-Nganga: La Cofradía de los Nganguleros.* Ediciones Maiombe (Madrid: R. Alpizar Valdés, 2019)

———. *Oráculos en el Palo Congo Mayombe: Mpaka; Cocos; Caracoles y Huesos.* Ediciones Maiombe (Madrid: R. Alpizar Valdés, 2019)

———. *Patimpembas: Símbolos Misticos y Esotéricos del Palo Congo Mayombe* (Madrid: R. Alpizar Valdés, 2019)

———. *Nsambia Mpungo* (Madrid: R. Alpizar Valdés, 2019)

Alpizar, Ralph, *Diccionario Razonado del Léxico Congo en Cuba* (Madrid: R. Alpizar Valdés, 2019)

———. *El Mundo De Los Brujos.* Ediciones Maiombe (Madrid: R. Alpizar Valdés, 2014)

———. *Palo Mayombe. El legado vivo de África en Cuba* (Madrid: Vision Net, 2012)

Álvarez Ferrer, Manuel, *Raíces del Palo Monte en Cuba* (Otros Ediciones, 2012)

Andreu Alonso, Guillermo, *Los Ararás en Cuba: Florentina, la Princesa Dahomeyana* (La Habana: Colección Echú Bi-Editorial de Ciencias Sociales, 1992)

Anghiera, Pietro Martire d", *De Rebus Oceanicis et Novo Orbe* (Coloniae: Apud Geruinum Calenium & haeredes Quentelios, 1574)

Apter, Andrew, "Herskovits"s Heritage: Rethinking Syncretism in the African Diaspora", *Diaspora: A Journal of Transnational Studies*, 1.3 (1991), 253–60 <doi:10.1353/dsp.1991.0021>

Argyle, William Johnson, *The Fon of Dahomey: A History and Ethnography of the Old Kingdom* (Oxford: Clarendon Press, 1966)

Artemi, Eirini, "Emperor Constantine And The Theology Of Christianity—1", *PEMPTOUSIA*, 2017 <https://pemptousia.com/2017/10/emperor-constantine-and-the-theology-of-christianity-1/>

Ayorinde, Christine, *Afro-Cuban Religiosity, Revolution, and National Identity* (Gainesville, Florida: University Press of Florida, 2004)

Badawi, Zeinab, *Ancestors, Spirits and God—History of Africa with Zeinab Badawi*, online video recording, YouTube, 2020 <https://www.youtube.com/watch?v=GlKSp2HoVow>

———. *Kongo and the Scramble for Africa—History of Africa with Zeinab Badawi*, online video recording, YouTube, 2020 <https://www.youtube.com/watch?v=Wov_SwObQns>

Badejo, Diedre L, Òsun Sèègèsí: The Elegant Deity of Wealth, Power, and Femininity (Trenton, New Jersey: Africa World, 1996)

Bairon, Sérgio, and José da Silva, Congo em Cuba: Regra de Palo Monte, online video recording, YouTube, 2012 <https://www.youtube.com/watch?v=lyTDPkK8Cac>

Balandier, Georges, and Helen Weaver, Daily Life in the Kingdom of the Kongo: From the Sixteenth to the Eighteenth Century (New York: Pantheon, 1968)

Basso Ortiz, Alessandra, Los Gangá en Cuba: La Communidad de Matanzas (La Habana, Cuba: Fundación Fernando Ortiz, 2005)

Bataille, Georges, and Mary Dalwood, Erotism: Death & Sensuality (San Francisco, U.S.A.: City Lights, 1987)

Bataille, Georges, and Robert Hurley, The Accursed Share: An Essay On General Economy. Volume I-Consumption (New York, NY: Zone, 1991)

———. The Accursed Share: An Essay On General Economy. Volume II-The History of Eroticism & Volume III-Sovereignty (New York, NY: Zone, 1991)

Bellegarde-Smith, Patrick, Claudine Michel, and Guérin C. Montilus, Haitian Vodou: Spirit, Myth, And Reality (Bloomington, Indiana: Indiana University Press, 2006)

Bentley, Rev. W. Holman, Dictionary and Grammar of the Kongo Language: As Spoken at San Salvador, the Ancient Capital of the Old Kongo Empire, West Afrika [And Appendix]; Compiled and Prepared for the Baptist Mission on the Kongo River, West Africa (London: Baptist Missionary Society, and Trübner & Co., 1887)

Benzecry, C.E., Deener, A. & Lara-Millán, A. Archival Work as Qualitative Sociology. Qual Sociol 43, 297–303 (2020). https://doi.org/10.1007/s11133-20-09466-69.

Bockie, Simon, Death and the Invisible Powers: The World of Kongo Belief (Bloomington, Indiana: Indiana University Press, 1993)

Bolívar Aróstegui, Natalia, and Valentina Porras Potts, "Cuba. Una Identita in Movimento—Ifá: Su Historia en Cuba", ArchivoCubano, 2009 <http://www.archivocubano.org/ifa_historia.html>

Bolívar Aróstegui, Natalia, Carmen González, and Natalia del Río Bolívar, Ta Makuende Yaya y Las Reglas de Palo Monte (El Vedado, La Habana: Ediciones UNIÓN, 1998)

Bostoen, Koen, and Inge Brinkman, The Kongo Kingdom: The Origins, Dynamics and Cosmopolitan Culture of an African Polity (Cambridge, U. K.: Cambridge University Press, 2018)

Bourne, Edward Gaylord, Columbus, Ramon Pane, and the Beginnings of American Anthropology (Worcester, Mass.: American Antiquarian Society, 1906)

Brandon, George, Santeria from Africa to the New World (Bloomington, Indiana: Indiana University Press, 2000)

Bravo, Ernesto, Manejo de los Chamalongos Desde los Tiempos de la Colonia (Florida: Las Tres Potencias Publisher, 2014)

Brooke Persons, A., "Reconsidering the Guanahatabey of Western Cuba", Proceedings of the 21st Congress of the International Association for Caribbean Archaeology, (St. Petersburg, Florida: Cultural Resource Solutions, 2007) < https://dloc.com/AA00061961/00914>

Brown, David H., The Light Inside: Abakuá Society Arts and Cuban Cultural History (Washington, D.C.: Smithsonian Institution, 2003)

Brown, Karen McCarthy, and Claudine Michel, Mama Lola: A Vodou Priestess in Brooklyn (Berkeley, California: University of California Press, 2010)

Cabrera Suárez Òkàmbí, Frank. Ilé Tüntun: La Nueva Tierra Sagrada (Barberà del Vallès: Humanitas, 2010)

Cabrera, Lydia, and Isabel Castellanos, *Vocabulario Congo* (Miami, Florida: Ediciones Universal, 2001)

Cabrera, Lydia, *El Monte* (Miami, Florida: Ediciones Universal, 2006)

———. *La Regla Kimbisa Del Santo Cristo Del Buen Viaje*, Second edition (Miami, Florida: Ediciones Universal, 1986)

———. *La Sociedad Secreta Abakuá: Narrada por Viejos Adeptos* (Miami, Florida: Ediciones Universales, 1998)

———. *Reglas De Congo Mayombe Palo Monte* (Miami, Florida: Ediciones Universal, 1986)

Cajón Pa"l Muerto- Los Indios, online video recording, YouTube, 2022 <https://www.youtube.com/watch?v=pIwFbZXG7pU>

Cañizares, Raul, *The Book on Palo: Initiatory Rituals and Ceremonies* (Old Bethpage, New York: Original Publications, 2002)

Carbonel, Walterio, *Secreto del Palo Monte* (Revista Unión, 1990)

Caren Fernandez, Ninette, "From the Love Story Between Ashikuelu and Afokoyeri the 4 Seasons Are Born", *Ashé Pa Mi Cuba*, 2022 <https://ashepamicuba.com/en/ashikuelu-y-afokoyeri/>

———. "Who Is the Deity Ashikuelu? The Eshu de Ifá that Guides the Eggunes", *Ashé Pa Mi Cuba*, 2022 <https://ashepamicuba.com/en/eshu-ashikuelu/>

Carr, Greg, *Ki Kongo Cosmograph, Historical Memory and Perspective of Time*, online video recording, YouTube, 2015 <https://www.youtube.com/watch?v=ZtDA7FADdLA>

Castellanos, Jorge, and Isabel Castellanos, *Cultura Afrocubana: El Negro en Cuba, 1492-1844*, Tomo I (Miami, Florida: Ediciones Universal-Coleccion Ebano y Canela, 1998)

———. *Cultura Afrocubana: El Negro en Cuba, 1845-1959*, Tomo II (Miami, Florida: Ediciones Universal-Coleccion Ebano y Canela, 1998)

———. *Cultura Afrocubana: Las Religiones y las Lenguas*, Tomo III (Miami, Florida: Ediciones Universal-Coleccion Ebano y Canela, 1998)

———. *Cultura Afrocubana: Letras, Música, Arte*, Tomo IV (Miami, Florida: Ediciones Universal-Coleccion Ebano y Canela, 1998)

Chatelain, Daniel, José Betancourt, and Patrice Banchereau, *Un Plante Abakuá—Documental/Documentaire*, online video recording, YouTube, 2018 <https://www.youtube.com/watch?v=2_Df4cSGkzg>

Chinea, Jorge L., "Diasporic Marronage: Some Colonial and Intercolonial Repercussions of Overland and Waterborne Slave Flight, With Special Reference to the Caribbean Archipelago", *Revista Brasileira Do Caribe*, 10.19 (2009) <doi:1518–6784>

Christopher, Emma, "Josefa Diago and the Origins of Cuba's Gangá Traditions", *Transition*, 111 (2013), 133–44 <doi:10.2979/transition.111.133>

Coart, Émile Jean Baptiste, and Alphonse de Haulleville, *Notes Analytiques sur les Collections Ethnographiques du Musée du Congo*, (Bruxelles, Belgium: Musée Royal de l'Afrique Centrale, 1902)

Conybeare, F. C., "The Testament of Solomon", *The Jewish Quarterly Review*, 11.1 (1898) <doi:10.2307/1450398>

Covington-Ward, Y., *Gesture and Power: Religion, Nationalism, and Everyday Performance in Congo* (Durham, North Carolina: Duke University Press, 2018)

Cunha, A., "Muerte, muertos y "llanto" palero", *Ateliers d'anthropologie*, 38 (2013) <https://journals.openedition.org/ateliers/9413>

De La Torre, Miguel A., *Santeria: The Beliefs and Rituals of a Growing Religion in America* (Grand Rapids, Michigan: William B. Eerdmans Pub. Co., 2004)

De las Casas, Bartolomé, and Manuel Serrano y Sanz, *Apologética Historia de las Indias* (Madrid: Bailly, Bailliere e hijos, 1909)

De las Casas, Bartolomé, José Miguel Martínez Torrejón, and Gustavo Adolfo Zuluaga Hoyos, *Brevísima Relación de la Destrucción de las Indias* (Antioquia, Colombia: Editorial Universidad de Antioquia, 2006)

Deren, Maya, *Divine Horsemen: The Living Gods of Haiti* (Kingston, New York: McPherson & Co, 2004)

Desmangles, Leslie Gâerald, *The Faces Of The Gods: Vodou And Roman Catholicism In Haiti* (Chapel Hill & London: The University of North Carolina Press, 2000)

DeVito, Joey, "Cigars Vital to Religious Practice in Cuba", *Mario's Cuban Cigars*, 2016 <blog.marioscubancigars.com/blog/cigars-vital-to-religious-practice-in-cuba>

Dianteill, Erwan, "Kongo in Cuba: The Transformations of an African Religion", *Archives de Sciences Sociales des Religions*, 117 (2002), 59–80 <doi:10.4000/assr.2480>

Diaz Castrillo, Luis, Iyami Oshoronga, *Los Ancianos De La Noche: El Culto A Los Ancianos De La Noche* (La Habana Cuba: Colección: En La Tierra De Oshá, n.d.)

———. *Tratado Enciclopédico de Palo Monte* (Caracas: Inversiones Orunmila C.A., 2004)

Diaz Fabelo, Teodoro, *Diccionario de la Lengua Conga Residual en Cuba* (Vista Alegre, Santiago de Cuba: UNESCO ORCALC, 2007)

Edmonds, Ennis Barrington, and Michelle A Gonzalez, *Caribbean Religious History* (Manhattan, New York: NYU Press, 2010)

Ekholm, Kajsa, *Power and Prestige: The Rise and Fall of the Kongo Kingdom* (Uppsala, Sweden: Skriv Service AB, 1972)

Elias, Norbert, and Edmund Jephcott, *Civilizing Process: Sociogenetic and Psychogenetic Investigations* (Malden, Massachusetts: Blackwell, 2000)

Ellis, A. B., *The Yoruba-Speaking Peoples Of The Slave Coast Of West Africa; Their Religion, Manners, Customs, Laws, Language, Etc. With An Appendix Containing A Comparison Of The Tshi, Ga, Ewe, And Yoruba Languages* (London: Chipman and Hall, ltd., 1894)

Enamorado Rodríguez, A., "Los mitos terapéuticos dentro de la regla conga o palo monte: significación social y aportes a la cutura popular en el municipio Holguín" (master"s thesis, Universidad de Holguín, 2013)

Erichsen, Gerald, "Where Did The Word Hurricane Come From?, *Thoughtco*, 2019 <https://www.thoughtco.com/etymology-of-hurricane-3080285>

Escalona, A., *Tratado de Orun* (Raleigh, North Carolina: Lulu, Inc., 2008)

Espinosa Morales, Luis Alberto, *Zambia Palo-Monte* (México, D.F.: Cacelin, Impresores, 1981)

Espírito Santo, Diana, *Developing the Dead: Mediumship and Selfhood in Cuban Espiritismo* (Miami, Florida: University Press of Florida, 2015)

Eucherius de Roy, Pere, *Le Congo: Essai su l"Histoire Religieuse de ce Pays Depuis sa Découverte (1484) Jusqu"à nos Jours* (Huy, Belgium: Charpentier & Emond, 1894)

Falola, Toyin, and Ann Genova, *ORISA: Yoruba Gods and Spiritual Identity in Africa and the Diaspora* (Trenton, New Jersey: Africa World, Inc., 2006)

Falola, Toyin, *ÈṢÙ: Yoruba God, Power, and the Imaginative Frontiers* (Durham, North Carolina: Carolina Academic Press, 2013)

Fatunmbi, Awo Fá"Lokun, *Egun: The Ifa Concept of Ancestor Reverence*, The Metaphysical Foundations of Ifa, Volume 3 (Columbia, South Carolina: CreateSpace Independent, 2013)

———. *Ori: The Ifa Concept Of Consciousness*, The Metaphysical Foundations Of Ifa, Volume 4 (Columbia, South Carolina: CreateSpace Independent, 2014)

Feraudy Espino, Heriberto, *Irna: Un Encuentro con la Santería, el Espiritismo y Palo Monte* (Santo Domingo, República Dominicano: Editora Manatí, 2002)

Fernández de Oviedo y Valdés, G., *Sumario de la Natural Historia de las Indias* (Toledo: Biblioteca Nacional de España, 1526)

Fernández Olmos, M., Murphy, J. M., & Paravisini-Gebert, L., *Creole religions of the Caribbean: An introduction from Vodou and Santería to Obeah and Espiritismo* (NYU Press, 2011)

Flanders Crosby, Jill, and J. T. Torres, *Situated Narratives and Sacred Dance: Performing the Entangled Histories of Cuba and West Africa.* (Gainesville, Florida: University of Florida Press, 2021)

Forde, M., *Obeah and other powers: The Politics of Caribbean religion and healing* (Duke University Press, 2012)

Forte, Maximilian C., "Extinction: The Historical Trope of Anti-Indigeneity in the Caribbean", *Issues in Caribbean Amerindian Studies*, 1.4 (2005)

Frisvold, Nicholaj de Mattos, *Ifá: A Forest of Mystery* (London: Scarlet Imprint, 2016)

———. *Palo Mayombe: The Garden of Blood and Bones* (Dover: Scarlet Imprint, 2011)

Fromont, Cécile, *The Art of Conversion: Christian Visual Culture in the Kingdom of Kongo* (Chapel Hill, North Carolina: University of North Carolina Press, 2017)

Fuentes Guerra, Jesús, and Armin Schwegler, *Lengua y Ritos del Palo Monte Mayombe. Dioses Cubanos y sus Fuentes Africanas* (Madrid: Iberoamericana, 2005)

Fuentes Guerra, Jesus, *El Médico-Adivino en el África Bantú* (Madrid: Ediciones Maiombe, 2014)

———. *Estudios de Bantuidad. Malongui ma bantu* (La Habana: Editorial de Ciencias Sociales, 2018)

———. *Los Negros Congos de Cuba* (El Vedado, Ciudad de La Habana: Ediciones UNIÓN, 2017)

———. *Lydia Cabrera y La Bantuidad Lingüística* (Cienfuegos, Cuba: Ediciones Mecenas, 2006)

———. *La Regla de Palo Monte. Un Acercamiento a la Bantuidad Cubana* (El Vedado, La Habana: Ediciones UNIÓN, 2012)

———. *Nzila Ya Mpika (La Ruta del Esclavo). Una Aproximación Lingüística* (Cienfuegos, Cuba: Ediciones Mecenas, 2002)

Gámez Osheniwó y Águila de Ifá, Leonel, *Comprendiendo Nuestras Tradiciones* (Distrito Federal, México: Sociedad Yoruba de México y Águila de Ifá Foundation, 2012)

———. *Defendiendo Nuestras Tradiciones*, Tomo I (Distrito Federal, México: Sociedad Yoruba de México y Águila de Ifá Foundation, 2012)

———. *Defendiendo Nuestras Tradiciones*, Tomo II (Distrito Federal, México: Sociedad Yoruba de México y Águila de Ifá Foundation, 2012)

———. *Defendiendo Nuestras Tradiciones*, Tomo III (Distrito Federal, México: Sociedad Yoruba de México y Águila de Ifá Foundation, 2012)

———. *Enseñanzas de un Amigo un Hermano, un Mastro* (Distrito Federal, México: Sociedad Yoruba de México y Águila de Ifá Foundation, 2015)

———. *Teología en Ifá: Nuestra Visión de Olodumare y los Orishas* (Distrito Federal, México: Sociedad Yoruba de México y Águila de Ifá Foundation, 2014)

Giral, Sergio, *Rancheador*, online video recording, YouTube, 1976 <https://www.youtube.com/watch?v=dq9aPz8pWGY>

Gómez, Francisco Javier, *El Impacto De Las Religions Indígenas Americanas En La Teología Misionaria Del S. XVI* (Bilbao: Desclée De Brouwer, 2000)

Gonzales-Wippler, Migene, *Santería: Magia Africana en Latinoamérica* (New York: Julian, 1973)

———. *Santeria: The Religion: Faith, Rites, Magic* (Woodbury, Minnesota: Llewellyn Publications, 2010)

Gran Tratado de Briyumba, Tomo I, n.d.

Handler, Jerome S., "Slave Medicine and Obeah in Barbados, circa 1650 to 1834", *New West Indian Guide/Nieuwe West-Indische Gids*, 74.1–2 (2000), 57–90 <doi:10.1163/13822373–90002570>

Hartman, Joseph, "The Ceiba Tree as a Multivocal Signifier: Afro-cuban Symbolism, Political Performance, and Urban Space in the Cuban Republic", *Hemisphere: Visual Cultures of the Americas*, 4.1 (2011), 16–41

Hechizos y Firmas de Palo, n.d.

Hernandez, Lorenzo, *Manual del Mayombero* (Rincon, Puerto Rico: Botanica 7 Rayos, 1993)

Heywood, Linda M., *Central Africans and Cultural Transformations in the American Diaspora* (New York: Cambridge University Press, 2002)

Hilton, Anne, *The Kingdom of Kongo* (Oxford: Clarendon Press, 1985)

James Figarola, Joel, *Cuba La Gran Nganga* (La Habana: Editorial José Martí, 2012)

———. *La Brujería Cubana: El Palo Monte, Aproximación al Pensamiento Abstracto de la Cubanía* (Santiago, Cuba: Editorial Oriente, 2009)

Janzen, John M., and Wyatt MacGaffey, *An Anthology of Kongo Religion: Primary Texts from Lower Zaïre* (Lawrence, Kansas: University of Kansas, 1974)

Josephs, K. M., "A Descriptive Grammar of Kalinago", (doctoral thesis, University of Arizona, 2019)

Kardec, Allan and Anna Blackwell, *The Spirits" Book: According to the Teachings of Spirits of High Degree and Transmitted Through Mediums* (Valley Cottage, New York: Discovery Publisher, 2017)

———. *The Mediums" Book: the Mediums" and Evokers" Guide* (Valley Cottage, New York: Discovery Publisher, 2019)

Kardec, Allan, *Genesis: Genesis-Miracles and Predictions According to Spiritism* (Rio de Janeiro, Brazil: International Spiritist Council-FEB Publisher, 2011)

———. *Heaven and Hell* (Rio de Janeiro, Brazil: International Spiritist Council-FEB Publisher, 2008)

———. *The Gospel According to Spiritism* (Rio de Janeiro, Brazil: International Spiritist Council-FEB Publisher, 2011)

Kerestetzi, K. and Fornal, G., *Les Morts du Palo Monte*, online video recording, YouTube, 2019 <https://www.youtube.com/watch?v=_cQHCT9fJlU>

Kerestetzi, K., "Fabriquer une nganga, engendrer un dieu (Cuba)", *Images Re-vues Histoire, anthropologie et théorie de l'art*, 8 (2011) <http://journals.openedition.org/imagesrevues/478> [accessed 11 November 2020]

———. "Making a Nganga, Begetting a God. Materiality and Belief in the Afro-Cuban Religion of Palo Monte", *Ricerche di Storia Sociale e Religiosa*, 87 (2015)

———. *Vivre Avec les Morts À Cuba: Réinvention et Transmission Religieuse dans le Palo Monte* (Paris: Karthala, 2016)

Kia Bunseki Fu-Kiau, K., *African Cosmology of the Bantu-Kongo: Tying the Spiritual Knot, Principles of Life and Living* (Astoria, New York: African Tree, 2014)

Klieman, Kairn A., *The Pygmies Were Our Compass: Bantu and Batwa in the History of West Central Africa, Early Times to C. 1900 C.E.*, Social History of Africa Series (Portsmouth, New Hampshire: Heinemann, 2003)

Kopytoff, I., *The African Frontier: The Reproduction of Traditional African Societies* (Bloomington, Indiana: Indiana University Press, 1989)

Krämer, Gudrun, and Graham Harman, *A History of Palestine: From the Ottoman Conquest to the Founding of The State of Israel* (Princeton, New Jersey: Princeton University Press, 2011)

La Rosa Corzo, Gabino, *Los Cimarrones de Cuba* (La Habana, Cuba: Editorial Ciencias Sociales, 1988)

LaGamma, Alisa, *Kongo: Power and Majesty* (New York: Metropolitan Museum of Art, 2015)

Lage Entuala Kongo, Domingo B., *El Libro De Tratados Y Pactos Del Palo Mayombe* (Bloomington, Indiana: Palibrio, 2011)

——. *Que Me La Hace Me La Paga* (Bloomington, Indiana: Palibrio, 2012)

——. *Secretos Intensos Del Palo Mayombe* (Bloomington, Indiana: Palibrio, 2013)

Law, Robin, "Dahomey and the Slave Trade: Reflections on the Historiography of the Rise of Dahomey", *The Journal of African History* 27.2 (1986), 237–67 <doi:10.1017/s0021853700036665>

Lawrence, Raymond, and Roselyn Paul, "The Kalinago Language", *Division of Culture*, 2021 <http://divisionofculture.gov.dm/creole-languages/7-the-kalinago-language>

Lippold, Adolf, "Theodosius I | Biography, Accomplishments, & Facts", *Encyclopedia Britannica*, 2022 <https://www.britannica.com/biography/Theodosius-I>

Lopes, Duarte, Margarite Hutchinson, and Filippo Pigafetta, *History of the Kingdom of Congo: Filippo Pigafetta, Rome 1591* (London: John Murray, 1881)

Lovejoy, P.E., *The "Middle Passage": The Enforced Migration of Africans across the Atlantic* (York University, Toronto, 2007)

Lugo Aikulola Iwindara Fewehinmi, N., "Diferencias entre Santeria Cubana y la practica de Nigeria", *Asociacion Cultural Yoruba de Canarias*, 2014 <https://yorubacanarias.com/3/post/2014/07/diferencias-entre-santeria-cubana-y-la-practica-de-nigeria.html>

Malongo Sarabanda, Tata Nkisy, *Manual Basico De Palo Monte* (Miami, Florida: Independently published, 2003)

Mampuya Batsîkama, Patrício Cipriano, *As Origens Do Reino do Kôngo* (South Luanda, Angola: Mayamba, Colecção: Biblioteca da História, 2010)

——. *O Reino Do Kôngo E A Sua Origem Meridional* (Luanda, Angola: Universidade Editora, 2011)

Martinez, Milton, *EWE for the New Diaspora: Plants in REGLA CONGA* (Miami, Florida: Independently Published, 2020)

Martínez-Ruiz, Barbaro, *Kongo Graphic Writing and Other Narratives Of The Sign* (Philadelphia, Pennsylvania: Temple University Press, 2013)

McKenna, Amy, "Maya | People, Language, & Civilization", *Encyclopedia Britannica* <https://www.britannica.com/topic/Maya-people> [accessed 10 April 2022]

Mercier, P., "The Fon of Dahomey", *African Worlds: Studies in the Cosmological Ideas and Social Values of African Peoples*, 2.1 (1954), 210–34 <doi:0852552866>

Métraux, Alfred, Hugo Charteris, and Sidney W. Mintz, *Voodoo in Haiti* (New York: Pantheon, 1989)

Mignolo, Walter D., *The Darker Side of Western Modernity: Global Futures, Decolonial Options* (London: Duke University Press, 2011)

Miller, Ivor L., *Voice of the Leopard: African Secret Societies and Cuba* (Jackson, Mississippi: University Press of Mississippi, 2012)

Millet Batista, José, *Espiritismo, Variantes Cubanas* (Los Teques, Venezuela: Ediciones Fundación Casa del Caribe-Cuba-Espiritismo, 2018)

Millet Batista, José, *Regla Konga Palo Mayombe en Santiago de Cuba: Y Recuperación de la Memoria de los Musundis* (Los Teques, Venezuela: Ediciones Fundación Casa del Caribe, 2018)

Montejo, Esteban, and Miguel Barnet, *Biografía de un Cimarrón* (México: Siglo Veintiuno Editores, 1975)

Morejón, Jorge Luis, "From the Areíto to the Cordon: Indigenous Healing Dances", *Revista Brasileira De Estudos Da Presença*, 8.3 (2018), 563–91 <doi:10.1590/2237–266069826>

Moreno Fraginals, Manuel, "Africa in Cuba: A Quantitative Anaylsis of the African Population in the Island of Cuba", *Annals of The New York Academy Of Sciences*, 292.1 (1977), 187–201 <doi:10.1111/j.1749-6632.1977.tb47743.x>

———. *El Ingenio: Complejo Económico Social Cubano del Azúcar*, Tomo I (La Habana, Cuba: Editorial Ciencias Sociales, 1978)

———. *El Ingenio: Complejo Económico Social Cubano del Azúcar*, Tomo II (La Habana, Cuba: Editorial Ciencias Sociales, 1978)

———. *El Ingenio: Complejo Económico Social Cubano del Azúcar*, Tomo III (La Habana, Cuba: Editorial Ciencias Sociales, 1978)

Muñoz-Pando, Roberto G., and Sebastian Robiou Lamarche, *Creencias Mortuorias De Los Aborígenes Antillanos, Taínos Y Caribes: Estudio Etnohistórico Y Social. Análisis de los Taínos y Caribes: etnohistoria, arqueologia y literature oral* (San Juan, Puerto Rico: Centro de Estudios Avanzados de Puerto Rico y el Caribe, n.d.)

Murrell, N. S., *Afro-Caribbean religions: An introduction to their historical, cultural, and sacred traditions* (Temple University Press, 2010)

Ochoa, Todd Ramón, *Society of the Dead. Quita Manaquita and Palo Praise in Cuba* (Berkeley, California: University of California Press, 2010)

Ogunsina Adewuyi, Chief Olayinka Babatunde, *Ifá: The Book of Wisdom* (Nigeria: River Water, 2018)

Olupona, Jacob K., and Rowland O. Abiodun, *Ifá Divination, Knowledge, Power, and Performance* (Bloomington and Indianapolis: Indiana University Press, 2016)

Olupona, Jacob K., *City of 201 Gods: Ilé-Ifè in Time, Space, and the Imagination* (Berkeley, California: University of California Press, 2011)

Orche García, Enrique, "Españoles y Hoja de Coca a Mediados del Siglo XVI en El Antiguo Perú- I: Contacto con la Coca", *De Re Metallica: Revista De La Sociedad Española Para La Defensa Del Patrimonio Geológico Y Minero*, 29 (2017), 53–64

Ortiz, Fernando, and Bronislaw Malinowski, *Contrapunteo Cubano Del Tabaco Y El Azúcar: Advertencia de sus Contrastes Agrarios, Económicos, Históricos y Sociales, su Etnografía y su Transculturación*, Second edition (Santa Clara, Cuba: Direccion de Publicaciones Universidad de las Villas, 1965)

"Paganism—New World Encyclopedia", Newworldencyclopedia.org, 2022 <https://www.newworldencyclopedia.org/entry/paganism>

Pals, Daniel L., *Nine Theories of Religion* (New York: Oxford University Press, 2015)

Pané, Ramón, José Juan Arrom, and Martí Soler, *Relación Acerca de las Antigüedades de los Indios* (México, D.F.: Siglo Veintiuno, 2004)

Pell Alimany, Narciso, and Leonardo Prohenza Osoria, *Mango Kutesya ya Ntoto ti Bilongo ya Kimbanda: Oráculo Geomántico y Medicina de Palo Monte* (Mexico City: Biblioteca de las Sombras, 2004)

Penyak, Lee M., and Walter J. Petry, *Religion In Latin America* (Maryknoll, New York: Orbis, 2006)

Pérez Obá Ecún, Cecilio, *Itutu: El Libro De Los Muertos* (Miami, Florida: Obá Ecún, 1995)

———. *Mayimbe: Como Fabricar Una Nganga* (Miami, Florida: Obá Ecún, 2001)

Pérez, Blas Nabel, *Las Culturas Que Encontró Colón* (Quito, Ecuador: Abya-Yala, 1992)

Peters, F. E., *Judaism, Christianity, and Islam: The Classical Texts and Their Interpretation, Volume I: From Covenant to Community* (Princeton, New Jersey: Princeton University Press, 1990)

———. *Judaism, Christianity, and Islam: The Classical Texts and Their Interpretation, Volume II: The Word and the Law and the People of God* (Princeton, New Jersey: Princeton University Press, 1990)

———. *Judaism, Christianity, and Islam: The Classical Texts and Their Interpretation, Volume III: The Works of the Spirit* (Princeton, New Jersey: Princeton University Press, 1990)

Ramos Ilarí Obá, Miguel Willie, *Adimú—Gbogbó Tén"unjé Lukumí* (Miami, Florida: Eleda.org Publications, 2012)

Ramos Ilarí Obá, Miguel Willie, and Jorge R. Brito Santana, *Curamagüey: Enclave Lucumí en Matanzas* (Miami, Florida: Eleda.Org Publications, 2014)

Ramos Ilarí Obá, Miguel Willie, *Asé Omó Osayín . . . ewé Ayé* (Miami, Florida: Eleda. Org Publications, 2012)

———. *Obí Agbón: Lukumí Divination with Coconut* (Miami, Florida: Eleda.org Publications, 2012)

———. *On The Orishas Roads and Pathways: Oshun, Deity of Femininity* (Miami, Florida: Eleda.org Publications, 2014)

———. *On The Orishas Roads and Pathways: Yemojá, Mother of the World* (Miami, Florida: Eleda.org Publications, 2019)

———. *On The Orishas Roads and Pathways: Obatalá, Odúa, Oduduwá* (Miami, Florida: Eleda.org Publications, 2017)

———. *Orí Eledá mí ó . . . Si mí Cabeza no me Vende* (Miami, Florida: Eleda.org Publications, 2011)

———. *Oro Egungun . . . Las Honras de Egungun* (Miami, Florida: Eleda.Org Publications, 1982)

Refranes de Palo, n.d.

Rey, Terry, *Key Thinkers in the Study of Religion*, Second edition (London: Equinox, 2008)

Robiou Lamarche, Sebastián, and Grace M Robiou Ramirez de Arellano, *Tainos and Caribs: The Aboriginal Cultures of the Antilles* (San Juan, Puerto Rico: Editorial Punto y Coma, 2019)

Rodas, Josean, *La Guia Del Palero* (Puerto Rico: Independently published, 2012)

Rojas Calderon, Carlos Alberto, *Palo Brakamundo (El Palo Monte Cubano)*, Colección de los Congos en los Estados Unidos (Bloomington, Indiana: Palibrio, 2011)

Rubio, Juan, *Palo Monte y La Verdad Esotérica.* (Miami, Florida: Publicaciones Miami, 2014)

Said, Edward W., *Orientalism* (New York: Vintage—Random House, 1978)

Sanpal, Oscar, *Soy Tata Nganga Enriquito Hernandez Armenteros*, online video recording, YouTube, 2016 <https://www.youtube.com/watch?v=tF9n6FGISmY&t=120s>

Schmelz, Bernd, Gabriele Lademann-Priemer, and Julia Dombrowski, *Kubas Afrikanische Geister = Cuba''s African Spirits* (Hamburg, Germany: Museum für Völkerkunde, 2016)

Sebag Montefiore, Simon, *Jerusalem: The Biography* (New York: Vintage—Random House, 2012)

Shultz, Sophia Kelly, and Tata Rodriguez, *Seeking the Spirits of Palo Kimbisa: Exploring the Mysterious World of the Afro-Cuban Religion* (Atglen, Pennsylvania: Schiffer, 2021)

Souza Hernández, Adrián de, *Echu-Elegguá: Equilibrio Dinámico de la Existencia (Religión Yorubá)* (La Habana: Ediciones Unión, 1999)

———. *Los Orichas en África: Una Aproximación a Nuestra Identidad* (La Habana: Ciencias Sociales, 2008)

Stahl, A., *Los Indios Borinqueños. Estudios Etnográficos* (Puerto-Rico: Impr. y Libr. de Acosta, 1889)

Tedlock, Dennis, *Popol Vuh: the Definitive Edition of the Mayan Book of the Dawn of Life and the Glories of Gods and Kings* (New York: Simon & Schuster, 1996)

ter Haar, Gerrie, and Stephen Ellis, "The Occult Does Not Exist: A Response To Terence Ranger", *Africa*, 79.3 (2009), 399–412 <doi:10.3366/e0001972009000874>

Thompson, Robert Farris, *Flash of the Spirit: African & Afro-American Art & Philosophy* (New York: Random House-Vintage, 1984)

Thornton, John K., *The Kongolese Saint Anthony: Dona Beatriz Kimpa Vita and the Antonian Movement, 1684–1706* (Cambridge: Cambridge University Press, 1998)

———. "The Kingdom of Kongo and Palo Mayombe: Reflections on an African-American Religion", *Slavery & Abolition*, 37.1 (2015), 1–22 <doi:10.1080/01440 39x.2015.1103524>

Tollebeek, Jo, *Mayombe: Ritual Statues from Congo* (Lannoo, 2011)

Torrealba, Wilmer, *Tratado de Nkunia Nfinda (Pino Nuevo)*, n.d.

Trabajando Con la Nganga. Fundamentos, Firmas, Trabajos, Resguardos, Palo, Plantas, n.d.

Tratado de Zarabanda. Nzo Mboumba Loango Mayombe, n.d.

Tukuenda, "Nsunga, Tabaco, Caribbean Spirituality and Understanding in the Diaspora, 2010 <https://caribbeanspiritualityandunderstanding.blogspot.com/2010/11/nsunga-tabaco.html>

Ulloa Hung, Jorge, and Roberto Valcárcel Rojas, *Indígenas e Indios en el Caribe. Presencia, Legado Y Estudio. Serie Los Indígenas Más Allá De Colón* (República Dominicana: Editora Búho, S.R.L, 2016)

Ulloa, Alfonso, *Historie di Europa, Nella Quali Principalmente si Contione la Guerra Fatta in Ungheria Tra Massimiliano Imperatore et Sultan Solimano Re De''turchi* (Venetia: Bolognino Zaltieri, 1570)

van Wing, Rev. P. Joseph, *Études Bakongo* (Bruxelles, Belgium: Librairie Falk fils, Georges van Campenhout, Successeur, 1921)

Varona, Arnaldo, Santeria: A Brief History of the Babalawos (Babalaos) in Cuba + Santeria: Breve Historia de los Babalaos en Cuba, *The Cuban History*, 2021 <https://www.thecubanhistory.com/2015/12/santeria-a-brief-history-of-the-babalawos-babalaos-in-cuba-santeria-breve-historia-de-los-babalaos-en-cuba/>

Villaverde, Cirilo, Alberto Batista Reyes, and Enrique Martinez, *Diario del Rancheador* (Habana, Cuba: Letras Cubanas. Testimonio, 1982)

von Worms, Abraham, Georg Dehn, Steven Guth, and Lon Milo DuQuette, *The Book of Abramelin: A New Translation-Revised and Expanded* (Lake Worth, Florida: Ibis, 2015)

Wilson Nin, Leonardo, "Language of the Voiceless: Traces of Taino Language, Food, and Culture in the Americas From 1492 to the Present" (master"s thesis, Harvard University, 2020)

Wilson, Samuel Meredith, *The Indigenous People of the Caribbean* (Gainesville, Florida: University Press of Florida, 1999)

Wright, M., "WORKING OSHOOSI", *Oshoosi*, 2015 https://oshoosi.com/oshoosi-details.html

www.ingramcontent.com/pod-product-compliance
Lightning Source LLC
Chambersburg PA
CBHW061727270326
41928CB00011B/2136